DEDICATION

To Jesus Christ: My Lord and Savior, to Jehovah God the Father of all, and the Holy Spirit the Third Person of the Holy Trinity who guides, leads and directs every step we take as believers in the risen Christ and has given all believers the power to attain Christlikeness.

To my beautiful wife, Lena: my ever present loving "Joy" of my life, she is my support and the controlling influence that keeps me grounded and in control of my ugly, stinking thinking and emotions while teaching me to pick my battles before I open my mouth.

To my children Christopher who is serving in the U.S. Air Force, Anthony and Matthew both are attending colleges who have taught me to listen to their points of view with respect in order to receive it in return as young men. I am so proud of the men each of you are becoming.

To my mother and father for showing unconditional love to my wife, children and me when we most needed it to stay a family with dignity and purpose in the face of possible tragedy.

To my late friends Diane Bricker and Pastor Bev Hills who taught me to face the trials of this life with grace as they both handled physical ailments with dignity and a smile on their face with the peace of our Lord Jesus Christ evident in their hearts. I can't wait to see my beautiful sisters in Christ again in heaven.

To my two mentors I've been so fortunate and blessed to learn from Al Schorpp and Tom Perz who both in their boldness and desire to proclaim the good news of Jesus Christ to any and every person the Holy Spirit leads them to speak to. Thank you both for putting up with me with patience and true brotherly love. I am honored and truly blessed to know you both.

To John Goulandris my good Greek friend who while I thought I was teaching you, you were actually teaching me the simplicity of the Gospel and Finally to Chuck Arena, John Pavlish, Jerry Schill and Dave Weber thank you for your kind generosity in continuing to assist my family and me after the diagnosis of Multiple Sclerosis. You were truly a God sent blessing to us Thank You again; you are all in my prayers.

You Might Be Right, but You *Aint* Right with the Word of God!

Dimitri Yanuli

WESTBOW
PRESS

A DIVISION OF THOMAS NELSON

WestBow Press books may be ordered through booksellers or by contacting:

WestBow Press
A Division of Thomas Nelson
1663 Liberty Drive
Bloomington, IN 47403
www.westbowpress.com
1-(866) 928-1240

Because of the dynamic nature of the Internet, any web addresses or links contained in this book may have changed since publication and may no longer be valid. The views expressed in this work are solely those of the author and do not necessarily reflect the views of the publisher, and the publisher hereby disclaims any responsibility for them.

Any people depicted in stock imagery provided by Thinkstock are models, and such images are being used for illustrative purposes only.

Certain stock imagery © Thinkstock.

ISBN: 978-1-4497-7379-3 (sc)
ISBN: 978-1-4497-7380-9 (hc)
ISBN: 978-1-4497-7378-6 (e)

Library of Congress Control Number: 2012920969

Printed in the United States of America

WestBow Press rev. date: 12/19/2012

"For we wrestle not against flesh and blood, but against principalities, against powers, against the rulers of the darkness of this world, against spiritual wickedness in high places." (Ephesians 6:12)

"That if thou shalt confess with thy mouth the Lord Jesus, and shalt believe in thine heart that God hath raised him from the dead, thou shalt be saved. For with the heart man believeth unto righteousness; and with the mouth confession is made unto salvation." (Romans10:9–10)

"But ye shall receive power, after that the Holy Ghost is come upon you: and ye shall be witnesses unto me both in Jerusalem, and in all Judaea, and in Samaria, and unto the uttermost part of the earth." (Acts 1:8)

In the beginning was the Word, and the Word was with God, and the Word was God. The same was in the beginning with God. All things were made by him; and without him was not any thing made that was made. In him was life; and the life was the light of men. And the light shineth in darkness; and the darkness comprehended it not. (John 1:1–5)

And I say unto you my friends, Be not afraid of them that kill the body, and after that have no more that they can do. But I will forewarn you whom ye shall fear: Fear him, which after he hath killed hath power to cast into hell; yea, I say unto you, Fear him. (Luke 12:4-5)

CONTENTS

Chapter 1

GOD'S CALL

The premise of this book is to help give you an understanding of the process that mankind has had to go through in order to reconnect and have intimacy with the God of creation again after the fall of Adam. The Judeo-Christian Bible is the only account that tries to completely answer and explain creation from the beginning of time to the end of mankind here on earth. It alone explains his eternal destination that is based on this life's actions, done while we are alive and assessed at our death. With its account of the creation of the universe and all the life on this earth to all the calamities and consequences of evil actions done by people in this life, only the Bible answers completely the questions of mankind's purpose and his eternal destination after death.

I will venture to show and prove to the best of my ability, with clarity from the written Word of God, that it is God's desire to call man—all of mankind—into fellowship with Him again on the same level they had in the garden of Eden. I will try to show that every scientific discovery made only validates and proves God's existence and that the destination and purpose for man is explained in His Word alone. From the God of Adam at creation to the keeping of a pure bloodline for the Messiah to be born to heal and save a corrupt humanity—only in the Judeo-Christian biblical Scriptures are all the failures and victories of mankind recorded in detail. Only in the Jewish Torah and the complete Christian Bible do we see the purpose, failures, and restoration of mankind given continuously as examples for us to grow spiritually and achieve our fullest eternal potential. It alone tells us that you must believe in the only Creator, Jehovah God, who designed all that we see, taste, hear, touch, and smell, and that the consequences of our thoughts and actions are dealt with only at the cross of Christ. The Bible alone sets parameters that will determine our destination for eternity, and it alone warns us of potential losses in that eternity. The God of the Torah is the same God who sent His only begotten Son Jesus Christ as Messiah to Hebrew's and believing Gentiles as their perfect Redeemer so that all who believe in Him can be saved for eternity. The complete Bible alone explains that Jesus Christ of Nazareth is the Messiah and has fulfilled every requirement of the Old Testament as High Priest, perfect sacrifice, and King of Kings. It alone tells us of man's fall and that Jesus currently is seated at the right hand of the Father, interceding for us as our advocate and mediator in our times of need. Jesus is seated because His work is done and completed. There is nothing else needed for you or me to do to receive salvation other than to believe that Jesus is the great I AM spoken of to Abraham in Genesis17:1 and to Moses in Exodus 3:14

Thus my dilemma. As I read the Scriptures, I read sections that didn't seem to apply to my rigid Greek Orthodox denominational upbringing. So much of what I was reading had to do with the Jews, and even more than that, Jesus said He didn't even come for us Gentiles (see Matthew 10:5 and Mark 5:19). What I read didn't line up with my traditional understanding of who God and Jesus were in relationship to me individually or to the church as I understood it. What about the Virgin Mary the mother of Jesus, the dead saints, the book of James, and the books of Acts and Hebrews? Who were they talking about, and how can they help us now? Who were these books in Scripture written by, and why the confusion and rejection of the Jewish people who wrote them? The Word says that you must verbally confess that Jesus is Lord to be saved but doesn't say anything about where to attend a specific church or follow the specific doctrines of a particular denomination. It just says to believe with all your being—spirit, soul, and body. We will differentiate and explain their individual attributes and significance in our eternal quest throughout this book.

As I searched the Bible for the definitive salvation Scriptures, I studied the obvious one we all know: John 3:16, spoken by Jesus.

> For God so loved the world, that he gave his only begotten Son, that whosoever believeth in him should not perish, but have everlasting life.

The next most authoritative Scripture was written by the apostle Paul in Romans 10:9–10 for you to personally confess Jesus:

> That if thou shalt confess with thy mouth the Lord Jesus, and shalt believe in thine heart that God hath raised him from the dead, thou shalt be saved. For with the heart man believeth unto righteousness; and with the mouth confession is made unto salvation.

You don't have to do anything more than believe that Jesus is the only way to God the Father, that He is the Messiah, and that God raised Jesus from the dead for you to enter His presence. Throughout the Pauline Epistles, Paul emphasizes that after a person confesses Jesus as Lord and Savior of their life, they are a new creation. He says that old things have passed away, and all things have become brand-new.

> Therefore if any man be in Christ, he is a new creature: old things are passed away; behold, all things are become new. And all things are of God, who hath reconciled us to himself by Jesus Christ, and hath given to us the ministry of reconciliation. (2 Corinthians 5:17–18)

Once born again, your spirit is renewed and is as perfect as it will ever be for all eternity. You are clean and forgiven.

> Even the righteousness of God which is by faith of Jesus Christ unto all and upon all them that believe: for there is no

difference: For all have sinned, and come short of the glory
of God. (Romans 3:22–23)

We need to be cleaned and that can only be done through the blood sacrifice
of Jesus Christ the Messiah, our kinsman Redeemer on the cross. The process
begins for rebuilding the walls of your soul that protect your spirit, and in the
context of this revelation, each person is constantly building or destroying the
walls of their soul in their daily walk. The purpose of rebuilding those soul
walls is to then rehang the gates that access and lead to your believing spirit
to protect it from attacks of the Enemy. Let me explain.

My pastor had asked me to teach a class on a book written by the leader of
our denomination: *Rebuilding the Real You* By Jack Hayford. It is based on
the book of Nehemiah in the Old Testament, and it speaks of his desire to
rebuild the walls and rehang the gates surrounding the newly rebuilt temple in
Jerusalem. The walls were necessary for protecting the temple. We had many
great discussions on the difficulties, opposition, and process of rebuilding
the walls and rehanging the gates to protect the new temple in Jerusalem.
Similarly, as you grow in the Lord after your salvation experience, your newly
rebuilt temple needs to be protected by your soul walls, regardless if they're
damaged or not through this life. Because of the Holy Spirit being in you
and communing with your soul and spirit at salvation, we need to rebuild and
fortify our soul's walls to protect our newly "born again" spirit temple.

As we continue on in this book, I will explain all the obstacles and hindrances
that arose with Nehemiah as he rebuilt the temple walls, and I will discuss
the similarities to the obstacles I faced because of my desire for knowledge
through salvation. Jesus is the foundation, the "cornerstone" of our faith, and
everything we believe in after salvation is then based on this rebuilding of the
walls and gates to our soul, protecting our born-again spirits. All you have
to do is believe in Jesus and begin to change your mind (repent) from your
learned life (habits) that are detrimental to our eternal position and rewards
in the kingdom.

I will venture to explain what is necessary to receive after believing in this
priceless gift of eternal life we have been given through Jesus Christ. In my
personal quest to find God and be where I am today—saved, sanctified, and

filled with the Holy Ghost—I had to go through a whole transformation and reprogramming process of my mind and soul. The obstacles and ridicule I had encountered were very similar to those outlined in the book of Nehemiah as he was determined to rebuild the walls around the temple in Jerusalem. The striking similarities in the newly born-again believer's struggles with the acquisition of resources for rebuilding protective barrier walls is the heart and core of this book. It completely opened my eyes to all of my damaged walls and emotional strongholds I had built to protect my spirit temple with my damaged soul. This transformation has taken twenty-five-plus years since a (feta cheese) salesman brought me to the Lord at my mom's deli store in 1986. That's when the process began for me, and it continues to this day.

As I acquire resources of knowledge and wisdom from the Word of God, it removes the strongholds of racism and prejudice and refills the voids with the Godly fruit of the Spirit. I am a project in progress, continually learning and continually growing in the Lord. Scars and battle wounds are all part of the process in the pulling down of strongholds and the mending of broken walls which are all part of the restoration process. The Holy Spirit revealed this to me, and I realized that most of the soul wounds protecting my spirit were self-inflicted. This became more and more apparent to me the more I read about Jesus and His Father, Jehovah God. Many of these soul wounds I didn't even know I had.

I realized that I was responding to everyone around me with crude, snide comments that were really protective barbs repelling others to protect my wounded soul. These reactions had become so second nature with me that my family and friends expected them as my normal behavior. As my ugly, vulgar personality took over, this condescending ridiculing humor became second Nature to me and I found myself making jokes about everything. Many of the jokes and comments were really just a way for me to be accepted, and over the years, the jokes became filthier and the comments more hurtful to the people I really cared about. Not only was I struggling with what the Word called coarse jesting, but my spirit ached from the contradictions as I read Scriptures. Jesus was alone in His actions, and His teachings were diametrically opposed to the natural fleshly desires of the common man or woman. I'm in good company, because the apostle Paul tells us in his epistles that he battled his flesh as well.

> For the good that I would I do not: but the evil which I would not, that I do. Now if I do that I would not, it is no more I that do it, but sin that dwelleth in me. (Romans 7:19–20)

Wow! In learning that this earthly battle was experienced by all men, I began to understand that I was in a process that was entirely up to me to continue or to stop. I could delay it or completely stop this process on the road to physical and spiritual destruction, or I could choose my soul's restoration through Jesus with the help of the Holy Spirit. It was my decision and mine alone, just as yours is your choice alone. Contrary to the philosophers and gurus of antiquity, God has given us free will, and with it, we choose our eternal destination. I chose Jesus, I chose to study and show myself approved by rightly dividing the Word of Truth. I choose to teach, I choose to learn, I choose to obey Him, and I choose to write this book because His Word says He wants no one to perish but all to come to the knowledge of Jesus Christ. I choose to teach what I believe coincides with the Word of God: that science validates Scripture in the Old and New Testaments. I choose to preach and teach the good news of my Lord and Savior Jesus Christ of Nazareth in humility and grace to the Hebrews and the Gentiles alike. Finally, I choose to teach on the weapons of our warfare available to *all* believers with the baptism of the Holy Spirit *today*!

Remember, you can be right about astronomy, archeology, physics, and all the other sciences of time and space, but you ain't right about your rejection of the Bible. You can be right about biblical religious rules and traditions, but you ain't right in the ways you treat other people because of the color of their skin, their social economic status, or people's scientific conclusions deduced from undeniable facts. So it is my contention as I write this book that the combinations of all these scientific proofs and reasons for personal maladies are outlined only in the biblical Judeo-Christian Scriptures for all of mankind's edification and instruction for eternity. They are not mutually exclusive to each other but validation of a creator God and His endless love for every single soul who has ever lived or shall ever be conceived and born before Jesus' return.

Chapter 2

RESOLUTION: CHANGE ME, LORD

here were three hurdles I had to accept and pass over in order to return to the position of intimacy and fellowship with God the Father that I know He desires from us all. That's what I wanted, and I wanted to have what Adam had before his fall in Genesis 2:25–3:10. The three hurdles in my life that I needed to overcome were my notions of ethnic and racial superiority and the deep-seated anti-Semitism that was taught to me from childhood—none of which I could keep and reach my goal of serving the Lord Jesus Christ (a "Jew"). We will discuss in detail the purpose and reasons for the undefiled Hebrew lineage of Jesus through the Hebrew girl Mary, the significance of His virgin birth, and the legal priestly order of His stepfather, Joseph, all the way back to Abraham. Matt. 1-17 KJV.

These truths of Jesus' sinless humanity are paramount for the complete eradication of humanity's sin nature so as to never return again unless we legally invite it in. This is what the rest of this book is about. That every believer is not destined to suffer in torment, but through the sacrifice of Jesus on the cross and the baptism of the Holy Spirit, God has provided all the tools necessary for the believer's life here on earth and for eternity.

Scripture also promises us that Jesus will split the eastern sky; will then raise the dead in Christ first; then as the Word says, we will all be caught up in the clouds to meet the Lord and be with Him for a thousand years as fellow heirs, kings, and priests in the New Jerusalem of His kingdom. I want to be ready, and I knew I couldn't be ready with all the hate, prejudice, and anger in my heart. I had to take my ethnically racist and anti-Semitic blinders off and read Scripture without these prejudices for the first time.

> But I would not have you to be ignorant, brethren, concerning them which are asleep, that ye sorrow not, even as others which have no hope. For if we *believe that Jesus died and rose again*, even so them also which sleep in Jesus will God bring with him. For this we say unto you by the word of the Lord, that we which are alive and remain unto the coming of the Lord shall not prevent them which are asleep. For the Lord himself shall descend from heaven with a shout, with the voice of the archangel, and with the trump of God: and *the dead in Christ shall rise first: be caught up together with them in the clouds, to meet the Lord in the air: and so shall we ever be with the Lord.* Wherefore comfort one another with these words. (1 Thessalonians 4:13–18, emphasis added)

The *arpaxo*, or snatching away of the believers, to be caught up in the clouds, to meet the Lord in the sky, was revealed first to us as a shadow of this *arpoxo* in the Old Testament with Enoch being translated in Genesis 5:24 and again with Elijah being taken in a whirlwind and chariot of fire in 2 Kings 2:11.

> Enoch walked with God: and he was not; for God took him. (Genesis 5:24)

> And it came to pass, as they still went on, and talked, that, behold, there appeared a chariot of fire, and horses of fire, and parted them both asunder; and Elijah went up by a whirlwind into heaven. (2 Kings 2:11)

Many believe that these two men are the two witnesses of the book of Revelation 11:3–12 because they were both translated and did not die natural deaths as the rest of humanity does. This is what the apostle Luke spoke of in Luke 21:36.

> Watch ye therefore, and pray always, that ye may be accounted
> *worthy to escape* all these things that shall come to pass, and
> to stand before the Son of man. (emphasis added)

You have to understand that the things I'm telling you have nothing to do with your salvation. What they refer to is His promise to all believers that we will not experience the wrath of God, but because of our faith, we'll be translated (escape) through the rapture. When I think this will occur will be discussed in later chapters in detail. But suffice it to say that, without a doubt, once you receive Jesus and confess Him as Lord and Savior with your mouth and believe in your heart He is risen, you'll escape the wrath coming upon this earth:

> That if thou shalt confess with thy mouth the Lord Jesus, and
> shalt believe in thine heart that God hath raised him from the
> dead, thou shall *be saved*. For with the heart man believeth
> unto righteousness; and with the mouth confession is made
> unto salvation. (Romans 10:9–10, emphasis added)

You can pray this with me and be sure of your eternity. Repeat this now regardless of orthodox Christian denomination:

> *Father God, I repent for my sins, Lord. I'm sorry, and I'm*
> *willing to change the way I think and live. I believe You raised*
> *Jesus from the dead, and I am now ready to trust my whole*
> *life under the lordship of Your Son, Jesus the Christ. By faith, I*
> *receive Jesus Christ as my Lord and Savior. Amen.*

> *Halleluiah!*

This salvation through Jesus is the first hurdle and is the only mandatory one of the three to know you're a sinner in need of redemption. But with this first hurdle I had to climb, I realized it was the most difficult one for me to believe and accept, because Romans 10:9–10 is a non-ethnic, nondenominational prayer, and denominational religion has nothing to do with it. To believe in my heart that God raised Jesus from the dead and then confess Him as Lord and Savior of my life was no big deal. This was easy since I believed that I was already a Christian, even if only a nominal one at the time. So confessing with my mouth was easy, but believing in my heart … that was a different story. Nothing I had done in my life up to that point differentiated me from the rest of the nonbelieving world. The way I lived, spoke, and thought contradicted everything I read that Jesus expected of a believer in the risen Christ.

The more I read the New Testament, the more I realized that it was an extension of the Old Testament, and I then could begin to see how far from Jesus I really was. Without the Old Testament, the New Testament made no sense to me and it seemed incomplete. I read that God is not a respecter of persons and wants none to perish but all to come to the knowledge of Jesus Christ. When I read in the Bible what Jesus would say on judgment day to professing believers, fear of not making it to heaven ran through my mind, and for the first time, I realized that everything I took for granted wasn't going to save me.

> But he shall say, I tell you, I know you not whence ye are;
> depart from me, all ye workers of iniquity. (Luke 13:27)

I knew Jesus, so "worker of iniquity" was not me—right? How could that be? My thoughts ran through my life: I'm a Christian; I go to church on Easter and Christmas. I've donated to the Greek Church for the festivals. I never killed anyone, I should be okay … I am okay … I think I'm okay. There are a lot worse people than me. I'm really a good person. I really love people and I'm really a good person! God wouldn't punish me, would He?

In my mind, I was trying to justify my life's actions, my prejudices, and my hates. The more I read the Bible, the more I was convicted of my prejudice, bigotry, and intolerance of non-Greeks and nonwhites; this was my second major hurdle to cross. I needed to work on my walls and gates even though I didn't know it at the time. I just knew that I fell really short of what I was reading on how I should be as a believer in the risen Christ. Then I was confronted with the third hurdle: all the histories of the writers, their lives, their deaths, and their commitment to die for the Word were written by Jews. How they copied the words that Moses received from God exactly. How when even one mistake was made, the whole book was not kosher and was discarded. Every jot and every tittle had to be perfect. Then I had to acknowledge that Jesus was a Jew, and the apostles were all Jews. Every last one of them was Jewish. They wrote about the Jews. The history in the Bible was about the Jews. Prophecy was for the Jews.

Wait a minute. I hated the Jews; I even beat up a kid once because he was a Jew. The only people I hated more than the Jews were the queers and black people. I'm not proud of that, but I even used to go out with my cousin, looking for gays to beat up. In the army, this black queer kid beat the snot out of me for my prejudice toward blacks and gays. He kind of convinced me to change my opinion about them a little, but in my heart, I hated them all and I was still prejudiced, still racist, and still an anti-Semite. I never knew any Jews, queers, or black people, but I just knew I hated them all. Never really knew why; I just knew I did. They were my enemies. I was better, smarter, whiter, and of course, I was a Greek, so I justified my actions and opinions. If I saw any person of color—or even worse yet, a white girl with a black man in a store or restaurant—I would snicker and prejudge her as being a whore in my mind. I never really would say anything, but my heart was darkened with false accusations and the preconceived ideas of superiority over them was there. She was a white-trash whore. Or if the person she was with was what I deemed as beneath my class of people, they were white-trash hillbillies too.

This was the mind-set I had before my dad died when I was eleven years old, and it had stayed with me until I got saved at twenty-six and began reading the Bible. I had learned most of this from hearing my dad, family, and neighbors talk about the race wars in the sixties. The lady across the street from us had married a black policeman after her first husband died from cancer, and they of course became the topic of many neighborhood discussions. My father's ugly racial comments planted the seeds of racism and prejudice in my heart. Never mind that this lady was left alone with four kids to care for and that her second husband loved her. She was white and he was black—end of discussion. This was a time when many of the stereotypes of the sixties were running rampant, and tolerance of interracial marriages did not really exist (not in my family). Hearing them ridicule her and the other families in the neighborhood helped shape my racism and prejudices that I carried with me until I prayed the day my "white" niece married a black man. I prayed, and I distinctly remember the Holy Spirit telling me that they were doing the right thing by getting married and that I was wrong to snub them by not going to the wedding.

The second hurdle of racism was tied in with my sense of ethnic superiority that was intertwined with anger, forming hatred and intolerance of anyone different than white Greeks. There was a family that lived down the street from us that helped instill that racist Greek superiority complex even further. The fact that they had twelve kids—I think they were from West Virginia—also helped form my opinions. I remember my mom and dad calling them filthy hillbillies for years; you would think I grew up with Archie Bunker. Their house was only two houses away, and it really stunk; they were always dirty and nasty. Not only did the house stink from the cats and dogs defecating inside and out, but there was garbage everywhere. There weren't even screens on any of the house windows, which only added to the ridicule. It was my mission in life to beat up the oldest boy and his friends whenever possible.

No wonder when I grew older I had so many issues that had to be dealt with, especially in the false sense of superiority I had. In a way it seems cruel, but as I look back at every issue, every one of them was absolutely necessary for me to identify and remove to grow spiritually. I needed to understand from experience the shame and ridicule I contributed by inflicting this cruelty toward others, but the realization of the root planted was what was necessary.

The pain, shame, and remorse for the things I had done as a child and later as a young adult were brought to light the more I read Scripture. I am very ashamed and very sorry for how I acted and thought and the way I made fun of people. I couldn't even go to my twenty-year high school reunion because of my shame on how I treated some girls in high school. As a born-again believer, we're to be ambassadors for Jesus, and as a new creation in Christ, I could see that I was a miserable failure.

I now know that I was a very hypocritical, angry, and a very bitter man. How could I not be? It only makes sense since when I was a boy, I was filled with so much fear, hate, and anger about who I thought I was and who I thought everyone else was. It has taken Jesus twenty-six years to change me into the man I am today, and I thank God that what the Devil has designed for my destruction, God has transformed into victory. Had not a born-again Greek olive–and–feta cheese salesman come into my mother's deli and witnessed to me the good news of Jesus Christ and then taken me to a church youth meeting, I would not be where I am today. Because of my asking Jesus into my life, I am convinced that I would never have met the pretty youth group leader who later became my wife. She was yelling at the youth to get their act together because they only had a couple of weeks left until the Christmas play. I remember thinking how mean she was—good-looking, but mean.

The process had begun with my willingness to freely choose Jesus. As I look back, there really was no way I could have had such a heart transformation without Jesus. Only Jesus could have taken this wicked and hateful man that I had become and remold him even with all the scars, scrapes, and bruises into a man willing to admit failure and change the hates into the love of Jesus Christ. I was a hateful and angry man who still doesn't understand how or why anyone could or would fall in love with me—especially since I never even told my future wife that I loved her until after we were married. Go figure.

Have you ever seen the movie *My Big Fat Greek Wedding*? It's a pretty accurate depiction of my Greek family life growing up, once you get past the phony introductions and family-acceptance parts of the movie, which is another story. You know how the church is set up on the wedding day with the bride's family on one side and the groom's on the other? Well, mine looked a little different. My future wife Lena's side was full of family and friends; my side was completely empty except for my mom's best friend, Christine, and Uncle Peter who married an American girl and probably had sympathy for my situation. They were the only people on my side of the church (which seated about five hundred people). Because of my Greek Orthodox mutiny to my family, they disowned me for marrying an Italian-Polish-Jewish girl. Hmmm! Not only were they upset that their firstborn son wasn't marrying a Greek girl, but they were also upset for my going to another church. I even lost my job at my mom's deli store as well.

Not only did I get disowned by my family, but my soon-to-be mother-in-law stood at the entrance of the church on our wedding day, holding the keys to her car and telling my future wife she could still leave if she wanted to. She said, "It's not too late to leave!" No kidding! We had no money, my new wife was in debt, I didn't have a job, and we didn't even have a real honeymoon. We couldn't even keep the diamond wedding ring I bought her, because we needed the money to turn the electricity back on at our house. Good thing my poker buddy owned the jewelry store where I bought the ring from, and he gave me the deposit money back when we returned it. The only good thing was that my sister and I had made an agreement that whoever got married first would get the house that our mother bought for us to live together in while we both worked in the family store.

A couple of months after Lena and I got married, my mother sent my sister to Greece for vacation, all because some American boy showed an interest in her and my mom didn't want what happened to me to happen to her daughter. It's been twenty-five years since she went there. She now has a husband and four kids, and she's only been back to visit twice. That's okay. She's happy and I'm very happy for her. I was a young man full of hate, anger, fear, prejudice, and ugly stinking thinking until I was twenty-six years old and I received Jesus as my Lord and Savior and He showed me grace.

The process began in November of 1986 and is still going on today. I learned the hard way that all those learned attitudes just don't disappear when you get saved. The first two hurdles of ethnicity and racism kind of led me to automatically fall into the next obstacle of anti-Semitism. This third hurdle for me to get over was to accept the Jewish people as necessary to reestablish a relationship with God. God had to separate a people from the rest of the corrupted bloodline of the now-pagan world. God had to find a group of people undefiled by generational and national curses and to set up a people that revered Him (Jehovah God) as their one and only true God. God needed to find a righteous and mindfully conscious people that would adhere to His commands and His future rules of family lineage, marriage, food, cleanliness, and the priesthood, and only the pre-Jewish Hebrew people led by Abram were willing to meet these criteria. This was necessary to have a royal, legal bloodline as well as a holy priesthood to usher in the Messiah. It was not only required that the Messiah be of the lineage of King David, but He had to also be a high priest after the order of Melchizedek. Hebrews 4:14-16

The God I believed in was inherently different from the God of Israel. Sure I believed in God, but I didn't know Him as Israel's God too. I knew He was the same God, but because of Jesus, He was different. Somehow He was just mine and just the Greek Orthodox God, but I couldn't put the two together. I ignored the fact that the whole foundation of our belief system in the Greek Orthodox church was based on what the Hebrews had recorded as the history of creation in the Torah (first five books of the Bible). Somehow He was different. He was the God that I saw on TV and in movies, but I owned Him because He was the Greek Orthodox God, and that Old Testament stuff was the ancient history of the Jews.

We Greek Orthodox church people were better than anyone else. We Greeks wrote the book. Come on now. We were first, we are the best, the closest to God because of who we were, and you know the Bible was written in Greek, by Greeks. My ignorance of biblical history is embarrassing now and smacks of replacement theology and anti-Semitism. You can replace any denomination in its place—Catholic, Methodist, Lutheran, or Baptist—it's all the same replacement theology, just a different denomination. The God of the Bible is not exclusive to any one Christian denomination but inclusive to all who receive Jehovah as creator God and Jesus as their Lord and Savior. The only stipulation is to ignore any of the added non-biblical Scriptures, such as the supplemental writings of *The Book of Mormon* by Joseph Smith (1829) and Jehovah Witnesses in *The Pain Truth* (1870s), both of which I believe are about a different God and a different Jesus respectively.

What both of these groups teach is a perversion of the true gospel, and they are not true Christians but imposters perpetrating their lies (another gospel) to truly hungry seekers of the truth.

> Neither give heed to fables and endless genealogies, which minister questions, rather than godly edifying which is in faith: so do. (1 Timothy 1:4)

> But though we, or an angel from heaven, preach any other
> gospel unto you than that which we have preached unto you,
> let him be accursed. As we said before, so say I now again, If
> any man preach any other gospel unto you than that ye have
> received, let him be accursed. (Galatians 1:8–9)

Everything written after the death of the last apostle is open to scrutiny and further examination as to its validity. Islam began in AD 670, the Mormon Church was formed in 1830, and the Jehovah Witnesses began in the 1870s. All three of these religions were started generations after the last apostle of Jesus died. The Jews wrote the Bible (Old Testament); Jesus was a Jew, and He spoke only to the house of Israel while on this earth. Every Christian denomination thinks that they are the only ones that got it right. The truth is that the early church was made up of converted Jews and pagan Gentiles who got the most important eternal truth correct in John 14:6: "Jesus saith unto him, I am the way, the truth, and the life: no man cometh unto the Father, but by me."

These other non-Christian religions all profess to have private knowledge of what to teach about Abraham (Islam) and later Jesus Christ (LDS and JW's) . Unfortunately, they all neglected to continue on from the gospel of John into the book of Acts as their guide on the gift of the Holy Spirit with the evidence of speaking in tongues: "And they were *all* filled with the Holy Ghost, and began to speak with other tongues, as the Spirit gave them utterance" (Acts 2:4, emphasis added). *All* in the Word of God means *all* people, converted Jews and pagan Gentiles who witnessed the miracles of Jesus and His ascension into heaven.

I do believe the subsequent early church leadership in the second and third centuries were too interested in power and control of the people to continue on with preaching the good news of salvation and eternal life as preached by Jesus, than to allow the common man and woman to receive this individual power and authority from on high promised in the Word of God. The baptism of the Holy Spirit is for all believers who repent and ask to receive. In Acts 1:8, Jesus says,

> But *you* shall receive power, after that the Holy Ghost is come upon *you*: and *you* shall be witnesses unto me both in Jerusalem, and in all Judaea, and in Samaria, and unto the uttermost part of the earth. (emphasis added)

It's kind of funny, because I don't think God says you receive power in His Word and then limits access of His promised gifts to a select few, but rather the God of creation gives liberally to all who knock and seek. Nowhere in the Word does it say that there is only one denomination or that only that particular church has the ability to interpret Scripture. Nowhere does it say in Scripture that Foursquare Pentecostals should stand over here, Baptists stand here, Greek Orthodox stand here, and Roman Catholics should be over there because you're special etc., etc.. As long as you receive Jesus as your personal Lord and Savior, you're in; the rest is up to you—which is what the rest of this book is all about.

I do believe that sincere men and women of God received revelation about a particular issue, and they then based their whole denominational belief system around it, regardless if that new perceived revelation was corroborated by Scripture or not. Whether it is on the clothing and jewelry worn by parishioners; the adherence to church rules and traditions mandated by church leadership; or prayers to angels, dead saints, and the Virgin Mary, none of these are repeated or validated in Scripture. Take special note of this statement: none of the above traditions are found in Scripture. None, nada, zero, zilch; they ain't there! There are a number of scriptures that the Catholic and Orthodox churches both chose to ignore like Matthew 23:9 "And call no man your father upon the earth: for one is your Father, which is in heaven".

I do believe that what the Holy Spirit–inspired Word of God is saying to every man, woman, and child is to read and learn on their own about Jesus, but I also believe that the Holy Spirit was telling these men and women in dreams and visions what to do with their own individual walls and gates of their souls. What they then did was to push their own personal sense of religiosity and private interpretation as god inspired revelation onto everyone else, becoming very legalistic, similar to what the Pharisees of Israel did. God does have requirements that you must adhere to, but you must first show love and humility in everything else you do in this life. I knew of the Father, Son, and Holy Spirit as the triune God from the Greek Church, but I didn't understand it all; I just accepted it as fact.

I was completely ignorant of the nature of God, of who Jesus was historically, or who or what the Holy Spirit was and is to us now. I had never been taught that Jesus was the express image of the Hebrew God, Jehovah, or that the Holy Spirit was the third person of the Trinity and given to us all who believe in Jesus and that at Jesus' ascension, the Holy Spirit became available to each of us today by just asking for Him.

> Then Peter said unto them, Repent, and be baptized every one of you in the name of Jesus Christ for the remission of sins, and *ye shall receive the gift of the Holy Ghost.* For the promise is unto you, and to your children, and to all that are afar off, even as many as the LORD our God shall call. (Acts 2:38–39, emphasis added)

Joel 2:28–29 tells us in the Old Testament,

> And it shall come to pass afterward, that I will pour out my spirit upon all flesh; and your sons and your daughters shall prophesy, your old men shall dream dreams, your young men shall see visions: And also upon the servants and upon the handmaids in those days will I pour out my spirit.

In 1 John 5:7 in the New Testament, the Trinity is explained to all believers "For there are three that bear record in heaven, the Father, the Word, and the Holy Ghost: and these three are one."

Regarding the Old Testament, I had never heard that not only was it prophesied some seven hundred years before the Messiah's incarnation as it spoke of His virgin birth in Isaiah 7:14 and 9:6–7 in the Old Testament, but it also prophesized that Jesus would be killed by a not yet invented form of torture and murder. "Crucifixion" as described in Psalms in the Old Testament one thousand years before the birth of Jesus.

Therefore the Lord himself shall give you a sign; Behold, a virgin shall conceive, and bear a son, and shall call his name Immanuel. (Isaiah 7:14)

For unto us a child is born, unto us a son is given: and the government shall be upon his shoulder: and his name shall be called Wonderful, Counsellor, The mighty God, The everlasting Father, The Prince of Peace. Of the increase of his government and peace there shall be no end, upon the throne of David, and upon his kingdom, to order it, and to establish it with judgment and with justice from henceforth even for ever. The zeal of the LORD of hosts will perform this. (Isaiah 9:6–7)

I am poured out like water, and all my bones are out of joint: my heart is like wax; it is melted in the midst of my bowels. My strength is dried up like a potsherd; and my tongue cleaveth to my jaws; and thou hast brought me into the dust of death. For dogs have compassed me: the assembly of the wicked have inclosed me: *they pierced my hands and my feet.* I may tell all my bones: they look and stare upon me. They part my garments among them, and cast lots upon my vesture. (Psalm 22:14–18, emphasis added)

And then He was also prophesied to heal us:

Surely he hath borne our griefs, and carried our sorrows: yet we did esteem him stricken, smitten of God, and afflicted. But he was wounded for our transgressions, he was bruised for our iniquities: the chastisement of our peace was upon him; and with his stripes we are healed. (Isaiah 53:4–5)

I was not only amazed at these prophetic writings in the Old Testament, but I was also a little upset that these Scriptures were never taught to us in the Greek church or that the New Testament was based on them. Why was the fact that Jesus was a Jew never really taught to us? Why was the truth of our belief in the Jewish Messiah ignored and overlooked, with no connection to the Jews of the Old Testament, or that the Father of Jesus we pray to had actually come to us through the Hebrew people? I never knew that the Old Testament was relevant today and that without it; the New Testament makes no sense as you read it. Through reading Scripture completely and without prejudice, I concluded that Israel was and still is the apple of God's eye.

> For thus saith the LORD of hosts; After the glory hath he sent
> me unto the nations which spoiled you: for he that toucheth
> you toucheth the apple of his eye. (Zechariah 2:8)

I don't understand their position in the New Jerusalem but I do know that His Word says that the Hebrew will be rewarded for their obedience. When I attended church, there was only a New Testament Bible in the pew. I have just learned that recently some Greek churches have now added the Old Testament. I just assumed that it wasn't needed and that the Old Testament was for the Jews' history only and not for us Christians. The pride and superiority of the Greek heritage and traditions of the church and family precluded me from ever entertaining the thought of marrying a non-Greek woman or attending a non-Greek Orthodox church—both of which I did and do now; thank You, Jesus. My eyes were gradually opened to the love and grace that God has for all men and women regardless of sex, race, or ethnicity. His Word says in Romans 3:22–23,

> Even the righteousness of God which is by faith of Jesus
> Christ unto *all* and upon *all* them that believe: for there is no
> difference: Even the righteousness of God which is by faith
> of Jesus Christ unto *all* and upon *all* them that believe: for
> there is no difference. (emphasis added)

And in the context of this thought, Romans 2:11 says, "For there is no respect of persons with God."

The more I read the Bible, the clearer and clearer it became to me that God had to find someone to listen to Him. There are three instances in Romans 11 alone that state that God is not finished with the Jews, and because of their prejudice, God grafted the Gentile believers into that Jewish tree lineage. We need to understand that had not Abram listened to God and separated himself from his father and the people of Ur, God could not have begun the process of restoring His greatest creation of all—man. To the chagrin of our entire disillusioned, tree-hugging, insect-loving, global warming, Darwinian evolutionist intellectuals, there is an intelligent, loving designer God who has written in His Word a plan to return man to the place he was prior to the fall of Adam and Eve. God wants to prepare a people to rule and reign with His Son, Jesus Christ of Nazareth, during the prophesied millennium. The fact that the Jews wouldn't accept Jesus only opened the door for the gentiles and the Jew today is no different than any other non-believer needing salvation.

God would accomplish this by preparing a bride for the soon coming Bridegroom King, Son Jesus Christ, through whom I believe is with the preparation of our individually restored and healed souls that protects our born-again spirit temple. Had it not been for Abram hearing from God with his spiritual ears and obeying Him by separating himself from the rest of the world, we would not have been able to connect with the creator of everything. Because of his obedience, the Son of God could become the Son of Man so that the sons of men could become the sons of God.

This book is what I believe the Holy Spirit revealed to me on what is needed by all believers in Jesus Christ, regardless of denomination, to attain Christlikeness in the spirit to rule and reign with Him. I am well aware that many believers in the risen Christ discount many sections of Scripture because of their long-held denominational doctrines, but my contention in writing this book is for you to discard those denominational blinders. Take them off for a few hours and read what Scripture really says, and most of all what Jesus says about these last days we live in now. Read the truth of the Word, pray for the peace of Jerusalem, and most of all, prepare your hearts and prepare your household if the Lord tarries. Be strong, be ever learning, and most of all, be ever faithful to our Lord and Savior Jesus Christ of Nazareth.

Chapter 3

TAKE YOUR DENOMINATIONAL BLINDERS OFF

The first two thousand years outlined in Genesis 1–12 is the age of conscience, and because man could not live by his conscience alone, God needed to find a man to reestablish a theocratic government designed by Him (Elohim). It is really very simple: through this one man's obedience (Abram), we can believe in the one and only true God again. Thus began the process through Abram and his progeny to learn how we can again return to fellowship with God the Father. I believe the Bible to be the true, complete history according to the oldest and most complete account of mankind's original sin and his ability to spiritually connect and communicate with the God of all creation.

Torah, according to Jewish tradition, is the first five books of the Old Testament: Genesis, Exodus, Leviticus, Numbers, and Deuteronomy. These writings were dictated by God to Moses, word by word, in the forty years he and the Jews wandered in the desert. *Torah* translated is "The Light of God," and these historical records are the only real continuous account of the creation of this universe, this world, and man that is available to all of mankind. It alone takes into account all the aspects of man's thoughts and actions with the resulting consequences.

Not only was man created to use his five natural senses of sight, hearing, taste, touch, and smell, but I believe that God gave him at least these five senses in the spiritual realm as well. Using his five spiritual senses along with his five natural senses, Adam was able to communicate and commune with all his whole living "spirit" being with God. Since God is a Spirit, I believe that He intended for us to communicate with Him in spirit (Holy Spirit baptism), soul (verbal prayer), and body (physical service). When Adam and Eve sinned, their eyes were opened in the natural alone, and the glory Adam and Eve wore for their clothing in the Holy Spirit departed. Through this so-called enlightenment, Satan had enticed Eve to rebel and disobey God's only rule. Rebellion's consequence was nothing like she had supposed, and after convincing Adam to rebel with her, it was quite the opposite of what Satan had promised, with immediate and eternal consequences for each of them and all of mankind as well. Their spiritual senses were diminished with their sin, resulting in God's plan being delayed for some two thousand years by Satan's scheme. The result of their rebellion left them feeling dirty, humiliated, and ashamed. Man cowers in the presence of a Holy God, and if not for His Son's shed blood on the cross, man could not stand before Him. God could see Adam and Eve's shameful guilt, and their fear was evident as they tried to cover themselves and hide from God.

> And they heard the voice of the LORD God walking in the garden in the cool of the day: and Adam and his wife hid themselves from the presence of the LORD God amongst the trees of the garden. And the LORD God called unto Adam, and said unto him, Where art thou? And he said, I heard thy voice in the garden, and *I was afraid*, because I was naked; and I hid myself. (Genesis 3:8–10, emphasis added)

Rebellion, accusation, resentment, envy, and bitterness were the first sins I believe man committed, and after their rebellion, shame and guilt compounded them. Man has tried ever since then to hide himself from God. Man's feeble attempts to explain his now-excluded station with God was and still is to ignore Him or His very existence through his intellect and emotions.

This Adamic sin nature was next seen in Adam and Eve's first children, Cain and Abel, as they both brought an offering to God. The Bible says that both brothers brought offerings of their first fruits in Genesis 4:4–5, and Cain became angry when his offering was not received by God because, as the Bible says, "he had not respect." Cain had an attitude problem, and it seems as though he gave the offering from the first fruits of his labors grudgingly, and he became angry when God called him out on his attitude. God didn't want Cain's offering if he was going to give it resentfully and with disrespectfulness in his attitude. There was no honor, and his childish pride was very similar to the attitude that our children have when they are told to do something they really don't want to do.

Even today as adults, when we're told to work or do something we really don't want to do, when we've finished the task, it is either incomplete or done with the disrespectful disdain that Cain had. This attitude is precisely what displeased God with his offering. This is exactly how God sees our tithes and offerings when we give to the ministry grudgingly or from a false sense of obligation in service. Cain talked with his brother Abel and became angry; he allowed his thoughts to run wild with envy, pride, and jealousy—so much so, that his anger turned to rage and he killed Abel. God could smell Cain's vile perverseness, and hear his wicked and evil thoughts of jealousy, envy, bitterness, rivalry, strife, and murder. God could feel the pain of loss of Abel. Genesis 4:10 says, "And he said; What hast thou done? the voice of thy brother's blood cries unto me from the ground."

Everything we do in this life follows this same scrutiny with God. Our motives, our intents, our actions, and our reactions all follow this same story line written some six thousand years ago, and only the written Word of Jehovah God speaks to them. The Word of God alone covers every area of our lives, giving the consequences and solutions through examples and situations of a people ... the Hebrew people. God's desire was and still is for us to rebuild our relationship with Him first through acknowledging Jehovah God as Creator of this existence, and then through His Son, Jesus Christ our Redeemer, to carry us into eternity. It has taken six thousand years for mankind to live and learn to walk in the spirit again, to bring us to the point through our belief in the Father, the sacrifice of His Son, Jesus Christ, and the baptism of the Holy Spirit for us to be spiritually where I believe Adam was before the fall.

> If we live in the Spirit, let us also walk in the Spirit. Let us not be desirous of vain glory, provoking one another, envying one another. (Galatians 5:25–26)

When God created man, He created him "alone" and immediately put him to work. I don't really know how long he was alone, naming all the animals and plants, but some theologians believe that a portion of the missing 229 years of the 6,000-year total Hebrew calendar are found here in Scripture and were needed to round out the Jewish calendar of today's date which is now the year 5771 (2011). I too believe most of these years were spent with Adam in two time frames before the fall in Genesis 3:6. Firstly, Adam was alone to dress and have dominion Genesis 1:26 to keep and name everything, and the second part (Genesis 2:15, 19–20) was with Eve before they sinned in Genesis 3:6. I believe that this accounts for the 229 years needed to begin the first millennium of the Jewish calendar. I really don't know for sure, but I do know God's use of numbers is perfect, and any way you calculate all the years and genealogies from creation to now, you're still short +/- 229 years.

> And the LORD God took the man, and put him into the garden of Eden to dress it and to keep it. ... And out of the ground the LORD God formed every beast of the field, and every fowl of the air; and brought them unto Adam to see what he would call them: and whatsoever Adam called every living creature, that was the name thereof. And *Adam gave names to all cattle, and to the fowl of the air, and to every beast of the field*; but for Adam there was not found an help meet for him. And the LORD God caused a deep sleep to fall upon Adam, and he slept: and he took one of his ribs, and closed up the flesh instead thereof; And the rib, which the LORD God had taken from man, made he a woman, and brought her unto the man. (Genesis 2:15, 19–22; emphasis added)

> And when the woman saw that the tree was good for food,
> and that it was pleasant to the eyes, and a tree to be desired
> to make one wise, she took of the fruit thereof, and did eat,
> and gave also unto her husband with her; and he did eat.
> (Genesis 3:6)

Adam sinned for the same reasons we sin today, and that is because of our desire for the relationship, companionship, and approval from another person. He desired Eve more than he desired his relationship, companionship, and approval from God, and the Hebrew calendar, I agree, began 5,771 years ago when he first sinned and fell from grace.

I believe Adam didn't want to be alone again like he had been for two hundred plus years, seeing every creature with a mate except him. Not until Genesis 2:18 was Eve created to be his helpmeet and companion. Before Eve's creation, he had never experienced the love of another person, and Eve was created *from* him and *for* him alone, so he listened to Eve to please her. His love for Eve was selfish and shortsighted, and together their desire to have the unknown and forbidden caused the downfall of all mankind, even after God had warned Adam not to eat of this one particular tree in Genesis 2:16–17. Because of his sin, he could no longer have a spiritual personal relationship with God on the same level as before, for Jehovah is a Holy God. He would not allow Adam's now-sinful nature to enter His presence, and Adam could not remain in the garden.

> Therefore the LORD God sent him forth from the Garden
> of Eden, to till the ground from whence he was taken. So he
> drove out the man; and he placed at the east of the garden of
> Eden Cherubims, and a flaming sword which turned every
> way, to keep the way of the tree of life. (Genesis 3:23–24)

So, Adam and Eve were separated from God just like I believe that we will be inhibited from entering some areas of the future kingdom of Jesus because of our attitudes, moods and ulterior motives that we retain even after we're saved. This separation was further enhanced with Adam's children and many of these same choices to honor and worship of a God they could not see with their natural eyes only brought doubt and unbelief to enter in without Jesus and the Holy Spirit. The relationship and fellowship prior to the fall could never be attained again. With the reestablishing of knowing Jehovah God through Abraham, Jesus Christ, and the Holy Spirit as the predominate force in men and women's lives we all can begin to be reconnected with Creator God on a spiritual level. Adam and his future progeny were spiritually blind and corrupt, and it took four thousand years of the flood, Nimrod, Abraham, Moses, David, the coming of our Lord Jesus Christ with the baptism of the Holy Spirit to get us back to where Adam was before he forfeited his legal rights to what God had given him. Everything changed when man, the pinnacle of God's creation, had given Satan legal right and authority to the earth through his disobedience. The earth and everything in it was cursed because of Adam and Eve. Still, God tries to allow us to freely choose Him as God. Because God loves us so much, He has given us free will and the right to choose. Either to accept Him or not, we have been given the choice if we want to follow Him and His commands or not. It is your choice! Otherwise we would have been created as robots, worshipping Him without really a choice. As our spiritual Father, God desires us to love Him not from duty or obligation but rather for us to love Him because He first loved us.

If a man say, I love God, and hateth his brother, he is a liar: for he that loveth not his brother whom he hath seen, how can he love God whom he hath not seen? And this commandment have we from him, That he who loveth God love his brother also. (1 John 4:19–21)

As a child reciprocates their love to their parents because they want to, not out of a sense of requirement or obligation, we too are to love all our brothers in Christ as well that love God. When Abram first heard God's call, he did so in his spirit. Because of this obedience, he attained the ability to see and hear Jehovah God with his spiritual ears and eyes. This was an act of unparalleled faith. We are all designed with five natural senses and also with the same number of spiritual senses to commune with Him spiritually and the purpose of writing this is so that all believers in the risen Christ can reacquire all that was lost through Adam's fall, _regardless of Christian denomination_.

It has taken man almost six thousand years to return to the original state of Adam before the fall, when he could see, hear, taste, touch, and smell the goodness of God as he walked and talked with the Creator of all things in the Spirit. Through this process of six-thousand+/- years, there have been many spiritually righteous men and women who heard God and saw His angels, but their righteousness and faith had to be exceptional. Once Adam sinned, our spiritual hard drive was corrupted, very similar to how our personal home computers can be corrupted by a virus. We were all born in sin and have to be taught how to be good, not at all what the child psychologists of today say: "For all have sinned, and come short of the glory of God" (Romans 3:23).

You don't have to teach a child how to lie, cheat, steal, or to be bad, but you do have to teach them how to be good, compassionate, and sympathetic. Our minds and hearts are corrupted with the Adamic virus at birth, and through a lifetime of sin and tragedy, our hearts and thoughts get more evil and more corrupted as we experience life's tragedies. When Adam fell, he gave Satin legal authority to all the earth, including mankind, and Satan was given free rein to corrupt man's heart and his progenies' spiritual hearts. All of mankind's hard drives are corrupted at birth and have been diminishing spiritually ever since. Scripture calls this the Adamic nature: "Wherefore, as by one man sin entered into the world, and death by sin; and so death passed upon all men, for that all have sinned" (Romans 5:12).

When sin is introduced into our minds, it allows Satan to influence our hearts with the evil and corrupt thoughts he presents to our natural senses, which we then entertain. Now that Satan has found an access route to our minds, he can enter our hearts through the corrupted hard drives of our minds (soul walls). He now gives men and women thoughts of bitterness, accusation, rejection, fear, hatred, and perversion to corrupt everything that was and is pure.

Along with the process, God had to begin to teach us how to commune with Him once again in the Spirit. It has also taken this long for us to begin to learn how to clean our hard drives of the corruption of the flesh we each have learned and allowed to become a part of us. It has taken man these two thousand years to learn how to identify these problems and reboot all of our physical and spiritual senses with the teachings of Jesus. He alone can clean us up with the renewing of our minds. The blood of Jesus alone can evict the sin in our hearts and then fill us up with the Holy Spirit again, but we alone can initiate this. A study of the word *renews* reveals the only way man can ever commune again with a holy God on a spiritual level is when we're born again and filled with the Holy Spirit.

> That ye put off concerning the former conversation the old man, which is corrupt according to the deceitful lusts; And be *renewed* in the spirit of your mind. (Ephesians 4:22–23, emphasis added)

> For which cause we faint not; but though our outward man perish, yet the inward man is *renewed* day by day. (Colossians 3:10, emphasis added)

> I beseech you therefore, brethren, by the mercies of God, that ye present your bodies a living sacrifice, holy, acceptable unto God, which is your reasonable service. And be not conformed to this world: but be ye transformed by the *renewing* of your mind, that ye may prove what is that good, and acceptable, and perfect, will of God. (Romans 12:1–2, emphasis added)

It is so important; it is repeated over and over again. Once you get saved and are forgiven by the Father, then you can begin to rebuild and reoccupy the open areas of your soul and renew your mind with the Holy Spirit and the Word of God. You are called into the kingdom by the Holy Spirit, you reboot with the Holy Spirit, you are filled with the Holy Spirit, you are baptized by the Holy Spirit, and the Spirit will fall upon you after you are baptized in the Holy Spirit, renewing your mind by receiving your personal prayer language. You can now begin to rebuild the walls of your soul to protect your born-again spirit. Now we can commune and worship the lover of our souls in spirit and truth, the one and only living God, YHVH (Jehovah).

> And I appeared unto Abraham, unto Isaac, and unto Jacob, by the name of God Almighty, but by my name JEHOVAH was I not known to them. (Exodus 6:3)

You may not agree with this claim, but it is my desire that you do and regardless of denomination you personally correct your soul walls and learn to walk in Christ likeness. John 4:24 God is a Spirit: and they that worship him must worship him in spirit and in truth.

It is vitally important to completely remove any and all thoughts of racism, anti-Semitism, and any religious traditions that may influence your acceptance of this explanation. The King James Version of the Bible continuously says that the hearts of men are what God looks at and judges us on. What we see, hear, taste, touch, and smell influences the heart by way of the mind. The Bible alone tells us in both the Old and New Testaments that the hearts of man can be corrupted and deceived as well as be swayed and coerced by this world. Know that our natural senses dictate most if not all of our actions. We are taught and demanded of to adhere to the physical laws and dictates of men who govern over us but only God's Word speaks of the heart and its motivation and intents.

For the purpose of this writing, all references to Scripture are from the King James 1611 Version of the Bible. All study and references are based on the Hebrew and Greek translations of the Word in this translation, and I believe that every word, comma, and period is intended to be exactly where it is in this version. Of course, amplification and exposition of words only add to our understanding, and my greatest desire is to study the Word and show myself approved using this unadulterated translation. I am not a theologian or scholar in the Hebrew or Greek language in any stretch of the imagination; however, I am a child of the living God: saved, sanctified, and filled with the Holy Spirit. This same Holy Spirit who ministered to Stephen, Philip, Ananias, and Paul, is available to you and me today (Acts 7–9). These are the credentials I base these writings on. My entire life has led me to completely believe that the unadulterated 1611 version of these Scriptures are the Word of God. I believe it is entirely Holy Spirit–inspired and written, and that many of the newer translations may be academically correct, but not Holy Spirit–inspired. Over six thousand words have been changed or omitted from the NIV version and because of this it is unreliable for serious study. Out of all of the sciences and explanations, the theories and ideas given by so-called scholars, academics, and scientists, only the Holy Word of the living God has proven to heal any and every situation and problem. Only the Word (Jesus) can change a life without treatment and drugs or deliver us from them. Only Jesus can mend a broken heart, only Jesus teaches us to love our enemies, and only Jesus can lead us to the Father God Jehovah again.

> Jesus saith unto him, I am the way, the truth, and the life: *no* man cometh unto the Father, but by me. (John 14:6, emphasis added)

As we look for answers in creation, we are struck with two diametrically opposing explanations of how this life all began. One is the following of the tradition of the historic Judeo-Christian account of creation in Genesis, and the other is a relatively new theory called Darwinian evolution. I will try to explain later the reasons this theory is propagated today and so vehemently adhered to by secular academia and scientists of today.

This book "the Bible " is also a theory, but a theory based on the truth as I see it from the Judeo-Christian perspective, which is the basis of my belief system. When confronted with the idea of whether there is or isn't a God and if there is or isn't a purpose to this life we live, I choose to believe in the resurrected Jesus Christ of Nazareth for the answers to these questions. I have chosen to ignore the theory of evolution alone, and I cleave unto what I believe is confirmation of the Word of the living God and of all creation that is confirmed in science made by Him and for Him.

> In the beginning was the Word, and the Word was with God, and the Word was God. The same was in the beginning with God. All things were made by him; and without him was not anything made that was made. In him was life; and the life was the light of men. And the light shineth in darkness; and the darkness comprehended it not. (John 1:1–5)

I believe that Jesus Christ is the only begotten Son of the Father Jehovah (Judeo-Christian God), born of a virgin (Jewish girl), and that at His resurrection from the dead, He (the Jewish Messiah) ascended to heaven and is seated at the right hand of the Father (Hebrew God). That at His ascension (leaving earth), Jesus sent the Comforter (the Holy Spirit—the third person of the Trinity), who abides in us and with us.

> For there are three that bear record in heaven, the Father, the Word, and the Holy Ghost: and these three are one. (1 John 5:7)

Chapter 4

THE AGE OF CONSCIENCE

*T*his book, I believe, will show you the reader that God loves you and that His intent for us is to be complete in the Father, Son, and Holy Spirit—the triune creator God. Scripture tells us that God designed us both as physical and spiritual beings with a spirit and soul that are both held in a body. A triune being (spirit, soul, and body) and is an idea that is reiterated throughout Old and New Testament Scripture. Our spirit is eternal, our soul determines its eternal location, and what we do while in that eternal abode is determined while we are alive here on earth.

> And Hannah answered and said, No, my lord, I am a woman of a sorrowful *spirit*: I have drunk neither wine nor strong drink, but have poured out my *soul* before the LORD. (1 Samuel 1:15, emphasis added)

> And the very God of peace sanctify you wholly; and I pray God your whole *spirit and soul and body* be preserved blameless unto the coming of our Lord Jesus Christ. (1 Thessalonians 5:23, emphasis added)

> For the word of God is quick, and powerful, and sharper
> than any two edged sword, piercing even to the dividing
> asunder of *soul and spirit,* and of the *joints and marrow,* and
> *is a discerner of the thoughts and intents of the heart.* (Hebrews
> 4:12, emphasis added)

His Word shows us how to heal our broken and damaged souls and prepares us as the bride of Christ to then rule and reign with Him in the millennial kingdom.

God is not a man but is a spirit, and in the Spirit, He communes with man: "God is not a man, that he should lie; neither the son of man, that he should repent" (Numbers 23:19).

In the natural world, it is difficult for us to understand or even believe in the spiritual because our five natural senses are so completely in control of our being. God is considered abstract or supernatural, which is my point exactly. Prior to the fall of Adam and Eve, God (being spirit) communicated with Adam and Eve spiritually. It seems that Adam saw and heard God's glory with his natural eyes but heard His voice *spiritually.* I believe he communed with God supernaturally with his spiritual senses and could physically sense His presence. It seems as though they didn't need to communicate with God using any of the five physical senses at all and were only aware of them after they sinned. Once Adam and Eve disobeyed God and ate of the Tree of Knowledge of Good and Evil, that all changed, and time as we know it began and God's divine week began as outlined in Genesis.

Again, if you calculated all the years from the creation of Adam to now, it only adds up to 5,771 years, which means that if the year today is 2011, then we have 229 years left until the completion of biblical history. Like I said earlier, this means Adam lived for the most part of these two hundred twenty nine years on his own and then with Eve for the remainder of these years in a perfect world before they sinned and the Hebrew calendar began after they sinned. Their natural eyes were opened and their spiritual eyes were closing or closed completely, depending on how much of the natural fleshly lust dominated their soul.

> And the *eyes* of them both were opened, and they *knew* that
> they were naked; and they sewed fig leaves together, and
> made themselves aprons. And they *heard* the voice of the
> LORD God walking in the garden in the cool of the day:
> and Adam and his wife hid themselves from the presence of
> the LORD God amongst the trees of the garden. (Genesis
> 3:7–8, emphasis added)

Apparently Adam and Eve's natural eyes were opened to see in the natural
only and the rebellion and spiritual corruption that God could see was turning
off the spiritual senses, so to speak.

> And the LORD God said, Behold, the man is become as
> one of us, to know good and evil: and now, lest he put forth
> his hand, and take also of the tree of life, and eat, and live
> forever. (Genesis 3:22)

They still heard the voice of God walking in the garden, so their spiritual
senses were not completely shut off. They were afraid because they were
standing spiritually and physically naked before a God they now knew could
see their rebellious hearts. Adam could see and hear naturally, and they felt
fear and shame in their spirits for the first time in the presence of a Holy God.
Apparently God's presence could be heard naturally as well as seen spiritually.
Adam knew God could see through him and see his corrupted heart. Because
of Satan's taunts and tempting's, Adam and Eve had questioned God's
motivation for forbidding them to eat of the Tree of Knowledge of Good and
Evil or the Tree of Life.

Genesis 3:22

And the LORD God said, Behold, the man is become as one of us, to know
good and evil: and now, *lest he put forth his hand, and take also of the tree of life,
and eat, and live forever:*KJV

At that point, God tells us that because Adam chose to eat of the forbidden
fruit at Eve's prodding, he was now like a god in that he was able to choose
between good and evil. He had always been able to choose because he had
"free will," but I believe God allowed Satan to tempt Adam and Eve to choose

to disobey. Just like you and I are tempted today and must choose whom we will serve, God allowed Adam and Eve to choose freely. Free will isn't really free will unless you have the freedom to choose wrongly as well.

From this point on, they were to deal with the consequences, which included sickness, suffering, separation, and ultimately death. Free will had always been given to him, but now the consequences of these choices were their responsibility. This action changed everything; no longer was man provided for and fed or protected by God alone. He was cast out of the perfect garden; his supernatural senses were diminishing with each fleshly action taken. Now that his natural senses were increasing, all he had to direct his actions were his knowledge of the past and his conscience as his soul directed his flesh. He now lived in the natural world by which he had to use his natural senses to survive.

I say "alone" because he allowed his feelings and circumstances to dictate his behavior and decisions and not with a personal face to face with God like he had before the fall. God had given him a conscience, but that was limited to his knowledge and memory of right and wrong that he had learned while in God's presence. He had wondered what motivated God to keep two trees from him, and what he got was death.

Today we also have the choice of life or death, righteousness or evil, heaven or hell. There was and is no other way to give man free will without giving him the opportunity to choose freely. The resulting consequences of being good or bad are determined by the motivations of the heart of the living soul. Dealing with the choices made in this life (soul) is explained in Scripture alone, and these actions done with evil or selfish intentions lead to eternal damnation, or at the very least, the loss of eternal rewards if not done in godly love.

God could see the true intent of the heart of Adam and Eve, and He can see our motives and intentions as well. He could not allow their sin to be in His presence just as He can't allow ours either. God can see our true intentions. He can hear the words we speak in our hearts and minds, and we too will be judged accordingly by them. Not for our salvation but for our rewards at the "bema" seat for believers

2 Cor. 5:10. As a consequence of their disobedience and rebellion, Adam and Eve were cast out of the garden and punished—Adam to sweat and toil for sustenance, and Eve to greatly multiply her sorrows in bearing children.

> Unto the woman he said, I will greatly multiply thy sorrow and thy conception; in sorrow thou shalt bring forth children; and thy desire shall be to thy husband, and he shall rule over thee. And unto Adam he said, Because thou hast hearkened unto the voice of thy wife, and hast eaten of the tree, of which I commanded thee, saying, Thou shalt not eat of it: cursed is the ground for thy sake; in sorrow shalt thou eat of it all the days of thy life. ... Therefore the LORD God sent him forth from the garden of Eden, to till the ground from whence he was taken. (Genesis 16–17, 23)

Adam had to till the ground that was used to create him. Now in the eulogy given at funerals, "from dust you were taken and to dust you shall return" makes perfect sense. The hardest thing to get your arms around is that Adam was given perfect weather and perfect surroundings in which to live. No rain, cold, or heat. No death, disease, suffering, or pain to endure. Everything for him was perfect; he and Eve lived in a perfect world, had perfect minds, perfect bodies, and had a close loving relationship with the sovereign God Jehovah. Man was left to his own devices, and now Adam and his progeny didn't have God to communicate with on a physical or spiritual level.

Here is where I believe prayer began. Since Adam and Eve were cast out of Eden and physical/spiritual communication between God and Adam had ended, Adam cried out to Jehovah God and verbal prayer alone began. Through verbal prayer, he was able to tap into spiritual communication and commune somewhat with God again. They were left alone with no guidance except their individual consciences to guide them, and only when Adam spoke verbally to God with praise, worship, and homage did he receive an answer. No real issues arose until Cain and Abel were told by their parents to honor God with an offering of the first fruits of their labors.

And Abel, he also brought of the firstlings of his flock and of the fat thereof. And the LORD had respect unto Abel and to his offering: But unto Cain and to his offering he had not respect. And Cain was very wroth, and his countenance fell. And the LORD said unto Cain, Why art thou wroth? and why is thy countenance fallen? If thou doest well, shalt thou not be accepted? and if thou doest not well, sin lieth at the door. And unto thee shall be his desire, and thou shalt rule over him. And Cain *talked* with Abel his brother: and it came to pass, when they were in the field, that Cain *rose up* against Abel his brother, and *slew him*. (Genesis 4:4–8, emphasis added)

Why? What was it that caused God to be so displeased with Cain's offering? Genesis 4:5 tells us, "But unto Cain and to his offering he had not respect. And Cain was very wroth, and his countenance fell." Cain's problems of resentment and rebellion that had begun in his own head and are exactly where your and my problems usually originate from, these soul issues are as old as man. His thoughts and questions in his rationalization and justification for his actions originated in his own thoughts and mind like you and me today. God is omniscient (knowing all things), and He knew what Cain's thoughts were. God not only knows our thoughts, but He knows what the motivation is behind every one of them. God knew that Cain's motivations when he gave alms to God that were not out of a thankful heart for his bountiful harvest but rather from what he thought was a sense of obligation from his parents giving to God and not from him. Genesis tells us in 4:5 that "Cain and to his offering he had no respect. And Cain was very wroth [angry, incensed] and his countenance fell." With Cain, his grain offering came from the labors of his hands (works) and thus was the first aspect as to why his offering was not accepted by God. Secondly, it wasn't *what* he gave but rather *how* he gave the offering to God. He first thought and asked why he should have to give an offering anyways (doubt, uncertainty, reservation, rebellion), and when he thought that God didn't think his offering was good enough, resentment and pride set in.

I believe that this same rational is spiritually present in us today in our tithes and offerings to God. Although today we have Scripture for instruction and a greater advantage than Adam and Cain did respectively because of Jesus' shed blood and atoning sacrifice at the cross, we better understand the price that was paid for our salvation.

Because of Abram's obedience, the lineage of Isaac, Jacob, Joseph, Moses, and the Law were given to the Hebrew nation. Jesus as our High Priest fulfills all the requirements of that law and prepares us spiritually to receive the Holy Spirit. Only after being washed in the blood of Jesus to remit our sins can we be allowed to enter into the Father's presence again (atonement). As I wrote these words and meditated on these Scriptures, I realized that I am also guilty of these same offences that Cain committed with my countenance to my friends, family, and coworkers. To allow your countenance to fall is to carry your heart on your sleeve.

For years I would telegraph my unhappiness, anger, and annoyance with my facial expressions to anyone I came in contact with. Unfortunately, I still do at times to the embarrassment of my wife and the displeasure of my God. I often bragged about how everyone could tell how I felt with family, friends, and employees simply by my facial expression and fallen countenance (not pretty). My boys tell me that my facial expressions are mean and very intimidating (a bad habit) and that as teenagers and young adults, they would tune me out when I ranted, raved, and raised my voice. At work and home, I acted the fool until I had realized that these actions were not pleasing to God. Not only that; but the way I acted destroyed my testimony as a believer to strangers and, more importantly, to my family. The method of how I would get things done with the guys at work really didn't work so well at home (go figure). To my own detriment, the stress and anger I had was slowly killing me and contributing to the deterioration of my immune system. I had lost all my friendships and was a terrible witness of Jesus Christ because of my countenance and short fuse. Stress, anger, jealousy, and pride had telegraphed my displeasure and annoyance of things around me, and the Holy Spirit let me know that these were the same issues that lead Cain to murder his brother Abel.

And the LORD said unto Cain, Why art thou wroth?
and why is thy countenance fallen? If thou doest well,
shalt thou not be accepted? and if thou doest not well, sin
lieth at the door. And unto thee shall be his desire, and
thou shalt rule over him. And Cain talked with Abel his
brother: and it came to pass, when they were in the field,
that Cain rose up against Abel his brother, and slew him.
(Genesis 4:6–8)

In my case, I believe that these same toxic thoughts were what damaged
the myelin sheath of my brain, and only through the grace of God can
I see, walk, talk, and write this book. I knew that the same power that
raised Jesus from the dead, saved me and could heal my soul and body.
I needed to pray, and I needed to pray with power and the authority
of Jesus. As I read the Scriptures of the Old Testament and the New
Testament, it taught me that the God I claimed in the Greek Church
was first claimed by Israel, and if I in my distress needed to get closer
to Jesus, I first needed to get to know who His Father was. I knew that
I had committed my heart to Jesus and invited Him into my heart at
salvation, but I also knew that I had issues and prejudices that were not
pleasing to God the Father, and that my body was in pain and I needed
Him. Everywhere I read in the Word of God, it spoke of the heart, and
in everything I read in the New Testament, I found the same messages
referred to back in the Old Testament.

Jesus said unto them, If God were your Father, ye would love
me: for I proceeded forth and came from God; neither came
I of myself, but *he* sent me. (John 8:42, emphasis added)

For thus saith the LORD of hosts, the God of Israel. ...
Then shall ye call upon me, and ye shall go and pray unto
me, and I will hearken unto you. And ye shall seek me, and
find me, when ye shall search for me with all your heart. call
upon me. (Jeremiah 29:8, 12–13)

If thou prepare thine heart, and stretch out thine hands toward him; If iniquity be in thine hand, put it far away, and let not wickedness dwell in thy tabernacles. (Job 11:13–14)

And he spake a parable unto them to this end, that men ought always to pray, and not to faint. (Luke 18:1)

Let us draw near with a true heart in full assurance of faith, having our hearts sprinkled from an evil conscience, and our bodies washed with pure water. Let us hold fast the profession of our faith without wavering; (for he is faithful that promised). (Hebrews 10:22–23)

You pray from deep within your heart. God sees the true intent and motivation of your heart, and He calls us to come with humility in truth to Him. To ignore the Old Testament because of traditions and prejudice only shows your ignorance of the Word of God and your shortsightedness in your walk with Jesus. The Word of God tells us that He yearns for man to call on Him. Everywhere you read in Scripture, God is calling for His creation to *not* elevate creation above the creator but to honor and revere Him as the great I AM.

If my people, which are called by my name, shall *humble* themselves, and pray, and seek my face, and turn from their wicked ways; then will I hear from heaven, and will forgive their sin, and will heal their land. (2 Chronicles 7:14, emphasis added)

Confess your faults one to another, and pray one for another, that ye may be healed. The effectual fervent prayer of a righteous man availeth much. (James 5:16, emphasis added)

Call unto me, and I will answer thee, and shew thee great and mighty things, which thou knowest not. (Jeremiah 33:3)

Be careful for nothing; but in every thing by prayer and supplication with thanksgiving let your requests be made known unto God. And the peace of God, which passeth all understanding, shall keep your hearts and minds through Christ Jesus. (Philippians 4:6–7, emphasis added)

In every thing give thanks: for this is the will of God in Christ Jesus concerning you. (1 Thessalonians 5:18, emphasis added)

Jesus taught His apostles to pray, and I needed to pray. I then asked the Holy Spirit to show me how to pray, and almost instantly, He showed me the mark of Cain and the comparison of my countenance to Cain's. We will discuss later the power of prayer and how these same principles taught to the apostles applies to our souls today as we speak and explain the blessings afforded all believers through the fruit of the Spirit in our daily walk in that Spirit of God.

The words of Cain in Genesis 4:13 concerning the mark given to him by God for punishment in killing his brother Abel were more of a complaint to God than a prayer. It occurred to me that most prayers are really the same sort of speech to God with us today. Complaining and not repenting for our actions is the usual way we talk to God. God gets blamed for everything, especially for the consequences of our actions. It really isn't prayer; it's complaining about the situation we're currently in and that we can't figure out why God let this happen to us is really our prayer. The fact that Cain did something wrong or that he wasn't sorry for what he did never came up at all; all he did was have a pity party for himself.

Behold, thou hast driven *me* out this day from the face of the earth; and from thy face shall *I* be hid; and *I* shall be a fugitive and a vagabond in the earth; and it shall come to pass, that every one that finds *me* shall slay *me*. (Genesis 4:14, emphasis added)

Me, me, me, I, I, I—poor boy. Can you imagine why this selfish, cold, black-hearted man would think someone would want to kill him in retribution for committing murder? Huhmmm! I asked what the mark was that Cain received, and I saw his dead, dark heart. The simplest and most repulsive explanation is the race one. This narrow-minded, uneducated, and racist explanation for trying to explain the existence of the black race is a totally unfounded theory from the Mormon lie. It was first introduced by the apostate Mormon church in 1847 and later rescinded in 1978 when not corroborated by science or biblical Scripture. My God is not a respecter of persons, and any form of racism or eugenics discounts the individual soul's value to God.

> Then Peter opened his mouth, and said, Of a truth I perceive that God *is no respecter of persons*: But in *every* nation he that feareth him, and worketh righteousness, is accepted with him. (Acts 10:34–35, emphasis added)

In every nation, those who fear God and live in righteousness are accepted by Him. That means that the children of the living God can be brown, red, white, yellow, or any combination of races. To claim that the color of a man's skin is somehow the curse of Cain's actions doesn't take into account the fact that God protected him from any revenge or retribution. Secondly, that all of man was destroyed by the flood save eight souls defuses that thought. To think that somehow Cain's sin was passed on to his innocent progeny beyond the flood is ludicrous.

> And the LORD said unto him, Therefore whosoever slayeth Cain, vengeance shall be taken on him sevenfold. And the LORD set a mark upon Cain, lest any finding him should kill him. (Genesis 4:15)

To believe that a curse was handed down in Scripture can only be seen occurring with Noah's third son, Ham, who dishonored his father's nakedness in Genesis 9:22. Because of that sin, his progeny would be subservient to his two brothers Shem and Japheth (Genesis 9:24–28), and any curse was only in stature at birth and not in free will to rise individually above lesser socioeconomic stature in wealth and education. The mark that was placed on Cain was to protect him, not to curse him. The curse was an even further separation from God than that of his parents, and that was unbearable for him (Genesis 4:13). God still gave him time to think and repent, but I believe God gave him grace and mercy and waited for him to change his mind and repent (like He would with David), but he didn't; his heart was black and remained empty.

This is exactly how the Lord is with us today. He is patient and waits on us to repent and change our minds, moving away from sinful thoughts and actions. One night while meditating on these verses and wondering what the mark of Cain really was, I saw a vision of the people in the movie *Pleasantville*. As they acted out the lust of the flesh in the movie, they turned from black-and-white into vibrant, beautiful colors. In the vision I had, rather than lighting up with colors as the movie characters did when they were "enlightened" and practiced the desires of the flesh (adultery, selfishness, anger, and fornication), people who experienced these things actually lost color. The opposite happened in my vision: evil, hateful bitterness turned the hearts of every sinful man into an ugly, black and white void. The hearts of sinners were blackened, and their black hearts degraded the hues of their natural colors. I could see the pale colorless emptiness of their soul.

It's funny how some of the expressions given to cruel, evil people are actually true—"cold as ice," "heart of stone," "he has a black heart," etc. etc. There is an aura of evil around them just as with Cain's soul. Now his pure-evil heart emitted an aura around him for all to see. This is what I believe happened to Cain—and only Cain, not his children. He was a marked man in that the anger and rage he had for his brother was visible as a void or emptiness for all to see as a warning by God for committing the first murder. I also believe we can sense this evil today as one of the Gifts of the Spirit with the gift of a discerning spirit when the Holy Spirit warns us of impending dangers. 1 Cor. 12:8-11

When the children of Adam and Eve were born, they were born like you and me with a spirit and soul in a living body led by conscience alone with a much lower spiritual understanding than their parents. Every generation since is less spiritual then the previous one until virtually nonexistent, and the flesh completely dominated man's thoughts, heart and soul. Not until Jesus' ascension and the advent of the Holy Spirit with the spiritual baptism are all people able to commune and communicate again in spirit and truth with the God of creation, like I think Adam did before the fall.

Every man and every woman is born a triune being, consisting of a spirit, soul, and a body. The body contains the spirit and soul until the body dies and returns to the dust it was created from. The spirit is the innermost of the three, and our spirit is who we really are. It will never cease to exist; therefore, it is the most important of the three. This is the part of us that is saved at confession. Our soul consists of our thoughts, intellect, knowledge, emotions, and feelings, which together direct and influence our intentions and motivations of the heart. This compilation brings all the aforementioned together, forming our soul, which in turn determines the eternal destination of our eternal spirit. Our temperament and attitudes become habits with all the other aspects of our soul influences and are what direct our thoughts and ultimately our will to act in the flesh if not broken from this vicious cycle. Our will is the formulation of all our thoughts and emotions, and together these two frame our choices to act on which is our free will. This mental and emotional part of our soul's fruit influences our actions and ultimately determines our eternal destination. These feelings can completely dominate our spirit and soul if we allow the flesh to dominate us.

The men and women born between Adam and Noah were much more intelligent than we are today because of their longevity and experiences handed down from generation to generation. Sin in disobedience has shortened man's life span from 900-plus years to less than 120 years, and the wisdom of previous generations is lost. After the fall, man's longevity, intelligence, and spirituality have continually diminished to where we are today. There were some 1,600 years between Adam (4004 BC) and Noah (2350 BC). Many generations of violent, perverted people had forgotten who God was, and as each generation died off they began to live entirely after the lust of the flesh. Murders, sexual perversion, war, and brute strength ruled society and the land.

> The earth also was corrupt before God, and the earth was
> filled with violence. And God looked upon the earth, and,
> behold, it was corrupt; for all flesh had corrupted his way
> upon the earth. (Genesis 6:11–12)

Corruption and rebellion continued to increase in men's hearts until the flood of Noah's time. The first sins that man committed were doubt, fear, and shame, but the number and manifestations of sin increased until all the works of the flesh were evident in all of man except Noah (Genesis 6:9-13). Today every person, male or female, is born into sin and has to be taught to be good and not bad.

> For all have sinned, and come short of the glory of God. … Wherefore, as by one man sin entered into the world, and death by sin; and so death passed upon all men, for that all have sinned. (Romans 3:23; 5:12)

And in 1 Corinthians 15:45–50 (emphasis added):

> And so it is written, The first man Adam was made a living soul; the last Adam was made a quickening spirit. Howbeit that was not first which is spiritual, but that which is natural; and afterward that which is spiritual. The first man is of the earth, earthy: the second man is the Lord from heaven. As is the earthy, such are they also that are earthy: and as is the heavenly, such are they also that are heavenly. And as we have borne the image of the earthy, we shall also bear the image of the heavenly. Now this I say, brethren, that *flesh and blood cannot inherit the kingdom of God.*

Sin reigned in the earth until Noah, when God had endured enough and destroyed all life on the earth and all of mankind, save eight souls. Every civilization has in its antiquity stories of one man building an ark to spare humans and animals from a devastating worldwide flood. Missionaries and sociologists have visited or explored some five hundred different places from around the world which all having similar flood legends. From ancient civilizations in Russia, China, Babylon, and the Americas, to remote areas in Sumatra, Peru, and Polynesia, all have accounts that are similar to the biblical account of Noah and the ark.

God tried again to allow man to live with their conscience and free wills alone, but the people forgot God once more in only 175 years (two generations);

righteousness had been lost, spirituality had died, and God had been replaced by man's brute force and natural idols. Men, animals, and nature were the replacement gods, and most of the history of creation was lost. Again, every civilization in the world today has in its history some record of the flood, which adds to the validity of Noah's flood as recorded in the Bible. Only the Bible speaks of this history as truth and the natural propensity of mankind is to live and yearn after the fleshly desires of the flesh alone. Only the Bible speaks of the perversion evident in Noah's son Ham as he saw his father's nakedness. Many ancient Hebrew scholars concur that verses 9:23–24 of Genesis also refer to one of three explanations of Ham's dishonor and shame brought upon his father.

> And Shem and Japheth took a garment, and laid it upon both their shoulders, and went backward, and covered the nakedness of their father; and their faces were backward, and they saw not their father's nakedness. And Noah awoke from his wine, *and knew what his younger son had done unto him.* (Genesis 9:23–24, emphasis added)

The first explanation is obvious, and that was to leave his father in his nakedness. The second was to announce his nakedness to all; mocking his indiscretion and bringing shame upon him. Thirdly would be the most vile and disgusting act of all, and that would be to take the word of what Ham had "done" to his father by having homosexual relations with him while he was drunk.

> And God saw that the wickedness of man was great in the earth, and that every imagination of the thoughts of his heart was only evil continually. And it repented the LORD that he had made man on the earth, and it grieved him at his heart. (Genesis 6:5–6)

Considering the state of the world prior to the flood itself, the perversion and wickedness of the people that would cause God to want to destroy man must have been evident in Ham as well and makes the latter explanation seem plausible. These writings of man's perversions that were manifest in the thoughts and hearts of man five thousand years ago are the same opinions and judgments God has today toward all manner of unusual sexual practices, and His warnings are just as applicable today.

The next major personalities spoken about in Scripture were the grandsons of Noah and the generations that followed. Nimrod, the great-grandson of Noah, hated God and built the tower of Babel so that he could try to kill God and also high enough so that God could never flood the earth again and destroy the population like He did some two hundred years earlier. He hated God for killing his ancestors, and he wanted to avenge their death. His mindset for rebellion and revenge only added to his hatred of the God of Noah who flooded the earth. His attitude only exemplified in his life that there will always be a person who wants to rebel against God's rules and try to control the whole world without Him. Nimrod was the first but he won't be the last to lust after such supreme earthly power.

I believe the hatred of the Jews (anti-Semitism) began in the Middle East and throughout the world because of his hatred of the God of Noah. As emperor of the Babylonian empire (Iraq), I'm sure he convinced all his serving court that the God of Noah killed all their ancestors in the flood. I'm also sure that those enslaved to build the Tower of Babel under his rule had learned to hate Him (the God of Noah) as well. Nimrod persuaded the people not to credit his kingdom or their happiness in their own lives to Jehovah God but to him. What he did do was to gradually change the government into a tyranny for the sole purpose of turning men from the fear of God and reliance upon Jehovah to be constantly dependent upon his own power and authority. Man had forgotten who the living God of creation was, and their supernatural senses were diminished to being nonexistent. All of creation had become hedonistic and pagan. The Word of God says in Romans that man worshipped creation more than the Creator.

> And changed the glory of the uncorruptible God into an image made like to corruptible man, and to birds, and fourfooted beasts, and creeping things. Wherefore God also gave them up to uncleanness through the lusts of their own hearts, to dishonour their own bodies between themselves:

> Who changed the truth of God into a lie, and worshipped
> and served the creature more than the Creator, who is blessed
> forever. Amen. (Romans 1:23–25)

Mankind is no different today; he refuses to believe in a God who is holy and doesn't allow sin into His presence or even believe that there is sin. God has always tried to speak to man, but the flesh got in the way just like it does today. The Word of God tells us that man was lost and that he had to start over. After the flood, God used a righteous man, Noah, to replenish the earth: "And God blessed Noah and his sons, and said unto them, Be fruitful, and multiply, and replenish the earth" (Genesis 9:1).

All of man except for Noah, his wife, his three sons and their wives, were lost in the flood. Any reference to the mark of Cain was destroyed in the flood, but the sin problem remained. How was God now going to have fellowship with man like He had with Adam prior to the fall? Man's whole being was corrupted. Every aspect of man's being was infected with the virus of sin and rebellion. The complexity of his psyche and the workings of his mind were corrupted by the lust of the flesh just like today and throughout human history. The Word of God calls this corruption "the works of the flesh." Since the fall, the supernatural senses of man had diminished to a point that the flesh dominated his whole being. All the thoughts and the pure intent of the spirit were corrupted, infected, or gone completely.

God had called many men and women through the millennia, but when they heard, they allowed the natural desires of the flesh to dominate the pure thoughts given by God. It had contaminated them with the desires of the flesh and for power; even a worldwide flood couldn't remove the sin and corruption of man's heart. It's no different for us today. The flesh dominated man after Noah, and the flesh dominates us today. Trying to hear from God is kind of like someone trying to whisper to you in a crowded stadium or bus terminal. All the thoughts in your mind of life are crowding out the thoughts coming from God and you are trying to hear His small, still voice through it all. Unless you can get someplace quiet and are able to meditate on His Word, you won't be able to hear Him consistently.

> And after the earthquake a fire; but the LORD was not in
> the fire: and after the fire *a still small voice*. (1 Kings 19:12,
> emphasis added)

God doesn't speak with lightning or thunder; He speaks to us in a small, still voice. Not that we have to empty our minds, but we should clear it up and prioritize our thoughts from any thoughts that might muddle or cause our thoughts to be confused and distracted. It is so easy to be distracted and preoccupied with the things going on around you in your life that your thoughts easily go off on rabbit trails, and before you know it, you're thinking about something completely unrelated to what you started thinking about. It's also easy to be so distracted and preoccupied with life in general that you sometimes don't have time to meditate on the things of God or God's solutions in His Word to the issues you're facing. Know there isn't an issue that God's Word doesn't touch on and or gives an answer to, no matter how difficult that answer may be.

The Devil has a whole arsenal of weapons that he uses to distract us with and get us to lust after the things of the flesh. Sometimes it's the dumbest, craziest things that just pop up in your head and you don't know why or where they came from. There are only three places a thought comes from: you, God, or the Devil. We continually give Satan ammunition by simply entertaining thoughts that are our weak areas in life and by emptying our minds of everything else; this only opens the doors of our thoughts to self and self-gratifying issues of the flesh. The Word of God alone tells us we can counteract these distractions by taking every thought captive and casting them down. Vain imaginings of grandeur and self-indulgences at the expense of others around you only bring short instances of relief but usually leave long-lasting consequences and unresolved issues in their wake.

> Casting down imaginations, and every high thing that
> exalts itself against the knowledge of God, and bringing
> into captivity every thought to the obedience of Christ. (2
> Corinthians 10:5)

Chapter 5

THE APPLE OF GOD'S EYE

The Word of God is unique in that every issue known to effect man's life from before birth to beyond death is all covered in the Judo-Christian Scriptures.

For thou hast possessed my reins: thou hast covered me *in my mother's womb.* I will praise thee; for I am fearfully and wonderfully made: marvelous are thy works; and that my soul knoweth right well. My substance was not hid from thee, when *I was made in secret*, and curiously wrought in the lowest parts of the earth. (Psalm 139:13–15, emphasis added)

The thing that hath been, it is that which shall be; and that which is done is that which shall be done: and *there is no new thing under the sun.* (Ecclesiastes 1:9, emphasis added)

And as it is appointed unto men once to die, but after this the judgment. (Hebrews 9:27)

The lust of the eye and the pride of life are explained in the Bible as the works of the flesh. The works of the flesh include but are not limited to adultery (infidelity), fornication (immoral sexual activities), uncleanness (filthy, dirty), lasciviousness (lewd/erotic actions), idolatry (worship idols or false gods), witchcraft (seductive charm), hatred (loathing), variance (conflict), emulations (duplicating or imitating), wrath (rage/fury), strife (friction), seditions (provoking rebellion), heresies (unorthodox beliefs), envying (jealousy), murders (not in self-defense), drunkenness (drinking in excess), and revelry (to party in excess).

These can be isolated as in one or two acts, but usually they are seen in combination of two or more works of the flesh; usually manifesting in combinations of six, seven, or more works; feeding off each other; building strongholds; and manifesting in our thoughts and actions. Please understand that as we explain and define each one of these works of the flesh, each one has a myriad of lesser seemingly inconsequential thoughts that open doors of desire to each of us. As we tolerate and allow them, usually through entertainment and coarse jesting, it isn't very long before we're enticed to participate and ignore the convictions of the Holy Spirit to not partake in thought or deed.

In His Word, it tells us in Galatians 5:25 that "if we live in the Spirit, let us also walk in the Spirit." God wants us to walk in the Spirit and to live in the Spirit. God desires us to deliberately think and meditate on His Word and to have us live completely in the Spirit of God, consciously choosing to live as He designed us to live prior to the fall of Adam. To be complete in His Spirit, soul, and body. To be in the Spirit is to be in a place of perfect contentment and perfect purpose, utilizing all the natural and spiritual tools God has given every person at salvation. More than that, we are to live in perfect righteousness before God in His will and way. To do this, we must put every natural work of the flesh under subjection of the feet of Jesus.

> I thank God through Jesus Christ our Lord. So then with
> the mind I myself serve the law of God; but with the flesh
> the law of sin. (Romans 7:25)

> Simon Peter, a servant and an apostle of Jesus Christ, to
> them that have obtained like precious faith with us through
> the righteousness of God and our Savior Jesus Christ. ...
> Whereby are given unto us exceeding great and precious
> promises: that by these ye might be partakers of the divine
> nature, having escaped the corruption that is in the world
> through lust. (2 Peter 1:1, 4)

Every thought and every subsequent action Adam and Cain had, had been contaminated and perverted by the desires of the flesh and the works of the flesh. Fear—even if only fleeting—planted the seeds of doubt, unbelief and rebellion.

The ulterior motives, the deep-seated resentments, the whys and why not's, the jealousy, the anger, hatred, rage, and bitterness were all evident. These all must be repented for and atoned for through Jesus, and by the renewing of our mind, we can then begin the process of restoration. We may never act upon these thoughts like Adam, Cain, Nimrod, David, Judas, etc., but the seeds of rebellion are planted there through this "life" we live. They're still there; they are evident in our countenance in our attitudes of lust, envy, resentment, bitterness, and un-forgiveness even after we are saved. The whole purpose of the journey we will encounter in this book is to return us to a position of holiness and righteousness before the Holy God and Ancient of Days in spirit and truth. To return us to a relationship in spirit and soul to our creator God and prepare us in these last days physically and spiritually to meet our fullest potential in service as kings and priests in the new kingdom as the bride of Christ.

The restoration all started with Abram's call to separate himself from his father, Terah, and the idol worshipping he embraced along with the rest of the world. This began a return to a monotheistic (single God) religion that was different from the pagan, hedonistic (self-indulgent), ritualistic religions that inundated the world at that time. Abram was told by God to leave his father's house and lands, and God would show him where to go.

> Now the LORD had said unto Abram, Get thee out of thy
> country, and from thy kindred, and from thy father's house,

unto a land that I will show thee: And I will make of thee a
great nation, and I will bless thee, and make thy name great;
and thou shall be a blessing. (Genesis 12:1–2)

Abram and his father, Terah, left the land of Ur and entered the land of the
Chaldees where Terah became involved with the idolatrous practices of that
land. Here Abram was chosen in place of his father and given knowledge of
the patriarch Shem (Noah's oldest son) of a single deity in opposition to his
father's new beliefs, one God that didn't require idols or human sacrifices as
the vast number of people groups had done after the flood. It was not the
common practice of man to adhere to the God of Noah and Shem his son.
God's spiritual rules of conscience for man to use contradicted the common
practice of using brute force and fear to conquer and rule the people. The
ritual killings of human beings were common at that time. Throughout
history, defeated kings, their heirs to the throne, slaves, and all foes were
customarily slaughtered to appease the new ruler's insecurity and rightful
paranoia. Along with the spoils of the conquered nations, the women were
considered the property of the new king. In many cultures, at the death of the
reigning king, his servants would not only be sacrificed to appease the gods,
but they were killed to quell any reprisal against the new monarch. It was not
an uncommon practice that the servants of the dead monarch would be killed
in order to continue serving their master in the afterlife. When Abraham
took Isaac and trusted God to provide for him even if his only son was to be
sacrificed he went counter to the other religions and customs in the area of
human sacrifice to appease the gods.

> And Abraham stretched forth his hand, and took the knife
> to slay his son. And the angel of the LORD called unto him
> out of heaven, and said, Abraham, Abraham: and he said,
> Here am I. And he said, Lay not your hand upon the lad,
> neither do thou anything unto him: for now I know that
> thou fearest God, seeing thou hast not withheld thy son,
> your only son from me. And Abraham lifted up his eyes, and
> looked, and behold behind him a ram caught in a thicket by
> his horns: and Abraham went and took the ram, and offered

him up for a burnt offering in the stead of his son. (Genesis 22:10–13)

By not killing Isaac, Abraham continued a bloodline of people that would keep it pure and undefiled from Adam to Seth, from Noah to Shem, Abraham, Isaac, and Jacob—all in order to usher in the Messiah Jesus Christ. For two thousand years, the bloodline was kept intact. Moses and Aaron gave man the Law, which separated the Hebrew even further from the rest of the world with their practices, precepts, and laws.

Once I started to read the Torah, I began to appreciate that it truly is the Word of the living God. I find it utterly baffling how three of the major religions of the world base their founding principles on Torah but don't even acknowledge its genealogical record, relevance, and wise teachings. Even those professing Christianity neglect to teach the importance of Torah and its instructions. Not that it should supersede the gospel of Jesus Christ, but that it should be given its rightful place of importance in the establishment of a people to usher in the Messiah. Contrary to all theories of replacement theology and anti-Semitism, the Hebrew people are still the apple of God's eye. The Hebrew patriarchs are the ones who established the basis for every Christian denomination we have today, and any prejudice toward the Jew only shows ignorance and the rejection of the love taught by Jesus Christ the Messiah.

> For thus saith the LORD of hosts; After the glory hath he sent me unto the nations which spoiled you: for he that toucheth you toucheth the apple of his eye. (Zachariah 2:8)

> And he said, It is a light thing that thou shouldest be my servant to raise up the tribes of Jacob, and to restore the preserved of Israel: *I will also give thee for a light to the Gentiles, that thou mayest be my salvation unto the end of the earth.* (Isaiah 49:6, emphasis added)

The Judeo-Christian faiths are the only faiths that have valued human life from before a person's birth to the time after their death. Torah teaches us that all people are valuable and that there is sanctity to all human life from conception to adulthood. The mentally challenged to the infirmed to those injured and incoherent—all have value to Jehovah. From the first chapter in Genesis, Torah teaches us that man is distinct from all other created beings on earth. Because of this, man was and is the only creation formed in the image of the living God, and he has more value than all other created things, contrary to what the atheists and Darwinian evolutionists might tell you. This premise is unfathomable to the enviro-naturalists when told that man is superior to other created beings, and they justify many of their actions by basing them on unfounded and erroneous ideas.

> And God said, Let us *make man in our image*, after our likeness: and *let them have dominion over* the fish of the sea, and over the fowl of the air, and over the cattle, and over all the earth, and over every creeping thing that creepeth upon the earth. So God created man, in the image of God created he him; male and female created he them. (Genesis 1:26–27, emphasis added)

Every single person ever born is special and created in the image of our Creator, Jehovah God. Only an unbelieving, fleshly minded man has differentiated the races and creeds of people because of culture, traditions, and the financial status that they have. Only man has devalued the human fetus to appease his immoral sexual appetites and perceived financial needs of a narcissistic self-absorbed generation. Because of Abraham, we have the Jewish people; and because of Moses, we have Torah and the Law; and because of Torah, we have a religion that believes in one God who loves us and cares enough about us to sacrifice His only begotten Son Jesus Christ to redeem us.

Through this four-thousand-year process, the Bible alone tells us how to live function and flourish in society. Many discount the Old Testament as cruel, brutal, unforgiving, and not relevant to a modern civilized society, and they equally discount the New Testament as a bloody intolerant book. But one has to understand that because of these laws and dictates imposed upon the people, these laws of the Old and New Testaments are what bring order to an otherwise ruthless and uncivilized society. Today's laws are based on the combination of both Testaments and are what we base all our secular laws on.

Torah is a covenant. It is really a legally binding, formal Jewish marriage contract between God (the Bridegroom) and His own people (the bride), the Jews. The Torah refers to itself several times as a covenant with the first passage reference in Exodus 34:27. The context of this passage is the giving of the first written revelation to man, which is introduced by Moses as the Ten Commandments, as well as other instructions for living peaceably and productively as a people.

God called Abraham to establish a unique nation among the otherwise pagan world around 2000 BC. From the beginning, God's purpose was not limited to Israel alone. He desired that these laws and blessings might be exported to all nations who had perverted God's plan of civil government into pagan-centralized monarchies. God established in Israel a centralized representative government where every group of ten, fifty, one hundred, and one thousand families could choose or elect someone to be their judge or ruler. All of their civil laws were based upon God's higher fixed law and not minorities. This makes it a republic and not a democracy (*America's Providential History*): "And the LORD said unto Moses, Write thou these words: for after the tenor of these words I have made a covenant with thee and with Israel" (Exodus 34:27).

The second reference is Deuteronomy 29:1. Moses is entering the end of his life, over forty years after the events in Exodus 34. Here he has recorded much more of God's teachings and instructions. Now, with his people soon to enter the Promised Land, Moses summarizes all the teachings from God and calls it, again, a covenant.

> These are the words of the covenant, which the LORD commanded Moses to make with the children of Israel in the land of Moab, beside the *covenant* which he made with them in Horeb. (Deuteronomy 29:1, emphasis added)

Since Torah is a covenant, both parties involved are subject to certain legal obligations. God, the one who initiated this covenant, legally binds Himself to keep His word which He spoke in the covenant; Israel is likewise bound to the same covenant. In a sense one could say that, understood in this light, Torah is really the national constitution for the nation Israel (Berkowitz). Because of the reception of the Torah by the people who fled Egypt with Moses, the regulations of this covenant are different than anything ever seen before or since by natural man. The Ten Commandments go against any of the normal structures or teachings of man when left to his own devices. Torah and its regulations made man accountable to a higher authority than himself—God. No man, king or queen, or their families who were to rule superseded God's omnipotence (all-powerful). Only the patriarchs and other men and women of the Old Testament were to be honored and revered for their obedience to God, and they were only to bring glory to (Jehovah), not themselves. The history of their life's failures and victories in personal and family issues were spoken of to show the similarities of their problems to any man alive then or now.

The God who spoke to Adam, Enoch, and Noah, is the same God who spoke to Moses when he received the law and is the same God who hears you and me when we cry out to Him for help. What Moses did was supernatural, not accomplished by human hand but by the inspiration and leading of the Holy Spirit. God is omniscient (all-knowing), omnipresent (always present), and omnipotent (all-powerful), and He accomplishes everything through the third person of the Trinity, the Holy Spirit. Just as I believe the angelic being seen in the fire with Shadrach, Meshach, and Abednego was Jesus, the second person of the Trinity. So too do I believe the pillar of fire, the manna from heaven, and the feeding of five thousand on a mountainside across the sea of Tiberias was the work of the Holy Spirit, the third person of the Trinity. That same Holy Spirit who raised Jesus from the dead and knocked Saul of Tarsus off his horse on the road to Damascus and is the same Holy Spirit who falls upon every believer in Jesus.

Still, the creator of everything seen and unseen needs you, His greatest creation (man), to participate by asking for His help. He is God; He is holy and He is righteous, but most of all, He is Spirit and He wants nothing to do with the flesh or what motivates it. The God of all creation speaks to men of today just like He spoke to the great patriarchs, judges, prophets, kings, and priests prior to the birth of Jesus. God reiterated and clarified His standards and requirements needed for man to have fellowship with God the Father again when Jesus taught here on earth. Instead of rejecting the Old Testament tenants as antiquated and no longer needed today, what Jesus did was clarify and define what truly is required of man yesterday, today, and forever to enter into the presence of the living God. We need to honor and adhere to His laws and live as a civilized, compassionate, holy people who honor Jehovah God more than His creation.

Because of the work of Jesus Christ on the cross, the Old Testament comes alive and makes perfect sense. Had the Jewish leaders not allowed the lust of the flesh and the pride of life to overtake and blind them to who Jesus was, they too could have humbled themselves to receive the good news of the gospel preached by Jesus Christ the Son of the living God Jehovah. Jesus is the complete fulfillment of all the requirements of the Law, and we the church are His bride and as His bride we can move on to the third and final requirement to have fellowship with God as Adam did in the garden. That is to be baptized in the Holy Spirit and operate in the spiritual gifts given freely to all believers in Jesus.

The God spoken of in the Old Testament is the Father, Son, and Holy Spirit taught by the disciples in the New Testament. The triune God spoken of throughout Scripture—Old and New Testaments alike—is the great "I AM THAT I AM" and is the Jesus of the New Testament along with the Holy Spirit (1 John 5:7). This needs to be taught completely from Genesis to Revelation to make perfect sense. The God of the Old Testament is the Father Jesus spoke of in Matthew 5:16–17;; Luke 4:18–19; and John 5:17 10:30 ,16:32 as He was about His Father's business.

> In the beginning was the Word, and the Word was with God, and *the Word was God*. The same was in the beginning with God. All things were made by him; and without him was not anything made that was made. (John 1:1–3, emphasis added)

That's Jehovah in the "beginning." That's Jesus as the "Word." That's the Holy Spirit in the "made." Father, Son, and Holy Spirit are three in one.

As we learn to walk in the Spirit of God, we will see that same hate that some so-called believers of Jesus have toward the Jewish people is the same attitude that the Jewish believers of Jehovah have toward Christians. We will see that this attitude needs to be removed from every believer who professes Jehovah as God or Jesus as Messiah. I know that I am over-simplifying the importance of Torah and what it is all about, but the unwarranted hatred man has toward the Jewish people with the brutality perpetrated upon them is, I believe, demonically inspired and the third obstacle for us as believers to overcome is anti-Semitism. A non-believer in Jesus is still a non-believer in Jesus whether they are Jewish or any person alive they all need Jesus. We have to also acknowledge that because of the obedience of the Hebrew patriarchs and practicing Jewish people God the Father has a special place in His heart and kingdom for them. As believers in the first person of the Trinity only, I do believe that the Hebrew's of the Old Testament and the practicing Jew's of today will be able to enter into the kingdom as servants and not be able to enter into the inner courts, sanctuary or the Holy of Holies that only the priestly order as first born sons will be able to enter into. Only those that have received Jesus as Messiah will be able to enter there. Levidicus 25:55 For unto me the children of Israel are servants; they are my servants whom I brought forth out of the land of Egypt: I am the LORD your God. I Chronicles 6:49 But Aaron and his sons offered upon the altar of the burnt offering, and on the altar of incense, and were appointed for all the work of the place most holy, and to make an atonement for Israel, according to all that Moses the servant of God had commanded. Because of their unbelief Paul tells us in Galatians 4:4-6 But when the fulness of the time was come, God sent forth his Son, made of a woman, made under the law, To redeem them that were under the law, that we might receive the adoption of sons. And because ye are sons, God hath sent forth the Spirit of his Son into your hearts, crying, Abba, Father. All practicing Hebrew believers in Jehovah God were called servants under the law. Believers in Jesus as Messiah before His crucifixion are called friends. The Apostles and Jewish converts. John 15:15 Henceforth I call you not servants; for the servant knoweth not what his lord doeth: but I have called you friends; for all things that I have heard of my Father I have made known unto you. After Jesus' ascension all believers in the ascended Christ are called sons. Galatians 4:7 Wherefore thou art no more a servant, but a son; and if a son, then an heir of God through Christ.

Chapter 6

CONNECT THE DOTS

*T*hrough Abraham's obedience, man was reintroduced to God again after two thousand years of rebellion.

Now the LORD had said unto Abram, Get thee out of thy country, and from thy kindred, and from thy father's house, unto a land that I will show thee: And I will make of thee a great nation, and I will bless thee, and make thy name great; and thou shall be a blessing: And I will bless them that bless thee, and curse him that curses thee: and in thee shall all families of the earth be blessed. (Genesis 12:1–3)

Through Moses, we have the Law and an understanding of "covenant." The Law kept mankind civilized and reverent to one God who has stressed the superiority and value of human life over plants and animals. Most people think Torah is a book of dos and don'ts, but it's more than that. It is unique in that it is God's teaching of how man should act and treat family, friends, strangers, animals, and the earth. Unfortunately, not all professing people of

Jehovah or Jesus adhere to these precepts, and this has helped fuel ammunition and criticism by self-righteous agnostic beliefs and atheistic doubts to hurl at believers in the Word of God as they destroy each other.

The Word of God is unique in that it reveals that every thought causes our actions and that every action has eternal consequences. Every aspect of the Jewish man's life was regulated by the law in preparation for the Messiah. It took two thousand years to believe in one God again, another two thousand years to prepare the way through the law for the Messiah to come, and an additional two thousand years to prepare us to again utilize the gifts of the third person of the Trinity, the Holy Spirit. Once Jesus Christ the Messiah came, died, and ascended to the throne of God, He ushered in the Holy Ghost. The Father, Son, and Holy Ghost are perfect in unity and perfect in truth. It has taken these two thousand years from the ascension of Jesus to get us to the point where we can begin to understand and relate to God the Father through Jesus Christ in the Spirit of God, the Holy Ghost. It's so simple, yet it seems complicated: "For there are three that bear record in heaven, the Father, the Word, and the Holy Ghost: and these three are one" (1 John 5:7).

His desire is to return us each to a place where we can have fellowship with Him like Adam did in the garden prior to the fall, using all of his physical and spiritual senses together. The way we regain our spiritual senses is by conquering and defeating the works of the flesh in our life.

To regain the position spiritually, I asked the Holy Spirit to reveal to me how this was possible. I asked the Holy Spirit, and He showed me a vision of Jesus, and I could see His soul as a man (second Adam). His soul was the perfect representation of a perfectly protected, walled city and temple. As I looked at His perfection, I felt the anguish and longing to rebuild the city walls of my soul just as Nehemiah longed to rebuild the walls of Jerusalem in 446 BC.

In Jack Hayford's book *Rebuilding the Real You*, he explained the difficulties of rebuilding the temple walls and gates in the book of Nehemiah in the Old Testament. I knew that this story of Nehemiah meant much more than just a story of an ancient city. I saw the perfection of Jesus; His walls and His gates were perfect, and each and every block looked and seemed flawless. His gates were huge, but they still seemed perfectly proportionate to the walls. The gates were all labeled, not with letters or numbers, but rather I knew that they represented Jesus' perfect personality and character. Each gate was the perfect representation of His personage and depiction of the nine fruits of the Spirit (in Galatians 5:22–23).The apostle Paul refers to these attributes in Romans 12:1–2:

> I beseech you therefore, brethren, by the mercies of God, that ye present your bodies a living sacrifice, holy, acceptable unto God, which is your reasonable service. And be not conformed to this world: but be ye transformed by the renewing of your mind, that ye may prove what is that good, and acceptable, and perfect, will of God.

As I looked, I saw the side posts were all made of silver, and the roads leading to each gate were gold and were the perfect representations of Jesus. I knew at that instant that for you and me, the mantel and posts were covered with Jesus' blood for us at our salvation decision. The walls on either side of each fruit post were made up of many blocks, and each block was distinct from the ones around it. Its colors were variations of the gate colors, with the bricks on all sides influencing their tint and intensity of color as they got closer to the gate. These colors were of the rainbow, and each color of the spectrum was influenced by the love of Jesus. Each layer was representative of a color of the rainbow (red, orange, yellow, green, blue, indigo, and violet) and it corresponded to each individual wall of that particular fruit of the Spirit. They seemed to consist of all the character traits, hues, and colors of the gates of His walls. I don't know if the other two missing colors were actually two distinct separate colors or if they were just transitional colors that I didn't recognize or know the names for and were partially connected to the colors next to them.

I do know that I instantly knew His shed blood on the cross would dictate the deepness and intensity of our gate and wall colors. Just like the natural phenomenon where the sun shines onto droplets of moisture in the earth's atmosphere to produce a multicolored arc of color in a rainbow, I could sense that just as clouds and dust can hinder the formation of a rainbow, so too are the walls and gates of our soul influenced by our personal relationship with Jesus Christ and\or the world. I could also see that through the fruit of the Spirit that whatever spiritual fruit we do produce is influenced by our character and personalities. The Scripture that explains these fruit-labeled gates for us are spoken of in Galatians 5:22–23: "These are love, joy, peace, longsuffering, gentleness, goodness, faith, meekness, and temperance; against such action there is no law."

The only explanation I have of the seven colors versus the nine fruit written of in this Scripture is to combine longsuffering with temperance and meekness with gentleness; I don't know for sure. All I do know is that Jesus is our perfect example of the fruit of the Spirit, and they all transition seamlessly and flawlessly between and through each other. His life, death, and resurrection exemplify each one of these Fruit of the Spirit, and we individually need to emulate Him. Jesus is the sinless, faultless, flawless example of what our souls need to be reconstructed to be like (Christlikeness). Our personal pains and deep soul wounds discolor and destroy the walls to our soul that protect our eternal spirits; this in turn discolors, tarnishes, and damages our gates. The intents of our hearts and the motivations of our actions are evident as discolored cracks that traversed from fruit wall to fruit wall through the foundation blocks that connect the foundations and gateposts of the other fruit of the Spirit.

As I looked at the walls of Jesus, the first gate I saw in front of me was the Love gate, and it was goldish-yellow in color like the streets and foundations of the walls all around His Spirit temple. It was a translucent goldish-yellow as well, and I knew that all the fruit were connected and relied on each other for stability. I could see from the front that it encircled the temple with the other eight fruit, and I knew they depended on each other. The intensity of each of the nine fruits added to the pureness and the depth of His love. Jesus' love was also the first layer of each fruit block to the nine separate walls, and it was the foundation of all nine gateposts.

It was the footer of love so to speak, and it was the foundation on which all the gates were hung.

The next layer was joy, and it was as pure emerald green as the love layer beneath it was a goldish-yellow. The colors that encircled His spirit in the center of the temple were the same colors of the layers of the walls of Jesus' soul. I couldn't see any difference between the colors as they flowed so seamlessly from one to the next with what I knew was the love of God. Jesus' gates and walls were perfectly proportioned. The distance between the gates seemed to be perfectly spaced, one from another. Each brick of His walls was pure in color as that of a perfect rainbow on a clear blue sky after a spring rain. So pure in color, it seemed at the same time to have a depth of intensity but was still translucent because of its purity. It seemed to have degrees of purity and depth of color, but at the same time, degrees of translucency which I could sense was because of His righteousness and selfless love. I then saw my soul compared to Jesus' perfection, and I saw the imperfections of my soul next to Jesus' perfect walls and gates in His excellence. Instantly I saw my impure thoughts of love and prejudice that influenced all my gates and how these impurities of hate and racism permeated through all of the other walls and gates of my soul as black cracks and shades of gray throughout—exactly like the vision I saw of Cain after he slew Abel.

I could see that this one block in my Love foundation was perverting the other gates and walls. I knew that my salvation was secure, but I also knew that if I continued on with these feelings of hatred and self-righteousness, I could be overpowered with them and lose it. This one cornerstone of Love was mislaid and not plumb causing the rest of the walls to not be straight and plumb. There were manifestations of these self-righteous thoughts that I knew were displeasing to the God I thought I knew. My perverted sense of superiority and self-worth flowed through my Joy, Peace, Goodness, Gentleness, and Longsuffering gates while cracking and crumbling the walls of Meekness and Temperance to rubble in places which opened doors to the Enemy of my soul.

There were areas almost completely gone in every one of the nine fruit of the Spirit, and as I scanned around looking at my tarnished and discolored gates, I saw that my faith gate was in the most disrepair and the reason for the other fruit wall damage. The faith blocks on either side of the faith gate seemed to be almost nonexistent in Goodness or Meekness. As each individual gate was one of the colors of the rainbow encircling my believing spirit, so too were the walls built on the foundation of Love (goldish-yellow) rising up with individual layers of joy (green), peace (blue), longsuffering and temperance (indigo), gentleness and meekness (violet), goodness (red), and faith (orange).

This faith block in all the fruit walls to my soul was damaged. I could see the hypocrisy of trying to show love, compassion, and mercy as a Christian while still being filled with prejudice, disgust, anger, and hate toward non-Greeks, nonwhites, and Jews. The distinction between believers in Jehovah God and Jesus Christ of Nazareth was blurred with a false sense of pride and superiority that was present in my soul.

I could sense that most of the damage had occurred because of my attitude toward different Christian denominations and Jews. My sense of superiority over them, especially toward fellow believers in the Messiah, was the worst. The displeasure and disapproval from God I felt was because of this mind-set and feelings of superiority in my heart. I knew that could be the cause of the loss of my future rewards in heaven, and if I acted upon them while alive, they could inhibit my entrance into parts of the kingdom. Instead of the perfect distance between the gates and the seemingly perfect height of each of Jesus' supporting walls, my walls and gates were disproportionate and discolored from layer to layer. Missing blocks, dark and blackened with hate, anger, and prejudice, were all evident in each of the walls. Some of my gates were hanging on by just one screw. Others were not even able to close, and the walls that were supposed to be straight, high, and formed with the colors of the rainbow were instead a shambles—crumbled, gray, and black. They were all disproportionate in distance from one another, and I knew that the reason for the walls' state of disarray was because of me. My thoughts, my fears, my hates, my bitterness, my racism, my anti-Semitism, and everything else that is contrary to Jesus and the Father were all evident in my soul's faith gate and foundation of love supporting the other fruit walls.

We will discuss these nine gates and the seventeen bricks of contamination in detail in the works of the flesh and the seventeen spirit-world realities that influence these nine walls and eighteen gateposts later. My walls and gates were nothing like those of Jesus', and a sense of great despair and disappointment came over me. My Love gate was very small, and my Joy gate was even smaller. Our soul has nine gates that protect our spirits. These gates are explained to us in Galatians 5:22–23 as the fruit of the Spirit. Just as Nehemiah saw a need for the walls to be rebuilt to protect the temple from marauders and thieves, so too, do our spirits need to be protected from the enemies of our souls.

Paul shows us in Galatians 5:19–21 that the works of the flesh can affect and destroy our souls from the inside out, very similar to carpenter ants or rust that can eat at the foundation of a home, weakening the foundation so when a problem comes, it falls apart.

These walls and gates are either built on the love of Jesus or the hate and prejudice of what the world teaches us. The whole process of rebuilding the walls and having the gates hung properly is exactly what God wants from us in these last days. The whole purpose is to learn how we are to rebuild our damaged walls and hang the gates of our souls to our spirit, producing spiritual fruit everywhere we go. When we get born-again, our spirits are renewed as the temple in Jerusalem was rebuilt prior to the rebuilding of their walls and hanging of the gates. Like I said before, the whole purpose of Abraham, Moses, David, Jesus, and the Holy Spirit was to teach man to overcome the flesh. We as believers are to rely on God and the Spirit and not to rely on the flesh alone. To trust in Him for everything and bring us back into fellowship with God the Father, through Jesus Christ the Son, in the Holy Spirit.

One of the first things I teach my students in our church's life support classes is the acronym of TRUST. It is simple to remember and easy to apply to any situation you find yourself in. Simply by praying through each of the letters of the word *trust*, you pray through the issue or question about what the will of God is. This is the method I use to asked the Holy Spirit for answers as I prayed on certain subjects. I heard this acronym on television some years ago, and I can't remember the preacher's name. But … thank you!

> **T**—I **thank** You, Holy Spirit, for who You are and for what You have done in my life. Thank You for calling me into the kingdom and in guiding me, leading me, and showing me God's love. Through the death, burial, and resurrection of Jesus Christ the only begotten Son, I am saved!

> **R**—Holy Spirit, reveal **revelation** to me through the Word of God and through the people I come into contact with throughout the day.

U—I ask You, Holy Spirit, to **use** me and to make me usable. Use me to help increase the kingdom and use me in this particular situation.

S—**Strengthen** my mind, my soul, and my body to do Your will through this.

T—**Teach** me in Your word, Your will, and Your way, Holy Spirit, through Jesus as you teach me to be Christ like in this situation.

After praying this prayer, close by thanking and praising God the Father for calling you into His kingdom and for everything else He's already done in your life. But most importantly, thank Him in the midst of any troubles you may be going through now.

> Blessed is the man that endures temptation: for when he is tried, he shall receive the *crown of life*, which the Lord hath promised to them that love him. (James 1:12, emphasis added)

Thank Him for how He's revealing Scripture to you through situations and circumstances you're living through. Thank Him for using you and for strengthening your mind and memory. Thank Him for teaching you godly truths and precepts to live by. You can use any time for your prayer time to talk to God, whether taking a shower, lying in bed, or driving to work.

During one of these times in prayer and meditating on Scripture, the Lord revealed to me this method of restoration for my wounded soul areas. It came to me after I had been diagnosed with MS. Issues and contradictions arose in my mind as I read the Word of God and my life was falling apart all around me. I was constantly at odds with my thoughts, and the fear for my wife and kids' futures brought me to my knees. All I knew was I had to hang on to Jesus. Jesus is the only hope I have, because there is no known cure for progressive multiple sclerosis, and all the medicine can do is slow down the progression but not cure it.

The promises of God and the reality of losing everything I had worked for strained my faith in God. I constantly had to repent for things I thought, things I had said, and things I didn't say. I was angry, frustrated, and stressed out with the diagnosis and the situation I found myself in. My inability to work anymore, my relationship with my wife and kids, along with my failing business only added to my problems and fears. There was a battle raging in my soul, and my body was the recipient of all the stresses—I didn't know why or what to do. My spirit was born-again and as perfect as it would ever be when I received Jesus as Lord and Savior of my life, but I was sick. My soul was in a tug-of-war between my faith in God and the doubt and unbelief of my mind was raging in my soul. The question of why this was happening to me tormented my every thought. My family has a history of MS, an aunt and a cousin had passed because of it and along with my diagnosis another cousin and a niece were diagnosed with MS. My wife and children's future was my greatest concern, and fear gripped my very core.

Unfortunately, the resulting stresses, fears, and anxieties only added to my body's loss of health and increased pain. It felt as if someone was running a hot skewer through my joints and muscles. I was constantly dizzy, I couldn't see with my left eye, and my stomach was in a ball of knots. All I could do was cry out to Jesus in prayer. I would close myself in the bathroom, turn the fan on, sit on the toilet, and pray with understanding and in the Spirit. The Holy Spirit began to reveal to me areas of hypocrisy in my walk with Jesus and issue by issue, point by point, attitudes followed by actions were revealed to me that were not pleasing to God.

It was not until I asked the Holy Spirit specifically what the issues were in my life that were displeasing to Him that they were revealed to me, and I was then able to begin to deal with the areas of anger, poor attitude, hatred, and frustration—but I had to ask before He would reveal them to me. This process is not instantaneous with our confession unless addressed along with our confession. Salvation only gives Jesus and the Holy Spirit legal authority to evict any manifestations and strongholds that had become squatters in my soul. I had to specifically call out the area revealed by the Holy Spirit; I then quoted Scripture promises from the Word of God and began regaining lost ground in my heart, mind and soul.

My financial stability and security was lost, and my sense of who I thought I was, was crumbling down before my eyes. Most of all, my health was gone. My relationship with my wife and family was strained, and our future was so uncertain that it was impossible for me to understand what to do next. We have all had things happen to us that adversely affect our plans and dreams, but this had shaken my whole world and caused me to reflect back on my life like never before. All the deep-seated issues of bitterness, anger, hatred, low self-esteem, and low self-confidence to name a few were becoming more apparent to me the more I read Scripture. I could see they had become a part of my personality, but more importantly, they were the cause of most of my symptoms.

As I read and meditated on the Word of God, the Holy Spirit let me see that these seeds of bitterness were planted in me many years ago. These rotten seeds of hate and anger were nurtured with the hurts and rejections that I had experienced as an adolescent and young adult. Our plans and dreams get dashed or crushed with these traumatic occurrences that help mold our attitudes toward the people we meet and everything we think about. Our reactions are a result of all the stuff we carry around with us through this life and they just don't disappear when we get saved.

My inability to show love was a direct result of my father's rejection of me and the false expectations that he placed on me at a very young age. These same false expectations were placed on friends and family in anticipation of future rejection or their inability to meet my false standards of what I thought they should be like. My wife and boys walked on eggshells so as not to aggravate me and cause an angry outburst. This, coupled with my newly diagnosed physical limitations, brought to light all my shortcomings and probably was the cause of most of my physical problems to begin with.

This calamity had actually given me time to reflect on the many areas of my soul walls that were destroyed and replaced with some very unappealing strongholds and principalities. The first thing I needed to work on was my countenance and how I reflected my Savior Jesus with my attitude and facial expressions as His ambassador of love and grace. With the rest of this book, I will hope to show and help you realize how much God knows and loves you and how the Creator of all things has put into motion everything needed for all mankind to reestablish their relationship with Him. Through knowing the Father, Son, and Holy Spirit, we can begin to allow the Holy Spirit to show us the areas of our soul walls that need the dismantling of manifestations and strongholds so we can begin to repair them with the fruit of the Spirit. It has been a long process for me that has been very humbling and very introspective, but was necessary for my personal healing and spiritual growth. Again, it is entirely up to you to choose to change your mind and lifestyle or not. I believe the Holy Spirit has shown me how to change my mind and heal my soul primarily through prayer, reading the Word of God, and adhering to His instructions in them so that He can then heal my body through His promises in the process of healing my soul.

The Word of God says in Proverbs1:23: "Turn you at my reproof: behold, I will pour out my spirit unto you, I will make known my words unto you." And in John 14:16–17, Jesus said,

> And I will pray the Father, and he shall give you another Comforter, that he may abide with you *forever*; Even the Spirit of truth; whom the world cannot receive, because it seeth him not, neither knoweth him: but ye know him; for he dwelleth with you, and shall be in you. (emphasis added)

Through the sacrifice of our kinsman Redeemer, our immaculately conceived King of David and High Priest, Jesus Christ of Nazareth, we can then begin the process of rebuilding the walls of our soul. With the help of the Holy Spirit to identify the areas needed for repair, He will then strengthen us spiritually and direct our path so we can hang the new gates on the rebuilt walls of our soul: "There is therefore now no condemnation to them which are in Christ Jesus, who walk not after the flesh, but after the Spirit" (Romans 8:1).

How do I walk after the Spirit to repair my soul? It is not by just going after religious things or customs of the church you attend, but it's by doing a combination of good works, prayer, witnessing, and studying the entire Bible. All are important, extremely necessary, and wonderful, but the real questions that need to be answered are; How do I now put order into my life? How does my behavior reflect my newly born-again beliefs? Walking after the Spirit is placing all your faith exclusively in Christ Jesus. You should also know that through sowing seeds of the fruit of the Spirit that you now walk in; that they are not seasonal but can be of harvested at any time of your life. The seeds must be planted at the foot of the cross of salvation in the freshly tilled ground of your heart. True repentance, regardless of the sin, cultivates the soil of your heart which in turn is nurtured by the combination of spiritual watering mentioned earlier and the Word of truth in the Bible.

It's a fight, and it's difficult because Satan is constantly putting up roadblocks and distractions (fleshly desires) to detour your thoughts and ultimately your eternity from what God has designed you for from before creation. The Devil believes there is a God and he trembles. His job is to convince you that he doesn't exist and that the God of the Bible is a fable or some form of mythological figure. You must understand that Jesus Christ is the source of all things we receive in this life, and that He is God, along with the third person of the Trinity the Holy Spirit He knows you personally the moment you are born again. The choices we make are eternal, and the most important one is to choose Jehovah as the Father, Jesus as Messiah, and the Holy Spirit as the third person of the Trinity.

In the beginning was the Word, and the Word was with God, and *the Word was God*. The same was in the beginning with God. All things were made by him; and without him was not anything made that was made. In him was life; and the life was the light of men. And the light shineth in darkness; and the darkness comprehended it not. (John 1:1–5, emphasis added)

To believe in Jesus Christ, you must first believe that Torah is true. You then must believe that the New Testament is an extension of the Old Testament and that Jesus was a Jew and came to do the will of the Father (the Hebrew God, Jehovah).

> Who hath believed our report? And to whom is the arm of the LORD revealed?
> For he shall grow up before him as a tender plant, and as a root out of a dry ground: he hath no form nor comeliness; and when we shall see him, there is no beauty that we should desire him.

He is despised and rejected of men; a man of sorrows, and acquainted with grief: and we hid as it were our faces from him; he was despised, and we esteemed him not.

Surely he hath borne our griefs, and carried our sorrows: yet we did esteem him stricken, smitten of God, and afflicted.

But he was wounded for our transgressions, he was bruised for our iniquities: the chastisement of our peace was upon him; and with his stripes we are healed.

All we like sheep have gone astray; we have turned every one to his own way; and the LORD hath laid on him the iniquity of us all.

He was oppressed, and he was afflicted, yet *he opened not his mouth: he is brought as a lamb to the slaughter,* and as a sheep before her shearers is dumb, so he openeth not his mouth.

He was taken from prison and from judgment: and who shall declare his generation? For he was cut off out of the land of the living: *for the transgression of my people was he stricken.*

And he made his grave with the wicked, and with the rich in his death; because he had done no violence, neither was any deceit in his mouth.

Yet it pleased the LORD to bruise him; he hath put him to grief: when thou shalt *make his soul an offering for sin,* he shall see his seed, he shall prolong his days, and the pleasure of the LORD shall prosper in his hand.

He shall see of the travail of his soul, and *shall be satisfied: by his knowledge shall my righteous servant justify many; for he shall bear their iniquities.*

Therefore will I divide him a portion with the great, and he shall divide the spoil with the strong; *because he hath poured out his soul unto death: and he was numbered with the transgressors; and he bare the sin of many, and made intercession for the transgressors.* (Isaiah 53:1–12, emphasis added)

This Scripture in the Old Testament book of Isaiah can only be a prophetic picture of the crucified Jesus that was to occur some eight centuries later, foretelling His birth, life's purpose, death, and resurrection.

> That all men should honor the Son, even as they honor the Father. He that honors not the Son honors not the Father which hath sent him. Verily, verily, I say unto you, He that hears my word, and believeth on him that sent me, hath everlasting life, and shall not come into condemnation; but is passed from death unto life. (John 5:23–24)

If Torah is true, then all other religions are false and Jesus Christ is the only way to the Hebrew Father, Jehovah. Jesus has not only fulfilled all the requirements of Torah but commanded the twelve apostles to not go to the Gentiles but to the Jews first, which is anathema to many self-proclaiming so-called Christians. The Holy Word of God testifies to this *fact* in the gospel according to Matthew.

> These twelve Jesus sent forth, and commanded them, saying, Go not into the way of the Gentiles, and into any city of the Samaritans enter ye not: But go rather to *the lost sheep of the house of Israel.* And as ye go, preach, saying, The kingdom of heaven is at hand. Heal the sick, cleanse the lepers, raise the dead, cast out devils: freely ye have received, freely give. (Matthew 10:5–8, emphasis added)

Chapter 7

TRUST IN JESUS ALONE

ccording to the Gospels, the Messiah and teacher of Torah, Jesus Christ of Nazareth, came for the children of Israel first, and because of their traditions and pride, they would not receive Him (Matthew 10:6; 15:24). So, God grafted in the Gentiles to receive their blessings instead of the stiff-necked chosen children.

It was about two thousand years from the fall of Adam to the call of Abram in Genesis 12:1—"Now the LORD had said unto Abram, Get thee out of thy country, and from thy kindred, and from thy father's house, unto a land that I will show thee." Then another two thousand years from the call of Abraham to the cross of Jesus: "But these are written, that ye might believe that Jesus is the Christ, the Son of God; and that believing ye might have life through his name" (John 20:31). The cross of Christ is the object of our faith, and it has taken an additional two thousand years to understand the baptism of the Holy Spirit and what the third person of the Trinity means to you and me today as we await Jesus' return.

> Know ye not, that so many of us as were baptized into Jesus
> Christ were baptized into his death? Therefore we are buried

with him by baptism into death: that like as Christ was raised up from the dead by the glory of the Father, even so we also should walk in newness of life. For if we have been planted together in the likeness of his death, we shall be also in the likeness of his resurrection: Knowing this, that our old man is crucified with him, that the body of sin might be destroyed, that henceforth we should not serve sin. (Romans 6:3–6)

For two thousand years, so-called Christians have blasphemed the third person of the Trinity (the Holy Spirit), and these so-called Christians have murdered, pillaged, and persecuted the founders of their own faith (the Jews) under the name of Christianity. The Old Testament has many claims and clues as to why this is. The first is the misunderstanding of the spiritual requirements of Scripture by ignorant people of Torah to separate from the pagan world, and then secondly the misunderstanding of the meaning of the grafting in of the Gentiles to the cultivated tree of Israel in the New Testament. The problem was and is the refusal of the Jew to accept Jesus as the Messiah and secondly the refusal of the Gentile to accept the people of Torah (the Jews) as the foundation of Christianity.

And in that day there shall be a root of Jesse, which shall stand for an ensign of the people; to it shall the *Gentiles* seek: and his rest shall be glorious. (Isaiah 11:10, emphasis added)

For from the rising of the sun even unto the going down of the same my name shall be great among *the Gentiles*; and in every place incense shall be offered unto my name, and a pure offering: *for my name shall be great among the heathen, saith the LORD of hosts.* (Malachi 1:11, emphasis added)

In Romans (11:17, 19), Paul uses the metaphor "contrary to nature" of grafting a wild olive branch (the Gentiles) into the good olive tree (Israel): that the unbelieving Jews of Jesus (branches of the good tree) were broken off so that the Gentiles might be grafted in (believers in Jesus as Messiah). Jews and Gentiles equally must enjoy the same divine blessings by faith alone of Jehovah God and Jesus Christ. The issue that we need to stress is that the God of the Gentiles (New Testament) is the same as the God of the Jews (Old Testament), and the two must embrace Torah as well as embrace Jesus Christ as Messiah in the New Testament.

There are two questions that need to be answered from each religious perspective: What are the requirements that the Jewish faith needs to complete for the Messiah to come? and What if any of these requirements were not met by Jesus Christ's birth, death, and resurrection? From the Gentile perspective, the questions are: When did God uproot the whole tree from the roots and replace the Jewish person with the Gentile believers, which leads many to accept the false theory of replacement theology that justifies their prejudice and hatred of the Jew? and If the Gentiles are grafted into the good tree to replace Israel like the Word says, then what are they grafted into if the roots are gone? Is not the whole belief in the Messiah (Jesus) based on the premise of Jewish roots and tradition? If God is done away with the uprooted good tree of Israel, then when and where in Scripture did God plant a new tree or vine separate from the existing believers in Jehovah?

From what I read, God doesn't replace anything; He only adds to the already existing root system. Only in the complete Holy Bible, Old and New Testaments, does His story (history) make sense. We can't cherry-pick the parts we don't like or believe in to still be true and applicable to this generation. From Genesis to Revelation, the story of mankind from his conception to his eternal abode after his death are all explained and clarified in the Judeo-Christian Bible. Only in the Judeo-Christian Bible is the individual person elevated in importance and accountability for their life choices are explained. There is now no condemnation to those which are in Christ Jesus who walk not after the flesh, but after the Spirit, for the love of the Spirit of life in Christ Jesus has made us free. There is nothing we could do to bring about the intended results that the cross could. The cross of Christ obliterates anything man has to offer for spiritual growth, and our eternal destination is completely dependent upon our belief and confession of Jesus Christ.

The alternatives are nothing short of foolishness and tickling of itching, self-absorbed ears of the true nonbeliever. The flipside to the arrogance of science and vain philosophies of the so-called intelligentsia is a form of Christian legalistic codes whether secularly based or ritualistic in their nature. In turn, this futility equals trying to live for a God we can accept by a system of laws and rules religiously that we have made up to pacify our selfish lifestyles and fleshly indulgences. For many Christians, church attendance, tithing and working for the church is right as long as the church leaders commend them for doing these things. Their motivation is in their service and obedience to the church canon but is not the selfless act as taught by Jesus. That's why a personal relationship with Jesus Christ is so important and supersedes any man-made organization or rules to a church. Service is given not out of guilt or a sense of false obligation, but rather a desire to serve and bless the Lord of Hosts out of our love for Him. With a humble and repentant heart, we enter into the presence of the Father with Jesus as our advocate, interceding on our behalf as He sits at God's right hand.

Our fasting and praying is always for direction and His perfect leading to strengthening our resolve and character. We need to use fasting and prayer to overcome the sin issues that are in our life. Most if not all of these consequences are the results of self-induced issues that we've given legal authority to Satan to use when we compromise God's morals and laws. The Holy Spirit will then give us answers in the Word of God only after we specifically ask Him to show us what the roots of these issues are. The Holy Spirit will give us specific ammunition for specific spirit-world realities in the Word of God for us to attack the root cause of that particular sin issue we have in our life. We open legal door points that when entertained, turn our thoughts of that sin issue into a part of our life, and the root is then masked by spirit-world realities that are accepted by a perverse society in this life.

The root sin issue becomes dormant until later when it rears its ugly head when you least expect it either by a cynical quip or in coarse jesting. Laws and rules are of no effect with God if the root goes deep in our core. God will not honor our weak attempts at morality and ethics, because we have allowed sin to become common habits and works of the flesh in our lives that have become accepted norms. We cannot live as Christians by the means of legalism any more than we can live with racism and perversion and still claim Jesus as our Lord and Savior. That would be to revert back to a worldly lifestyle and form of "survival of the fittest" religiously speaking; specifically to live your life trying to live by someone else's standards of the faith is ludicrous. Legalism is a spiral down to our base instincts and judgments that only leads to slavery in the lust of the flesh and power.

What that says is "Look what I have done; look what I'm doing for God; aren't I the greatest!" Listen … none of this affords you anything with the Lord. It doesn't make you righteous before God, it only magnifies your flesh, and the flesh only alienates God. Legalism says that what Jesus did at the cross was not enough and that we've got to add works with His atonement and His laws to be good enough. What rules and laws really do is only cause you to digress and bring pain to yourself or those around you with no real fulfillment once you've attained your self-proclaimed standards. It will make you burn out and want to quit and give up on Jesus altogether. You can't live this kind of life through your own abilities or your own mental strengths by trying to adhere to some man-made rules or traditions; all you do is set yourself up for failure. Know that you're only doing legalistic works of the flesh for yourself and not walking after the Spirit for God. By showing true humility and love in giving of yourself with no intentions of receiving any praise or glory, you glorify the Father. What Christ did at the cross was to pay for all the requirements needed in Torah to atone for our sins:

+ The God of the Jews is the God of the Gentiles.
+ The Messiah of the Gentiles is the Messiah of the Jews also.
+ The Holy Spirit of the Old Testament and of the apostles is the same Holy Spirit available to you and me today.

Compare the connection and continuity of these first verses in the beginning of Genesis with that of the first verse in the book of the gospel of John in the New Testament.

> In the beginning God [Jehovah] created the heaven and the earth. And the earth was without form, and void; and darkness [chaos] was upon the face of the deep. And the

Spirit of God [Holy Spirit] moved upon the face of the waters. And God [Jehovah] said, Let there be light [Jesus/ Holy Spirit]: and there was light [Jesus/Holy Spirit]. And God [Jehovah] saw the light [Jesus], that it was good: and God [Jehovah/Holy Spirit] divided the light [Jesus/Holy Spirit] from the darkness [order]. (Genesis 1:1–4, emphasis added)

In the beginning was the Word [Jesus], and the Word [Jesus] was with God [Jehovah], and the Word [Jesus] was God [Jehovah]. The same [Jesus] was in the beginning with God [Jehovah]. All things were made by him [Jesus/ Jehovah]; and without him [Jesus/Jehovah, Holy Spirit] was not anything made that was made. In Him was life; and the life was the light of men. And the light [Jesus] shineth in darkness [chaos]; and the darkness [chaos] comprehended it not. (John 1:1–5, emphasis added)

The concepts of the Trinity are expressed throughout the Old and New Testaments, linking them together supernaturally.

For there are three that bear record in heaven, *the Father, the Word,* and *the Holy Ghost*: and these three are one. And there are three that bear witness in earth, the Spirit, and the water, and the blood: and these three agree in one. (1 John 5:7–8, emphasis added)

Turn you at my reproof: behold, I will pour out my spirit unto you, I will make known my words unto you. (Proverbs 1:23)

And it shall come to pass afterward, that I will pour out my spirit upon all flesh; and your sons and your daughters shall prophesy, your old men shall dream dreams, your young men shall see visions. (Joel 2:28)

> And I will put my spirit within you, and cause you to walk in
> my statutes, and ye shall keep my judgments, and do them.
> (Ezekiel 36:27)

The Spirit of God is available to all believers of the Messiah in this present age, and God is pouring out His Spirit upon all flesh.

> And it shall come to pass in the last days, saith God, I will
> pour out of my Spirit upon all flesh: and your sons and
> your daughters shall prophesy, and your young men shall
> see visions, and your old men shall dream dreams: And on
> my servants and on my handmaidens I will pour out in those
> days of my Spirit; and they shall prophesy: And I will shew
> wonders in heaven above, and signs in the earth beneath;
> blood, and fire, and vapor of smoke. (Acts 2:17–19)

Whenever we accepted Christ and placed our faith in Him, we accepted what he did at the cross, and we were then literally placed into Christ. Jesus said in John 14:20, "And in that day you shall know that I am in my father and you in me and I in you."

The Holy Spirit will always lead you to the cross, without fail. He will lead you to the Word of God, and the cross of Christ will become more real to you. The Bible is the story of Jesus Christ and Him crucified. Now walking after the flesh is the person trying to live without God by means of what a human being can do with his intellect, his science, his education, philosophies, traditions, talents, abilities, efforts, personal strengths, etc. Man continually evaluates and compares himself to creator God whether he does it intentionally or not. That is by definition walking after the flesh, attributing everything we see to nature and chance as the only truth is what the world without God knows. You're not going to make it with that kind of ignorance, pride, and rebellion.

> For the invisible things of him from the creation of the world
> *are clearly seen*, being understood by the things that are made,
> even his eternal power and Godhead; so that *they are without*
> *excuse.* (Romans 1:20, emphasis added)

When Adam ate the fruit of knowledge of good and evil, he removed God from his life and filled the void with selfish thoughts of excuses and rationalizations. Today man fails to reach God for the same reasons of rebellion that Adam had thousands of years ago, finding condemnation and expulsion from God's presence as the result. The problem is in the Adamic sin nature of man, and his thoughts preclude him from understanding his original purpose or why his life is so messed up and if it really matters if he ever lived at all. This confusion or delusion can make a person do the things that they really don't want to do and do what they know is harmful to them. In fact, we react impulsively and contrary to our spiritual desires that are opposed to our conscience and desires.

> For we know that the law is spiritual: but I am carnal, sold under sin. For that which I do I allow not: for what I would, that do I not; *but what I hate, that do I.* If then I do that which I would not, I consent unto the law that it is good. Now then *it is no more I that do it, but sin that dwelleth in me.* For I know that in me (that is, in my flesh,) dwelleth no good thing: for to will is present with me; but how to perform that which is good I find not. For the good that I would I do not: but the evil which I would not, that I do. Now if I do that I would not, it is no more I that do it, but sin that dwelleth in me. I find then a law, that, when I would do good, evil is present with me. For I delight in the law of God after the inward man: But I see another law in my members, warring against the law of my mind, and bringing me into captivity to the law of sin which is in my members. (Romans 7:14–23, emphasis added)

The Holy Spirit plays into the finished work of the cross. The cross gives the Holy Spirit the legal right to do all that He needs to do in healing our lives just like the Devil gets legal rights to enter your life by your sinful actions. This fact only proves what is required of us in this life to heal our soul and that our faith must be exclusively in Christ and what Christ did at the cross—not a church or a person except Jesus Christ of Nazareth. The Holy Spirit works entirely within the framework of the completed work of Christ at the cross. The act of restoring the rubble of our souls is only through the victory in the blood of Jesus and our willingness to change our minds (conforming to Christlikeness) and repent for what we have done in rebellion to God. It is vitally important to make a distinction with the worldview of what sin is and the need to acknowledge the consequences of it for eternity as outlined only in the Word of God.

Only the Bible deals with sin specifically, the ramifications of sin to us individually, and what it does to our relationships with others as a result of them. Sin is only important to you if you believe that the God of the Bible is real and the consequences of your actions affect not only yourself but all those you come in contact with. Too many people try to justify their lifestyles and their actions by ignoring the existence of an afterlife and a belief in a God or sin. Many people think if there really is a God, He will understand and overlook their perversion and actions because He is a loving God. In the Bible, we are told that when we reach the "deadline," judgment comes and we must give account for our actions. This judgment is explained to us by Jesus in Luke as He spoke and explained the consequences of our life choices, the law, and the kingdom of God to the disciples.

> And it came to pass, that the beggar died, and was carried by the angels into Abraham's bosom: the rich man also died, and was buried; And in hell he lifted up his eyes, being in torments, and seeth Abraham afar off, and Lazarus in his bosom. And he cried and said, Father Abraham, have mercy on me, and send Lazarus, that he may dip the tip of his finger in water, and cool my tongue; for I am tormented in this flame. But Abraham said, Son, remember that thou in thy lifetime received the good things, and likewise Lazarus evil things: but now he is comforted, and thou art tormented. And beside all this, between us and you *there is a great gulf fixed*: so that they which would pass from hence to you cannot; neither can they pass to us, that would come from thence.

Then he said, I pray thee therefore, father, that thou wouldest send him to my father's house: For I have five brethren; that he may testify unto them, lest they also come into this place of torment. Abraham saith unto him, They have Moses and the prophets; let them hear them. And he said, Nay, father Abraham: but if one went unto them from the dead, they will repent. And he said unto him, *If they hear not Moses and the prophets, neither will they be persuaded, though one rose from the dead.* (Luke 16:22–31, emphasis added)

What this tells us is that praying to our dead relatives, dead disciples, and saints of the church or even the Virgin Mary can't help the situation you're in; and secondly, they're all dead. Not only can they not change or help you in this life, but the Bible tells us they can't even help themselves. It says there is only one person who mediates between you and God, and that is Christ Jesus and Him alone and only while you are alive. Once you're dead, it's over and then the judgment.

For this is good and acceptable in the sight of God our Savior; Who will have all men to be saved, and to come unto the knowledge of the truth. For there is one God, and one mediator between God and men, the man Christ Jesus. (1 Timothy 2:3–5)

And as it is appointed unto men once to die, but after this the judgment. (Hebrews 9:27)

When you're praying to dead loved ones or dead saints for help, they can't see you, and the Bible says that they can't help you. They're dead and their souls are either with the Lord in heaven like Lazarus with Abraham or in the torment of hell like the rich man. The spirits or paranormal entities that people see can only be one of two things: the vivid imagination of an overactive mind or the very real demonic character emulating a previously living person. That demon suppressed, oppressed, or possessed in the past is now looking for a body of flesh and blood to rest in. The apostles repeated Jesus in these passages:

> When the unclean spirit is gone out of a man, he walks through dry places, seeking rest, and finds none. Then he says, I will return into my house from whence I came out; and when he is come, he finds it empty, swept, and garnished. Then goes he, and takes with himself seven other spirits more wicked than himself, and they enter in and dwell there: and the last state of that man is worse than the first. Even so shall it be also unto this wicked generation. (Matthew 12:43–45)

> When the unclean spirit is gone out of a man, he walks through dry places, seeking rest; and finding none, he says, I will return unto my house whence I came out. And when he cometh, he finds it swept and garnished. Then goes he, and takes to him seven other spirits more wicked than himself; and they enter in, and dwell there: and the last state of that man is worse than the first. (Luke 11:24–26)

Why is it so easy for people to believe that there are ghosts and UFOs, but they have such a hard time accepting that there is a creator God, angels, and heaven or the Devil with demons that torment living men and women. The whole theory of evolution is so widely accepted today that anyone who questions its veracity is ridiculed and called unintelligent. The undeniable fact that there are no concrete transitional (missing links) examples of one species evolving into another doesn't deter academia from teaching evolution as fact in our schools even though it is only a theory.

The sad truth is that if the Bible were taught as fact in our public schools, then scripture from Genesis on would condemn 90 to 95 percent of the lifestyles society condones as normal today. The failure to heed the warnings of the oldest, most consistent and complete writings about creation and the afterlife is foolish and arrogant on man's part. The idea that man can ignore the confusion and chaos in his own thoughts and concentrate on the presently demonically infested world we live in now only masks the need for answers. Only a personal relationship with the Messiah, Jesus Christ of Nazareth, the only begotten Son of the Lord of Hosts Jehovah God answers these questions and warns us of these spiritual hazards. With personal deliverance and the restoration by the Holy Spirit of our soul's walls, we can then begin to be Christ-like in our thoughts and stop accepting the lies of demons and man's ignorant, vain imaginations.

We now have two issues that need to be resolved. First, when looking for answers from science for the creation of everything we see through Darwinian evolution, that it falls miserably short in trying to answer life-origin, species/creation–origins, and cosmos/order–systems origin. You have to have more faith in science than you do in a creator God. Secondly, in studying human nature one can't ignore that every single issue of human nature is covered and explained in the Torah, the Old Testament, and later in the New Testament (The Holy Bible). On both counts in my limited knowledge of science, history, and psychology, the Bible wins hands down. When studying Scripture, the issue of reliance and obedience to a creator God and the issue of sin and how we deal with it is the main theme throughout.

Like we have stated earlier, sin and temptations of sin are the fruit of the seeds sown in the lust of the flesh and have to be dealt with specifically in order to have fellowship with the Father. I am convinced that the biggest lie ever perpetrated upon a believing people is to think that once you get saved and believe, you never have to worry about being attacked by Satan again. Honestly, once you do make a commitment to serve Jesus, I really do believe that Satan tries every trick in the book to trip you up to sin, and he will if you open the door and let him in. Then the flipside is to have you so tied up in traditions and religious pretentious actions in an organized Church that you become spiritually powerless. Only through belief in one God, the remission of sin through the sacrifice and redemption on the cross of Jesus Christ can we have access to the third person of the Trinity, the Holy Spirit, and the gifts He provides.

The Holy Spirit is the gift from the Father and the Son to the church and to the individual believer. Jesus said, "I will pray the Father, and he shall give you another Comforter, that he may abide with you forever" (John 14:16). God the Father sent Jesus the Son of God to become the Son of Man so the sons of men could become the sons of God. He sent His Son to die for us and save us. The Father and the Son gave us the Holy Spirit to empower us for the spiritual war we face in this life.

> But ye shall receive power, after that the Holy Ghost is come upon you: and ye shall be witnesses unto me both in Jerusalem, and in all Judaea, and in Samaria, and unto the uttermost part of the earth. (Acts 1:8)

> And, behold, I send the promise of my Father upon you: but tarry ye in the city of Jerusalem, until ye be endued with power from on high. (Luke 24:49)

The Holy Spirit is the omnipotent, omnipresent one; very deity of very deity; very God of very God; coequal, coeternal, coexistent with the Father and the Son. He does the work of God on earth. Jesus is the architect of the church, and the Holy Spirit is the contractor. All blessings, works of grace, repentance, faith, and victory in our Christian lives are the result of the Holy Spirit working in us. The Holy Spirit baptism is the coming of the Holy Spirit to dwell in the heart and life of an individual, fulfilling the Scripture, John 14:16–17.

> And I will pray the Father, and he shall give you another Comforter, that he may abide with you for ever; Even the Spirit of truth; whom the world cannot receive, because it seeth him not, neither knoweth him: but ye know him; for he *dwelleth with you, and shall be in you.* (emphasis added)

If not for the Holy Spirit calling us to inquire about Christ, we would not or could not be part of His bride. The Holy Spirit leads us to serve Christ, and He leads us to correct the issues that have caused pain in our lives. In the baptism in the Holy Spirit, He comes with a definite experience in baptismal fullness of power in Jesus' name; He has His own personality, His own ministry, and He begins to give us His own fruit and gifts. The apostle Peter preached the baptism in the Holy Spirit in Acts 2:38–39 which says,

> Then Peter said unto them, Repent, and be baptized every
> one of you in the name of Jesus Christ for the remission of
> sins, and ye shall receive the gift of the Holy Ghost. For
> *the promise is unto you, and to your children,* and to all that
> are afar off, even as many as the LORD our God shall call.
> (emphasis added) (Courtney, 24–26)

Peter wasn't just preaching to the other apostles but to the multitude of new
converts like you and me who believe in Christ as Lord and Savior then we
all receive the gift of the Holy Spirit. The Holy Spirit abides in us when
we receive Jesus as Lord and Savior and then He falls upon us when we're
baptized in the Holy Spirit.

> Howbeit when he, the Spirit of truth, is come, he will guide
> you into all truth: for he shall not speak of himself; but
> whatsoever he shall hear, that shall he speak: and he will
> show you things to come. (John 16:13)

> I will pour out my spirit unto you; I will make known my
> words unto you. (Proverbs 1:23)

> And I will put my spirit within you, and cause you to walk in
> my statutes, and ye shall keep my judgments, and do them.
> (Ezekiel 36:27)

> That the blessing of Abraham might come on the Gentiles
> through Jesus Christ; that we might receive the promise of
> the Spirit through faith. (Galatians 3:14)

God doesn't condemn you of sin, because *all* your sins are forgiven at salvation,
but He does convict you and warn you of potential problems and that's exactly
what the gifts of the Spirit are for (1 Corinthians 12:1–11). He then gives you
weapons for battle and then all God's armor to protect your spirit temple
from attack.

> Finally, my brethren, be strong in the Lord, and in the power
> of his might. Put on the whole armor of God, that ye may

be able to stand against the wiles of the devil. (Ephesians 6:10–11)

The gifts of the Spirit and the armor of God are for you and me as born-again believers to do battle against the Devil and his minions. Satan is very subtle, devious, and cunning and would like nothing more than to convince a child of the living God that the psychological, physical, and emotional pains you're suffering are your fault or that you're in a hopeless situation. His whole purpose in tormenting you is to cause you to hurt yourself physically, psychologically, emotionally, and interpersonally. His ultimate goal is to cause you to kill yourselves or someone else, because Satan hates you. He hates you because you were created in God's image, and he wants to destroy anything and everything that resembles the living God Jehovah.

Since no sin can enter into God's presence, all Satan or his minions have to do is keep you from Jesus, and by keeping you in sin, he keeps you from Jehovah God. "Try it, you'll like it," or "just a little bit more won't hurt" and "you can stop at any time you want" are Satan's surefire reasoning's and methods to trap you into an addiction. Drugs, alcohol, sex, pornography, or any number of enticing lusts of the flesh that are his mode of operation, and he's had six thousand years to hone his craft of deception and trickery.

There is a seven-step process to sin and sinning whether intentionally or not. Condemnation does not come from God. It either is self-induced by your conscience from guilt, or it is the thoughts of suggestions by Satan and his minions.

> Let no man say when he is tempted, I am tempted of God: for God cannot be tempted with evil, neither tempteth he any man: But every man is tempted, when *he is drawn away of his own lust*, and enticed. Then when lust hath conceived, it brings forth sin: and sin, when it is finished, brings forth death. (James 1:13–15, emphasis added)

First is temptation, then you are drawn away with lust of the senses. Next (2) you are enticed until the lust that is conceived in your mind is then formed in your heart; (3) then you act upon these sinful desires; (4) which brings forth spiritual death (5). Spiritual death brings about the root of bitterness that in its initial stages begins with resentment and unforgiveness. If this unforgiveness is not dealt with, it can lead to feelings of anger and hate (6), which is the precursor to retaliation and violence, which ultimately leads us to Satan's primary goal: (7) to murder a person's life, whether spiritually or physically. Satan hates God so much that he wants to destroy anything that resembles God in any way, shape, or form—that means you and your testimony as well. Whether by word or deed, he wants to hurt us or provoke us to hurt, kill, or destroy the people around us.

There is so much involved with each person's life, that every individual's protective walls are constructed and influenced by every word or deed said in ridicule or jest. Satan uses any little offence to prod and provoke us to act, and he uses other people to plant seeds of doubt and unbelief to our foundations. The consequences of these thoughts and our responses to them determine how our spirit's defenses are built and maintained in this life and ultimately for the rewards in the next. Only the Word of God (the Bible) deals with every act and thought of a man from the age of accountability to death. From an individual's thoughts in seclusion; to our speech; to and from spouses, siblings, family members, neighbors, coworkers, and acquaintances; every word spoken has influence and affects the lives of these people and subsequently our saved souls' eternal rewards. Every word and every motivation behind them shall be judged by our Creator.

> And the tongue is a fire, a world of iniquity: so is the tongue among our members, that it defileth the whole body, and setteth on fire the course of nature; and it is set on fire of hell. (James 3:6)

> But I say unto you, That every idle word that men shall speak, they shall give account thereof in the day of judgment. For by thy words thou shalt be justified, and by thy words thou shalt be condemned. (Matthew 12:36–37)

God spoke and He created the worlds. When you and I speak, we create the world and environment that we and those around us live in. Every word we speak to the people we love in our lives or the ones we hate will either build them up or help destroy part or all of their walls. Spoken words can do the most harm to a person's psyche and self-worth, especially those spoken words by a parent or guardian to a child in their formative years can damage them for life (Prince). Even in our later years in adolescence or adulthood, spoken words by an authority figure, parent, or spouse can destroy the other person's resolve and tenacity for life.

Remember that the spirit of every man or woman is renewed at the point of salvation. When they receive Jesus as Lord and Savior and are born again, the walls that protect that born-again spirit remain in the same condition they were in before. Unfortunately, until dealt with specifically, being born-again doesn't resolve all the hurts and broken walls to our soul that are caused by the offences of un-forgiveness, bitterness, depression, or guilt. They need to be rooted out specifically and resolved specifically for complete healing and restoration of that fruit of the Spirit soul wall. This is where words spoken in anger, hatred, and ridicule in childhood open the door to the soul and plant seeds that start destroying and damaging the foundations of fruit walls as they begin forming strongholds of bitterness, guilt, and shame. The opposite occurs with approval and praise by parents as they begin building a good, strong self-esteem and a humble pride in a person, sowing healthy seeds in fertile godly hearts. Manifestations and seeds of evil begin festering wicked thoughts that grow as a child grows into adulthood, and they can only be rooted out through Jesus and the Holy Spirit.

> For we wrestle not against flesh and blood, but against principalities, against powers, against the rulers of the darkness of this world, against spiritual wickedness in high places. (Ephesians 6:12)

Spiritual wickedness in high places refers to your thoughts or your dwelling on thoughts of pleasure and lusting for material things. The Word of God says our spirits are as perfect as they ever will be when we make the decision to receive Jesus and confess Him as Lord of our lives. Our soul consists of the nine fruit of the Spirit that may need healing even after being saved.

> But the fruit of the Spirit is love, joy, peace, longsuffering, gentleness, goodness, faith, Meekness, temperance: against such there is no law. And they that are Christ's *have crucified the flesh* with the affections and lusts. If we live in the Spirit, let us also walk in the Spirit. Let us not be desirous of vain glory, provoking one another, envying one another. (Galatians 5:22–26, emphasis added)

Your spirit is as saved, sanctified, and as holy as it ever will be for eternity; it is who we are as individuals and what our rewards for eternity are based on. All we have to do now is catch our souls up to our spirits so we can receive our new bodies and full rewards in the kingdom of God. After our death and judgment, the only part of our triune being that will not enter the kingdom of God is our earthbound sinful bodies. Our newly born-again spirits and our rebuilt soul walls are what we present to Jesus at the foot of the cross. While here in the third part of our being—our bodies—we must all understand that the body is the frailest of the three and it will get diseased, it will get old, and it will ultimately perish.

Our job is to rebuild the walls of our souls by becoming more and more Christ-like in our character and behavior as we mature as Christians. We are to rebuild the walls (our soul) surrounding the temple of our spirit just as Nehemiah wanted to rebuild the city walls to protect the newly rebuilt temple in Jerusalem. You and I need to rebuild the walls protecting our born-again spirit temple by improving the nine Christ-like fruit of the Spirit, forming the walls surrounding it in us. When Jesus was begotten of the Father, He came into this world born of a virgin for the remission of our sins. He (second Adam) died as the Lamb slain from the foundation of the earth but also to show each one of us how to attain Christlikeness in this life. Mary was a virgin impregnated by the Holy Spirit of God so as to not contaminate her child with the sinful Adamic nature that all the rest of humanity has after the fall. Hebrew law demanded the payment for sin with the shedding of innocent blood. No naturally conceived man could have fulfilled this requirement because of the lust of the flesh that is within the heart of every man and woman during this life.

> Therefore the Lord himself shall give you a sign; Behold, a virgin shall conceive, and bear a son, and shall call his name Immanuel [God with us]. (Isaiah 7:14, emphasis added)

> Now all this was done, that it might be fulfilled which was spoken of the Lord by the prophet, saying, Behold, a virgin shall be with child, and shall bring forth a son, and they shall call his name Emmanuel, which being interpreted is, God with us. (Matthew 1:22–23)

Jesus' sinless nature and uncontaminated blood (innocent and pure) is the only way to atone, purify, cleanse, and heal man's sinful nature, and only the Bible's Old and New Testaments address this aspect of sinful human nature. The Word of God tells us in Hebrews 9:22–24,

> And almost all things are by the law purged with blood; and *without shedding of blood is no remission*. It was therefore necessary that the patterns of things in the heavens should be purified with these; but the heavenly things themselves with better sacrifices than these. For Christ is not entered into the holy places made with hands, which are the figures of the true; but into heaven itself, *now to appear in the presence of God for us*. (emphasis added)

As eternal advocate and perfect sacrifice for all those of mankind who confess the risen Christ Jesus as Lord and Savior, not only does He cleanse us of all unrighteousness, but when He shed His innocent blood for us before and during His crucifixion He covered every area of our sin areas. He hung on a tree to take the curse away from us and He became a curse for us: "Christ hath redeemed us from the curse of the law, being made a curse for us: for it is written, Cursed is every one that hangeth on a tree" (Galatians 3:13).

The shedding of His own innocent blood over every area is needed for us as believers to conquer and defeat the sin in our lives. Jesus is our only advocate to the Father on our behalf and is seated at His right hand. Jesus is seated because His work is completed. We don't need to go to any dead people— no mothers, no fathers, no saints or patriarchs, they're all dead. Only Jesus defeated the Devil and only Jesus rose from the dead and only Jesus is alive today to plead our case to the Father. Only Jesus can and will comfort and understand you in your troubles because His blood was shed to cover and defeat every area of pain and hurt to our souls.

I will explain the seven places where Jesus shed His blood and the significance of each area where He was wounded as to how those clarify and cover any sin that we could possibly ever have in our lives.

First, when Jesus was alone in prayer on the Mount of Olives: "And being in an agony he prayed more earnestly: and his sweat was as it were great drops of blood falling down to the ground" (Luke 22:44). Anticipation, fear, and worries as a man worries of the future with the expectation of the trial and the pain He would have to endure, were all there. We, through His victory, are now able to defeat the mental anguish and perverted imaginations before us. He did not act on them because that would be sin, and Jesus is sinless.

> Who, being in the form of God, thought it not robbery to
> be equal with God. (Philippians 2:6)

He was every bit a man and every bit God incarnate. The perfect sacrifice, the Lamb of God, the living manna from heaven, Jesus Christ is the Son of the living God (Jehovah) made flesh and is our perfect example of how we're to restore and rebuild the broken walls of our souls to protect our born-again spirits. Jesus endured the scourging on His back to signify the burdens of this life that He endured for us. He then was lead to Pilot's court where the mockery and ridicule of His personhood and purpose were questioned. The pummeling of His face and the pulling out of His beard was to conquer the evil facial expressions and contortions of our fallen countenance. Every thought entertained in our minds is defeated by the bloodshed of the crown of thorns worn by our King of Kings and Lord of Lords, Jesus the Christ. Both hands were pierced, shedding His blood for the things we touch and handle that are contrary to God's laws (and are still God's laws, regardless of what society says today). His feet were pierced and shed His blood for the places we go to act out our fantasies that are again contrary to God's ways. Finally, the humiliation and scorn of the crucifixion as He hung naked on the cross in shame only exemplified by the final piercing of His side to His heart that was broken for us.

Through each of these seven places that Jesus shed His innocent blood, we can see how Jesus has defeated every area that we can possibly be tempted and tormented in. Our anguish, guilt, depression, physical pains, emotional hurts, and shame are all covered by the shed blood of Jesus Christ at the cross. Every thought, temptation, act of rage and lust of the flesh can be conquered by Jesus and Him alone at the cross.

Chapter 8

EITHER THE BIBLE IS
TRUE OR IT'S NOT

*I*n this next section, I will show you how only the Bible tells us that the flesh will override the spiritual if not maintained and repaired through prayer, restoration, and deliverance. Corruption begins in our mind and thoughts, and it ends with our bodies and relationships reaping the consequences of these damaging thoughts and actions. Paul warns us in Ephesians 5:3–5 that the precursors to these works of the flesh are established in our thought life as spirit world realities and lusts of the heart.

> But fornication, and all uncleanness, or covetousness, let it not be once named among you, as becometh saints; Neither filthiness, nor foolish talking, nor jesting, which are not convenient: but rather giving of thanks. For this ye know, that no whoremonger, nor unclean person, nor covetous man, who is an idolater, hath any inheritance in the kingdom of Christ and of God.

These seemingly innocuous actions are really seeds of corruption that, if watered and nourished with consistent inappropriate toleration (political correctness), will grow into what Paul calls the works of the flesh. These works of the flesh are found in Galatians 5:19–21, and they consist of seventeen works or areas of involvement that if not addressed early can and will wipe out our salvation confession if you practice one or more of these.

> Now the works of the flesh are manifest, which are these; Adultery, fornication, uncleanness, lasciviousness, Idolatry, witchcraft, hatred, variance, emulations, wrath, strife, seditions, heresies, Envying, murders, drunkenness, reveling, and such like: of the which I tell you before, as I have also told you in time past, *that they which do such things shall not inherit the kingdom of God.* (emphasis added)

As I read further and meditated on this Word in my prayers, I could see the contradictions in my life with what I read in the Word of God. For we wrestle not against flesh and blood, but against principalities, against powers, against the rulers of the darkness of this world, against spiritual wickedness in high places. (Ephesians 6:12, emphasis added)

We will discuss each of these in detail later in chapters ten, eleven and twelve but know that these four areas are the high-level demons in charge—or the generals so to speak. I could see that my (soul) walls surrounding my (spirit) temple was constructed of individual bricks and that each one of these bricks was influenced by one of these four Powers, Principalities, Rulers of darkness and Spirits of wickedness that I had permitted in. These PPRSs of Ephesians 6:12 as I call them, were visible in each of my nine fruit of the Spirit to some extent, and I saw them as discoloration and areas of destruction. This unpleasant fading and damage to my born-again soul was not only because of them but they were also influenced by lesser but still damaging actions and thoughts. I knew that I was saved, but the fruit of my Spirit were marred by the cares of this world or spirit world realities. I could see emanating from thin cracks and crevasses around the base of each fruit a dirty, dark mold or mildew that grew slowly and oozed out deteriorating the stability of my fruit walls from within each foundation and I knew they were emotional strongholds and the lusts of my heart because of my prejudice, my hatred, and my anger.

These are followed by one or more of the seventeen lusts of the heart and are the next lower level demons that every human faces whether you believe it or not. Whether you are saved or not, they *are* real and they are there. Their purpose is to work in unison with each other like foot soldiers, sergeants, lieutenants, captains, or colonels of an army on a mission for the single purpose of destroying your soul's walls so as to allow access to your other fruit and corrupt us spiritually. There also are in addition to the seventeen works of the flesh, seventeen spirit-world realities which are linked with the seventeen lusts of the heart and these lower-level demons torment every human being, saved or not, with their suggestions and innuendos in your thoughts first.

It is one of Satan's greatest deceptions to a Christ-believing people to convince them to think that once they're saved, they will never experience trials and tribulation again. Know that if you do have troubles, you're powerless to combat them in the spirit. Ignorance of the teachings of Jesus is no excuse, because He has given us all the keys to the kingdom and the authority to combat and defeat these demons in His Word. Satan and his minions throw perverted ideas into your thoughts, taking you on different rabbit trails that lead you to contemplate and dwell on every wicked and evil scenario imaginable. They then use these to try to gain access to your spirit through that open door in your soul. Again, his purpose is to weaken areas of your soul and tempt you to entertain these sinful thoughts, building strongholds to then rise up when you least expect them. It could be at work, at the grocery store, on the way home from work, or even in the pew at church during the preacher's sermon; all he's trying to do is get you to entertain these thoughts.

Jesus is our perfect example of the perfect soul of a man or woman, and we have to not only know His Word to instruct us, but we have to utilize the third person of the Trinity to guide us through this life. The Holy Spirit had shown me Jesus' perfection earlier now He was revealing to me by comparison how God sees our individual imperfections in more detail along with the remedy the Word of God is giving us through the fruit of the Spirit and the baptism of the Holy Spirit.

In my vision, the nine fruit of the Spirit were labeled on each one of the nine gates (Galatians 5:22–23)) of my soul, and I could see my entire protective soul walls around my saved spirit. Each wall consisted of color-labeled bricks, and every brick varied in its size and intensity in color depending on the influence of each spirit-world reality to my soul fruit. Unlike the translucent purity of color in Jesus' walls, the bricks of my walls changed with the hue and translucency of the damaged brick's color next to it. The discoloration was extreme on some areas of my walls, and as I looked more intently at the first gate of Love (goldish-yellow), I could see it was missing areas of its supporting walls and it didn't look very stable.

As I looked at the walls on either side, I could see the gates on both sides as well. Some parts of the walls were built with bricks that were completely perverted and alien to God's original intent. The gates were Joy on the right and Temperance on the left, and I could tell that there was very little love to influence either of them. The walls on either side of the Love gate were terribly distorted and unequally proportioned by the works of my flesh and the spirit-world realities that had wounded my soul from my youth and adolescence. All the gates that I saw were based on the foundation of a perverted love; their base was built on love, but it was very thin in places, and it looked unstable and incomplete—nothing like the vision I saw of the walls of Jesus. The discoloration came from some of the bricks used to build the walls around them, and as I looked in the direction of the next gate, I saw large gaping holes and areas of crumbled heaps of rubble that came from preconceived and self-imposed ideas of love and faith. On the side of Temperance I could see a stronghold of a lack of self-control, self-righteousness and anger. The reasons that caused the anger cracks were based in hatred, racism, un-forgiveness, self-hatred and bitterness towards fellow believers in the risen Christ.

I could see and know the cause and effects of traumatic events that were so extremely painful and sorrowful that they had a very damaging effect to my soul walls, and every relationship I had was influenced by them. When they reached a certain point, they seemed to have exploded and destroyed everything around them, damaging and filling all the nine fruit with a sort of shrapnel, all that was left in the nine walls of the fruit of the Spirit were the remnants of true love. I could see the manifestation and subsequent strongholds of where my father humiliated me in front of my ten-year-old teammates at a football game.

The shame and embarrassment I felt when he brought a doll to the field and said that I should play with the doll because I sure didn't know how to play football like the other boys. The anger and hatred I felt toward him, wishing him dead as I ran home, cursing him all the way. I could see the stronghold of guilt that I had built when the following year, my dad died from cancer at thirty-nine years old. I have only recently dealt with these emotions and removed them through deliverance and prayer. The seeds of hate, self-hate, guilt, and an inability to show real love were planted firmly in my psyche, forming strongholds that the Devil would later use to cause turmoil and strife in every relationship I ever had. It amazed me how I knew that every brick in my walls had been influenced by this one event and that the size of my nine gates and their color, hue, and intensity were based on the foundation of this love-hate experience.

Love not only was the first gate that I saw, but I could also see that the side posts were silver and ran down and encircled the entirety of each of my fruit gates, forming a distinct characteristic to the walls protecting my spirit. Love was the foundation that led to the side posts for all the remaining eight walls and gates and each one was based on my distorted and perverted love foundation. Every single emotion, attitude, feeling of prejudice, and thought of hatred emanated from the love or the lack thereof. This fruit of love in my heart determined the thickness and stability of all the nine fruit walls. The building of each wall of my soul was and still is the basis for every attitude and opinion that comes out of my mouth and it contorts the expressions of my face into the countenance everyone else sees.

This is what God sees in our hearts when we die, and He determines our rewards which are based on them. Yes I'm saved and will go to heaven, but what I do there is hindered and determined by my countenance and lack of love in my heart. Today everyone says that we should love and show love regardless of their adherence to God's Word, but no one ever tells you of all the demolition and rebuilding that has to be done to our soul's walls in order to protect our spirit from pains and hurts and still be able to enter into the presence of a Holy God. Only the Word of God reveals specific areas of our lives that need to be destroyed, rebuilt, and corrected to solve all the issues in this life and prepare us for the afterlife. Only Torah teaches a barbaric and uncivilized people how to live, prosper, and believe in the one and only true God once again. Only the Bible tells of what was needed to keep the priesthood and the lineage pure and holy for the Messiah Jesus Christ to come. Only the Bible tells us of how to correct all the unrighteousness of man's heart, and only the Bible shows us what is needed to live a righteous and holy life that is acceptable and pleasing to our creator God (Genesis 1:1).

If you believe that this creator God is the Jesus Christ of John 1:1–5 and that what His Word says in the New Testament is true, then you as a Christian must also believe that the Law Jesus believed in is true and believe what He taught as a teacher of Torah in His ministry while here on earth is true. His Word is color-blind and nondenominational, but it most definitely adheres to Torah and the New Testament and builds upon its truths.

> Think not that I am come to destroy the law, or the prophets: I am not come to destroy, but to fulfill. For verily I say unto you, Till heaven and earth pass, one jot or one tittle shall in no wise pass from the law, till all be fulfilled. (Matthew 5:17–18)

Only the Word of God shows us the method for eternal salvation. This salvation is only through His Son Jesus Christ, the Messiah, and our growth is only through the third person of the Trinity, the Holy Spirit, who reveals to us the remedy to correct all the wrongs in our lives while we're still breathing. The Holy Spirit alone can guide and lead us to salvation, and the Holy Spirit alone can help us rebuild our damaged soul's walls. Remember: when you're dead, it's too late to change anything. We must change and rectify all the wrongs we can while we're still alive. He gives us His Holy Spirit to reveal these revelations to us through the cross of Christ in prayer: **TRUST**. Jesus tells us,

> The Spirit of the Lord is upon me, because he hath anointed me to preach the gospel to the poor; he hath sent me to heal the brokenhearted, to preach deliverance to the captives, and recovering of sight to the blind, to set at liberty them that are bruised, To preach the acceptable year of the Lord. (Luke 4:18–19)

> And he said unto them, It is not for you to know the times or the seasons, which the Father hath put in his own power. But ye shall receive power, after that the Holy Ghost is come upon you: and ye shall be witnesses unto me both in Jerusalem, and in all Judaea, and in Samaria, and unto the uttermost part of the earth. And when he had spoken these things, while they beheld, he was taken up; and a cloud received him out of their sight. And while they looked steadfastly toward heaven as he went up. (Acts 1:7–10)

God has brought man around full circle to this point in history to learn how to walk after the Spirit as I believe Adam and Eve did prior to the fall. Only now has man come to the point with the advent of the third person of the Trinity, the Holy Spirit of God, where we can begin to be the creation God intended us to be in spirit, soul, and body. Only now can we individually attack the strongholds of our lives and live a righteous and holy life which is our reasonable service.

> There is therefore now no condemnation to them which are in Christ Jesus, who walk not after the flesh, but after the Spirit. For the law of the Spirit of life in Christ Jesus hath made me free from the law of sin and death. For what the law could not do, in that it was weak through the flesh, God sending his own Son in the likeness of sinful flesh, and for sin, condemned sin in the flesh: That the righteousness of the law might be fulfilled in us, *who walk not after the flesh, but after the Spirit.* (Romans 8:1–4, emphasis added)

What an amazing verse! God through Paul in the Holy Spirit is telling you and me in these four verses that we can correct and rebuild our walls by walking in the Spirit. It has taken over six thousand years to get man spiritually to the place of humility and meekness to receive this correction, and it has taken me twenty-six years to admit my shortcomings and begin to walk in faith and the spirit, to begin learning how to reconcile with Jehovah God. Look what Galatians says in verses 22 through 24,

> But the fruit of the Spirit is love, joy, peace, longsuffering, gentleness, goodness, faith, Meekness, temperance: against such there is no law. *And they that are Christ's have crucified the flesh with the affections and lusts.* (emphasis added)

There is no law against living in the fruit of the Spirit, only when the works of the flesh are evident in these fruit and they begin taking over these fruit is there an issue with God. Then we are in trouble, and we produce nothing but rotten fruit. The ramifications of our actions are made apparent by the fruit we bear. Only at salvation does the battle really begin to rage within us, pitting our recreated spirits against our fleshy souls and bodies that have been in control our whole lives. Only Torah and the Old and New Testaments tell us the ramifications of our actions and the effects they have on our children and our children's children. Only the Old Testament tells us the curses and blessings in Deuteronomy 27 and 28 and of the law given to Moses at Mount Ebal.

> And it shall be on the day when ye shall pass over Jordan unto the land which the LORD thy God giveth thee, that thou shalt set thee up great stones, and plaister them with plaister: And *thou shalt write upon them all the words of this law*, when thou art passed over, that thou mayest go in unto the land which the LORD thy God giveth thee, a land that floweth with milk and honey; as the LORD God of thy fathers hath promised thee. (Deuteronomy 27:2–3, emphasis added)

And put on the stones all the words of this law, writing them very clearly. Then Moses and the priests, the Levites, said to all Israel, Be quiet and give ear, O Israel; today you have become the people of the Lord your God. For this cause you are to give ear to the voice of the Lord your God, and do his orders and his laws which I give you this day. (Deuteronomy 27:8–10)

Cursed be the man that maketh any graven or molten image [*idolatry, occultism, astrology*] …
Cursed be he that removeth his neighbour's landmark [*defrauding, stealing, fraud*] …
Cursed be he that maketh the blind to wander [*defrauding, mockery, pride*] …
Cursed be he that perverteth the judgment of the stranger, fatherless, and widow [*defrauding, mockery for amusement*] …
Cursed be he that lieth with any manner of beast [*perversion, bestiality*] …
Cursed be he that lieth with his sister, the daughter of his father, or the daughter of his mother [*incest, perversion*] …
Cursed be he that lieth with his mother in law [*incest, adultery, perversion*] …
Cursed be he that smiteth his neighbour secretly [*murder*] …
Cursed be he that taketh reward to slay an innocent person [*murder, debauchery*] …
Cursed be he that confirmeth not all the words of this law [*disobedience, rebellion*]. (Deuteronomy 27:15, 17–19, 21–26; emphasis added)

And put on the stones all the words of this law, writing them very clearly. Then Moses and the priests, the Levites, said to all Israel, Be quiet and give ear, O Israel; today you have become the people of the Lord your God. For this cause you are to give ear to the voice of the Lord your God, and do his orders and his laws which I give you this day. (Deuteronomy 27:8–10)

When I looked at these ten commands from God, I wondered what it was that made these commands so different than another leader's instructions to his people. I asked the Holy Spirit to reveal this revelation to me in my prayers before I went to sleep. The next morning when I awoke, what the Holy Spirit told me to do was to look at all of these curses and tell Him what the common denominators of them all were.

I noticed that the common factor of the all these commands was that all the curses were the result of a premeditated thought process of an individual and the action taken was long in the making. In other words, the thoughts to commit these acts were not spontaneous, unintentional, or by accident. They were conceived in thought premeditated, and in some cases planned way in advance from fear, hate, or greed.

Let's look at them individually and see what the Holy Spirit tells us. First there is the making of graven images of God (Jehovah). It is ill-conceived and tries to put the face of created things to represent the invisible creator God which is spirit. The concept of trying to put structure and form to a spirit is ludicrous and only leads to vain imaginations and self-grandeur. Man's greed and lust for power uses people's fears and ignorance to enslave and control them. Man can't imagine the splendor or brilliance of a truly holy God and only brings disgrace and dishonor to His name through his fleshly efforts.

Some may think the next command is irrelevant, but in light of man's need to protect his livelihood and possessions, the removing of a neighbor's landmark for selfish gain is fraud and thievery and still is the cause of many disputes and wars today. Mistreatment and abuse of the weak, innocent, and infirm, widows, strangers, and orphans for bullying or mockery was frowned upon by God. The plotting and scheming in deception for profit also brought a curse.

We will expound upon these in later chapters, but let us suffice it to say that the God of Torah gave laws to regulate and provide instruction for reasonable and fair treatment in human relations of all people. Contrary to the idea of political correctness, God's commands brought order and structure to an otherwise repressive and autocratically ruled civilization. The Ten Commandments are still relevant today and give us true security and the freedom God intended us to have.

The next curse is disgusting and abhorrent to God, and that is bestiality. The idea and perversion of the degenerate mind reduces God's finest creation to a subhuman form, and I believe Satan relishes this act of perversion. To coerce a man or woman who is created in the image of the living God to act and lust after an animal only dehumanizes them and gives demons cause for mockery and scorn.

God then warns against incest of family and stepchildren, which is self-explanatory, and the repercussions are evident for generations. Finally God commanded us not to kill or to murder the innocent. Killing and murder are not synonymous but rather quite different in that to murder is with intent for self-gain of property, to achieve status or position or for revenge. To kill someone because of war or self-preservation does not require restitution. If you kill someone by accident, some restitution is required. His Word explains these in Deuteronomy 19, delineating their differences and restitution requirements very clearly. God's Word even called for the establishment of cities for the express purpose of building places of refuge that would protect people who accidently killed someone and were sought after in retaliation by surviving family members. Quite often when speaking of the Ten Commandments, the destructive consequences of these actions are not explained but were stated with the expectation that most civilized people would understand their implication.

Along with these Ten Commandments are laws of human relations, marriage, laws on repayment of debts, on violence, war and retribution, the legal system, the treatment of servants and employees, how to build an altar for prayer, festivals, and how to worship the living God. All of which was to civilize and separate a people from the rest of the wicked world. When man was left to his own devices, it led him to fail miserably. Man tends to elevate himself and his accomplishments far above the reality of who he really is and begins to think of himself as superior. Beyond that, he begins to justify his opinions and prejudices by attributing them to God, or worse yet, raises himself to God status.

> The LORD shall establish thee a holy people unto
> himself, as he hath sworn unto thee, if thou shall keep the

commandments of the LORD thy God, and walk in his ways. And all people of the earth shall see that thou art called by the name of the LORD; and they shall be afraid of thee. (Deuteronomy 28:9–10)

This command has not been substituted or replaced but, rather, expanded and unfolded to reveal God's plan for all of man's restoration. We've all heard the phrase, "The Old Testament concealed is the New Testament revealed," and I am amazed how many professing Christians ignore the Old Testament and justify their actions of prejudice, racism, and murder to Jews and fellow Christians in the name of Jesus. When Jesus spoke and taught from the Law, He clarified and explained its precepts that guide moral behavior like no other religious leader, priest, or teacher of Torah could—because He wrote it. Not until the disciples of Jesus and later Saul of Tarsus saw the risen Christ did they fully understand why Jesus came or what He accomplished for all of mankind as the Messiah.

Chapter 9

WAS JESUS LYING?

When Jesus spoke to the people (mostly Jews), He delivered a message that had never been heard or told before. The Sermon on the Mount, better known as the Beatitudes, was a message that was characterized by the quality of God that was now available to all who believed Torah. Jesus spoke and taught as a man with the authority and knowledge of a learned man of Torah, yet with compassion for the multitudes of people, especially to those infirmed and considered unclean and outside the Law. He spoke on a soul-and-spiritual level rather than only a legalistic flesh-oriented set of laws that dominated the Hebrew culture of the day.

> Blessed are the poor in spirit: for theirs is the kingdom of heaven.
> Blessed are they that mourn: for they shall be comforted.
> Blessed are the meek: for they shall inherit the earth.
> Blessed are they which do hunger and thirst after righteousness: for they shall be filled.
> Blessed are the merciful: for they shall obtain mercy.
> Blessed are the pure in heart: for they shall see God.

> Blessed are the peacemakers: for they shall be called the
> children of God.
> Blessed are they which are persecuted for righteousness'
> sake: for theirs is the kingdom of heaven.
> Blessed are ye, when men shall revile you, and persecute you,
> and shall say all manner of evil against you falsely, for my
> sake. (Matthew 5:3–12)

Blessings weren't only conditional by strictly following the Mosaic laws alone, but these blessings spoken of here were considered by most of what society called human frailties or weaknesses and were actually who Jesus wanted to minister to. Jesus wanted believers to know that the final judgment of those who believed in Jehovah would have to represent the attributes of the fruit of the Spirit in spite of the difficulties they faced because of the lusts of the flesh and their trusting in traditions of men. Regardless of the particular law or rule you followed, you could be "right," but you ain't right in the big picture of eternity.

> Enter ye in at the strait gate: for wide is the gate, and broad
> is the way, that leadeth to destruction, and many there be
> which go in thereat: Because strait is the gate, and narrow is
> the way, which leadeth unto life, and few there be that find
> it. (Matthew 7:13–14)

Jesus is talking about salvation for all believers in Torah, and He was talking about the way we live after our confession of faith in Jesus as Messiah. I looked at it and asked the Holy Spirit to explain to me what happens after our confession of faith and what is expected of us regardless of our stated denomination. At the very instant we truly believe in our hearts and confess with our mouth that we believe that God raised Jesus from the dead, we're in and our spirits are as perfect as they ever will be for all eternity. Unfortunately, many professing Christians live by the laws of the flesh and the "church" and not by what the Word claims or requires, because they've never read it. They trust in other men's interpretations and traditions that have absolutely nothing to do with our spiritual walk and more with what someone else thinks is spiritual.

Through this confession of faith in Jesus and Jesus alone are we justified, and if we were to die, we would be permitted to enter into the kingdom of God and be with Jesus. It really doesn't matter what denomination of Christianity you belong to, the God of creation demands perfect righteousness, and only through the shed blood of Jesus Christ on the cross are we justified before a Holy God. Your sins or "works of the flesh" will be punished by God regardless of your denomination or the "good works" you think you've done in this life. The question is, will you be punished for your sins in hell forever because of your self-righteousness and hypocrisy, or are you going to receive your just rewards because of your overcoming the lusts of the flesh and changing your mind (repenting) and conforming to Christlikeness. Getting saved is not the end but the beginning, and our quest to be Christ-like has only just begun. Matthew 7:21–23 states,

> Not everyone that saith unto me, Lord, Lord, shall enter into the kingdom of heaven; but he that *doeth the will of my Father which is in heaven.* Many will say to me in that day, Lord, Lord, have we not prophesied in thy name and in thy name have cast out devils? And in thy name done many wonderful works? And then will I profess unto them, *I never knew you: depart from me, ye that work iniquity.* (emphasis added)

What does that mean? Does it ask you if you were really saved in the first place or if you were just going through the motions to get people off your back? It means to me that you really need to be very careful about your walk. Not only could you lose your salvation if you *practice* any of these works of the flesh, but you *can* also lose some or all of your rewards for eternity if you don't ever remove these emotional strongholds and rebuild your walls. I say this because either your salvation wasn't a real repentance and you never really were going to change the way you lived, or it was legit and Jesus came into your heart and saved you. Either way, your fruit will verify if your confession was truly real. I believe that if you ask the Holy Spirit to show you areas that need improvement, He will show you. God will not be mocked and will not allow sin in His presence, so you must remove the sinful issues in your life regardless of what the world says about your lifestyle, or you will be one of these people Jesus is speaking of.

> God forbid: yea, let God be true, but every man a liar; as it is written, That thou might be justified in thy sayings, and might overcome when thou art judged. (Romans 3:4)

You will be judged. I thank God every day that through all of these physical trials and difficulties in my life that I can still change my mind and truly learn to do the will of my Father which is in heaven, because when we die and cross that "deadline," it is too late to change anything from our life for eternity. After our true confession of faith, we are saved for eternity then we will be judged as to what our rewards will be. I am convinced that our motivations, thoughts, intentions, and conveyed attitudes will determine our rewards and duties in heaven. This life not only determines our eternal destination, but it determines how and what we will be doing once we get there. People tend to be disillusioned and lulled into a false sense of security about being saved. They just trust in the onetime act and don't worry or think about deliverance and restoration of our damaged soul walls.

Yes, we are saved with our confession of faith, but we still have issues that need to be addressed. Every traumatic event or hurt feeling in our life opens a door and damages the walls of our soul, which supports a gate to a fruit of the Spirit. Every single thought that we think and every single terse and rude word that comes out of our mouth will be the determining factors of our rewards. Every motive and every deep-seated reason for our sour attitudes and actions will be exposed by the light of Jesus Christ. I believe it is life after salvation that helps restore our walls, broken and destroyed by the words and actions of people in our lives.

The proof is in His Word, and unless you're willing to repent and change your life attitude, you will be limited in the kingdom. These limitations can be formed at a very young age, establishing lifelong habits of hate, rejection, or bitterness that rear their ugly heads at the slightest provocation. Many times an angry or frustrated attitude can be instigated by the mere presence of a person who reminds you of a past hurt or situation. You consciously really don't know why you're in a bad mood, but you are and your face shows it.

Your countenance has fallen, and everyone around you knows your disdain for them or the situation you've just put yourself into, and controlling your fallen countenance is almost impossible.

I have a few examples of my failures in my own life that, through the grace of God, I believe I have begun the process of rebuilding the walls of my soul. This has allowed me to grow spiritually and be more pleasing to God and my family. Until this realization that my walls were in need of repair, I was not able to really process my feelings or thoughts. Internally the stress and frustration of this spiritual stagnation helped, I believe, cause my immune system to begin to fail. If you don't take every thought captive and replace them with good thoughts, they will destroy you or your relationships. I had a business, status, money, a beautiful wife and kids, I was saved, sanctified, and filled with the Holy Ghost, and I was still dying inside—which is exactly what I believe many believers are doing today. They are saved and still suffering unbeknownst to family or friends or even themselves.

Up until this point in my life, I had been living the American dream. There weren't enough hours in the day to do what I thought was important to do. There wasn't anything my wife and kids wanted that I didn't try to get them. Like I said earlier, not until my world came tumbling down around me did I really cry out to God. I had lost my health, my job, and my business, and I was on the verge of losing my wife and kids. My wife, Lena, hadn't worked since the first year of our marriage, and now she had to find a job that offered health insurance and a decent wage. For that first year, the money she made as a receptionist paid for the car, food essentials, gas, and utilities. My medication deductible and COBRA insurance alone exceeded $960.00 a month, and that was nearly all my disability insurance check.

Thank God for my mom and dad who kept extra food in the house for us. They literally were a godsend when they came over unannounced with five or six grocery bags full of fruit, meats and cookies for the kids. Thanks be to God that He is Jehovah-Jireh, my provider, and all we lost was my perceived status, my pride, and the so-called friends that came along for the free ride. Once I got over feeling sorry for myself, I could then begin dealing with the reality of not being able to go back to work. I realized that I had to make the best of the situation. I was able to devote the majority of my time to studying the

Bible and reading books on it. I refused to accept the diagnosis of progressive MS and began pushing my body. The pain in my legs was excruciating, and it felt as if someone took a hot barbecue skewer and ran it through my legs. I then turned to apitherapy or honeybee venom therapy which is taking live honeybees, grabbing them with clamp tweezers, and allowing them to sting me at various acupuncture points or wherever it hurt. At one point, I had stung myself with the help of my wife some 2,500 times before I stopped. This really helped my drop foot but only temporarily.

There are two types of MS. One is remitting recurring and the medication at least helps reduce the exacerbation symptoms, and the second is my diagnosis that really has no cure. Progressive MS has no medication to relieve the effects of the disease; it only continues to get worse and never stops the blurred vision, fatigue or the dizziness. The doctors at the clinic said that at least if I took the medications that it might slow down the progression of the disease.

I rejected that diagnosis and will not receive that lie. The doctors don't even know what causes MS and there is no cure for it, so I choose to trust in Jesus and Him alone. Galatians 3:13 says,

> Christ hath redeemed us from the curse of the law, being made a curse for us: for it is written, Cursed is every one that hangeth on a tree.

I receive my healing just as I receive my salvation from the risen Christ. His Word says to confess things that are not as though they were, and I did and do what Abraham did. I believe God's promises that I am healthy, healed, and whole, and I am strong, stable, and full of stamina.

> As it is written, I have made thee a father of many nations, before him whom he believed, even God, who *quickeneth the dead, and calleth those things which be not as though they were.* (Romans 4:17, emphasis added)

Yes I struggle, but the Lord has given me the strength and the ability to climb up and down two flights of stairs daily to get to my office and do most of the laundry. I can see, walk, read, teach, type, and usher at church, and by the grace of God I will finish this book. Fourteen years ago I couldn't do any of these things, but God has called me to write down these visions. I firmly believe that the Devil has assigned his demons to try to stop me from sharing His truth about what every born-again believer has been given. That is, that you have the authority and power to destroy every stronghold and curse perpetrated against you and your family.

God has given us the operation manual for our lives, and that is the King James Version of the Bible—not the emasculated, bloodless, effeminate new translations that have taken out all the power and authority of the Word of the living God so as not to offend anyone. The so-called academics and biblical scholars have tried to discredit and eliminate all references of the Trinity, the blood, and sin. The Trinity is the whole purpose of the Word of God yesterday, today, and forever. What I believe is the cause of your and my infirmities, pains, hurts, and offenses is the Adamic curse. There are three types of curses that fall under the heading of the Adamic curse that can afflict us: the curse of the Law, generational curses, and word curses. The curse of the Law is expounded upon by the apostle Paul in Galatians 3:10–12.

> For as many as are of the works of the law are under the curse: for it is written, Cursed is every one that continueth not in all things which are written in the book of the law to do them. But that *no man* is justified by the law in the sight of God, it is evident: for, The just shall live by faith. And the law is not of faith: but, The man that doeth them shall live in them. (emphasis added)

Man is cursed from the fall of Adam. The consequences of the curse can not be ignored or kept under control, but we must defeat it by becoming an overcomer with the blood of the Lamb and the Word of God. If not seriously considered and dealt with, it will be fed by the lust of the flesh and completely devour and destroy the walls of our soul, ultimately killing us spiritually. One thing we must be reminded of constantly is that God has not left us without weapons to destroy the strongholds in our lives; He has given us the tools to rebuild the walls and rehang the gates of our souls.

YOU MIGHT BE RIGHT, BUT YOU AIN'T RIGHT

> This I say then, Walk in the Spirit, and ye shall not fulfil the
> lust of the flesh. For the flesh lusteth against the Spirit, and
> the Spirit against the flesh: and these are contrary the one to
> the other: so that ye cannot do the things that ye would. But
> if ye be led of the Spirit, ye are not under the law. (Galatians
> 5:16–18)

The first curse is the curse associated with the Law. It is better known as "legalism," which in reality is drowning in the works and lusts of the flesh. Wherever this curse is evident, you will see a hierarchy of a selected few who are determined by their own standards or the standards as they perceive them from God as to what the "law" is.

The second are generational curses, and these result from unbroken strongholds passed down from your parents, your grandparents, great-grandparents, and beyond to as many as ten generations. These curses have been written in your families DNA and make us susceptible to demonic oppression and are ignorantly called "family traits" that are taught to our children and accepted as the way it just is and you can't change it. When these thoughts are entertained by you or family members, they then grab hold, and they become a new stronghold that is not easily broken off the new generation.

The third and last is probably the most insidious and subtle of them all and it is the word curse. These word curses can be implanted into our minds and hearts so that they seem only natural for our actions and reactions to occur the way they do. Word curses can be spoken to us at a very young age and carried through our childhood, our adolescence and into adulthood. If not addressed, we can get married and unintentionally pass them on to our children, who could then pass it on to their children, and their children, and on and on becoming generational.

> Death and life are in the power of the tongue: and they that
> love it shall eat the fruit thereof. (Proverbs 18:21)

What a weapon of destruction or construction we have in the words we speak or that are spoken to us. There are two types of word curses that can cause soul wounds, planting seeds of destruction and opening doors to our spirits;

they are self-curses and (others) curses. Others curses are usually the basis for many self-curses that we inflict upon ourselves in a time of reflection or resentment toward actions previously taken by other people in our youth. These curses are filled with death, and at the very least, they are the causes of our stunted spiritual growth. Most of these "others" curses usually come from those closest to you—your parents, siblings, or other family members. Your parents can inflict the greatest damage to their children with the words they use like "you're stupid," "I wish you were never born," "you're a sissy (or tomboy)," and/or "you were a mistake." All of these statements can lead to major emotional and self-esteem issues. Even in pregnancy, talk of abortion, and complaining and arguing over the pregnancy can adversely affect the child's development by opening doors of rejection, self-worth issues, fear, and insecurity. Once older, it can become very difficult to form friendships and lasting relationships (Restoration Ministry of Ohio).

Chapter 10

THE DAILY BATTLES WE FACE

he Word of God is emphatic with its warnings about the battles we face. Ephesians tells us that the battle is not typical or natural in that it is not with flesh and blood that we war with but is spiritual in nature.

> For we wrestle not against flesh and blood, but against principalities, against powers, against the rulers of the darkness of this world, against spiritual wickedness in high places. (Ephesians 6:12)

These four PPRS's (principalities, powers, rulers of darkness and spirits of wickedness) combine with the next lower level enemy's to our soul being spirit-world realities that try to become strongholds as the works of the flesh and burrow into our lives and become the lusts of the heart spoken of in the book of James. These are the battlefields of our soul. These, all work together to destroy our soul walls and open doors to our saved spirit (Restoration Ministry of Ohio). They need to be fought, defeated, and removed with the spiritual weapons afforded every born-again believer at salvation. The Holy

Spirit has been given to us to help us win the lost ground that the Devil has taken from us in this life; all we have to do is ask Him.

It's not that God needs us to win the war—Jesus already has done that. What He really wants from us is to confront and defeat Satan at the points of attack in our daily walk so that we can taste the victory in battle and give Jesus our crowns of battles won. We by submitting to Jesus' authority lay these won crowns at the foot of the cross as our testimonies of His kingship over us and the world (flesh). Jesus in His mercy will show us through the Holy Spirit the strongholds in our lives that need to be conquered and removed. These strongholds are areas in our soul's walls which are our intellect, feelings, and will that we sometimes aren't even aware of having. Many don't believe that we as believers can be infected or influenced with sin because we have been taught erroneously that God won't let bad things happen to you once you get saved. Some people refuse to believe that after getting saved we can get attacked or worse yet they ignore the Word's warnings and indulge in politically correct actions that are anathema to God. To submit to the authority of the Lord Jesus Christ we need to understand that we're in a daily battle in a larger spiritual war. What we end up doing is using our worldly indoctrinated intellect, our hardened scarred heart, and our stubborn self-righteous will to protect our damaged soul from getting hurt again, but in reality what we are really doing is leaving ourselves defenseless and open to spiritual attack from the inside. Our fleshly motivated defenses come across as being either mean, legalistic religion or tolerant and accepting "love" but that's because we don't know or understand our enemy.

For me, the way I handled issues that made me feel vulnerable to my soul wounds was to be negative and say no all the time. As I looked at my soul's walls in the vision I had earlier seen, I saw the destroyed sections of my protection and support walls for my spirit and it wasn't pretty.

Along with the great potential of each of the gates in my life were the damaged and destroyed sections that had formed strongholds that were really enemy passageways and tunnels that led to foul and perverted roots coated over with fear, hate, and anger. My Love gate was very narrow, and I could see the walls on either side of Temperance and Joy. I could sense and know the potential God had intended for each of the gates in my life, but I could also see the destruction and emptiness that had retarded the growth of each section. What hindered the spiritual growth of each section were the works of my flesh and a refusal to open up for fear of ridicule and being laughed at like I had been as a young boy. I could tell that part of the hindrance also was the fear of rejection of my love and the disapproval of my efforts by others. A deep sadness overtook my emotions as I knew that the lust of the flesh had hindered my spiritual growth and that I could have changed the outcome to glorify Jesus, but I didn't know how to and that was the cause of my sadness.

The potential of each gate was unlimited, and I knew that God's love alone had helped build the walls to support the fruit of "my" Spirit. As I looked at the side posts and the footers to the walls supporting my Love gate, huge sections were missing and in their place were smaller blocks that formed strongholds of self-righteous indignation. These strongholds had suckers or roots that extended around to every fruit gate like a climber vine or tentacles from an octopus. Bitterness, accusation, pride, envy, jealousy, rejection, unloving, fear, addiction, and occultism were the causes of what kept me from being right with God. Not only were these coming from the Love gate, but these same tentacles or roots were extending out to all nine gates. These same roots were strangling all the nine fruit of the Spirit along with the self-righteousness that is not pleasing to God in my faith. These strongholds are actually legal open doors points where I gave Satan and his minion's legal right to enter into my life through my distorted outlook of faith in general.

> Now the works of the flesh are manifest, which are these; Adultery, fornication, uncleanness, lasciviousness, Idolatry, witchcraft, hatred, variance, emulations, wrath, strife, seditions, heresies, Envyings, murders, drunkenness, revelings, and such like: of the which I tell you before, as I have also told you in time past, that they which do such things shall not inherit the kingdom of God. (Galatians 5:19–21)

The influence from some of these seventeen works of the flesh are motivated by some of the seventeen real-world realities and the lusts of the heart that gives Satan legal right to cause continual confusion, anger, and anxiety in our life. Strife and continuous friction for no apparent reason are just a few of the symptoms that point to possible strongholds and manifestations that are in control of your life. Many people suffer from a combination of these lusts of the flesh and spirit-world realities causing frequent mood swings from anger and cynicism and physical sickness from headaches to nausea with a need for seclusion and a sense of depression overtakes them. These initial lower level demonic influences suggest lies and deceit that only add to double-mindedness and spontaneous evil actions. Traumatic experiences, rejection, and ungodly soul ties only fortify these strongholds and leave a person in such confusion and despair that drug abuse, alcohol, and sexual promiscuity occur to try to pacify these deep-seated soul wounds. (Restoration Ministry of Ohio)

Four PPRSs

Top-Level Demonic Forces (the Generals)
(Ephesians 6:12)

Powers: These spirit powers have great abilities to do, act, or affect, showing great influence of force or authority, usually in demeaning perverted sexual acts or by causing the embarrassment of other people. These powers plant seeds of discord amongst family members or coworkers (especially a spouse) to demean and subdue the will of God's greatest creation.

Principalities are territories that are ruled by a demonic prince who, once identified, will retaliate with the lust of the flesh physically with rage and aggression, trying to retain its control and dominance over a spouse, servant (employee), or child to try to prove superiority and dominance.

Rulers of darkness of this world are not earthly; they are spirit powers of this world that cause people to be wicked and do destructive things to themselves or any and everything they come in contact with that resembles Jehovah God and is rejected and scorned. They use fear through people to maintain control and shun all those who question their authority, perversion or deviance.

Spiritual wickedness in high places is the act of iniquity causing injustice to the innocent. These spirits entice the innocent into actions showing immorality and riotous lawlessness, and people are completely uncontrollable. This spirit promotes the desire to be malicious, mean, sexually perverted, promoting cruel actions that show uncontrolled rage with unquenchable sexual appetites. These include bestiality, lesbianism and homosexuality (sodomy)

These are not physical but spiritual strongholds that we battle in our life with that can have deep-rooted issues that involve any one or more of these next seventeen works of the flesh in combination to corrupt any one or all of our nine fruit of the Spirit.

Seventeen Works of the Flesh (the officers colonials-captains- lieutenants)

(Galatians 6:19–21)

1. *Adultery*: breaking of spiritual vows, mentally or physically
2. *Fornication*: illicit sexual relations (can include adultery)
3. *Uncleanness*: defiled, sensuality, and evil doctrine
4. *Lasciviousness*: no restraint, excesses, evils from the heart
5. *Idolatry*: heathen deity worship or loved more than God
6. *Witchcraft*: sorcery; use of drugs, spells, incantations, occult
7. *Hatred*: malicious, unjustifiable feelings toward others
8. *Variance*: to cut apart, be divisive
9. *Emulations*: to burn with jealousy, moved to envy
10. *Wrath*: hot anger, passionate, fierceness, to provoke
11. *Strife*: contentious, disputing, fighting

12. *Seditions:* dissentious, unsettling, divisive, asunder, set apart

13. *Heresies:* chosen, self-willed erroneous opinions of truth/God

14. *Envy:* feelings of jealousy toward another's prosperity

15. *Murder:* to kill in thought or deed

16. *Drunkenness:* intoxicated, not in right mind

17. *Revelings:* consequence of drunkenness to riot, carousing

These next lusts of the heart and spirit world realities together influence and provoke us to act out the works of the flesh to our spiritual demise. These spirit-world realities and lusts of the heart originate in our minds and are the exact opposite of the convictions of the Holy Spirit.

"Lusts of the Heart That War in Your Members" (the sergeants)

(James 4:1–4)

Un-forgiveness- is proof of a lack of genuine love in your heart; and the problem with the sin of un-forgiveness is that it is an on-going condition of a person's heart to an individual that has wounded your soul.

Separation: the act of causing division with intent and provocation or goading. to mark off; to limit; to cause divisions between people and family of faith with fear of misunderstood Scriptures (Ephesians 2:12)

Bitterness- to have latent anger and resentment towards someone. Often Bitterness is an outcome of persistent emotional imbalance from past soul wounds: to cut or prick; to irritate; of evil speaking and hatred toward family, neighbors, authority figures, religious leaders, and coworkers (Romans 3:14; Ephesians 4:31; Colossians 3:19; Hebrews 12:15)

Accusation: to charge wrongfully; to imply; to accuse falsely; planting seeds of distrust and unproven ulterior motivations through gossip and hearsay

DIMITRI YANULI

(Leviticus 19:11; Proverbs 18:17; Matthew 18:29; Luke 3:14; 1 Timothy 3:11; Revelation 12:10)

Envy and jealousy: feeling displeasure at another's success; moved to jealousy or connected heavily with covenant mates (Matthew 27:18; Mark 15:10; Romans 1:29; 13:13; 1 Corinthians 3:3; 13:4; Philippians 1:15)

Resentment-as a result of a real or imagined wrong towards a person or people.

Retaliation-a harmful action against a person or group in response to a grievance, be it real or perceived. It is also called payback, retribution, retaliation

Addiction: alcoholism and drugs, weight gluttony, anorexia, bulimia, self-mutilation with cutting, asphyxiation, masturbation, sexual promiscuity; usually associated with a low self-esteem and diminished self-worth

Occultism: to believe, seek, and search for ungodly occult forces and powers; a preoccupation with oaths(masons) and occult arts (horoscopes) that detract from the reality of who God really is (Deuteronomy 18:10–12; Psalm 90:10; Matthew 24:24)

Rejection:to discard or throw out as worthless, useless, or substandard; to pass over or cast off; to deny acceptance, care, or love, etc.; a rejected child of the living God (Mark 7:9; 1 Thessalonians 4:8; 1 Timothy 5:12)

Unloving: not giving or reciprocating love; not feeling or showing love and affection based in insecurity, self-hatred, and a broken heart (Matthew 22:37–39)

Fear: anxiety; phobias; an uneasiness of the mind of possible future events; that which causes one to be afraid and have night terrors; to have reverential awe, especially toward God; to be afraid of or for someone's safety (Hebrews 2:15; 2 Timothy 1:7; 1 John 4:18)

Seventeen Spirit World Realities

(1 Corinthians 6:9–10; Mark 7:21–23)
Lowest-Level Demons (1st attackers –
air-artillery-infantry-navy)

These demons are used to provoke, prod and promote irreconcilable discord among the Christ-believing brethren of the entire world through lust of the heart visual enticements and self-perceived unmet needs doubt and unbelief that bombard the mind.(used to muddy the water) They cause confusion, fear and uncertainty.

1. *Un-forgiveness:* a root record of past wrongs that are not forgotten

2. *Resentment:* the remembrance of unforgiven wrongs

3. *Retaliation:* after resentment has taken hold, we act on it

4. *Anger:* a strong feeling, a natural impulse or desire to show displeasure and your superiority

5. *Hatred:* a malicious, unjustifiable feeling toward others that are different than you or your self-imposed expectations

6. *Violence:* a forceful act causing suffering through intimidation or pain to gain power position or retaliation

7. *Murder:* to kill in word, thought, or deed

8. *Separation:* to mark off, to limit, or to cause divisions and strife

9. *Bitterness:* to cut or prick, to irritate, of evil speaking with hatred and resentment of past wrongs someone else's gains

10. *Accusation:* to charge wrongfully, to imply or to accuse falsely

11. *Envy:* feeling of displeasure at another's success, moved to jealousy, resentment or insecurity and debasing

12. *Jealousy:* the act of envy or overprotectiveness of one's items, success or loves

13. *Addiction:* alcoholism and drugs, weight gluttony, anorexia, bulimia, self-mutilation (cutting), asphyxiation, masturbation, sex

14. *Occultism:* belief in occult forces and powers, a preoccupation with occult arts

15. *Rejection:* to discard or throw out as worthless, useless, or substandard; to pass over or cast off; to deny acceptance, care, or love, etc.; a rejected child or spouse

16. *Unloving:* not giving or reciprocating love, not feeling or showing love and affection

17. *Fear:* anxiety, phobias, an uneasiness of the mind of possible future events, that which causes one to be afraid, to have reverential awe especially toward God, to be afraid of or for someone's safety

The only way to defeat the four PPRSs is with the Word of God through Jesus Christ of Nazareth and the Holy Spirit. With godly love, we spiritually grow and develop into our potential as a child of the living God. God knows who we are; He knows our thoughts, our ways, the words we speak and sees everything we do and the reasons why we do them. Psalm 139:1–4 best exemplifies His omniscience and omnipresence in our lives today!

> O LORD, thou hast searched me, and known me. Thou knowest my downsitting and mine uprising, thou understandest my thought afar off. Thou compassest my path and my lying down, and art acquainted with all my ways. For there is not a word in my tongue, but, lo, O LORD, thou knowest it altogether.

The influence of ungodly soul ties is so great and so powerful that God warns us again in 1 Corinthians 6:15–18.

6:15   Know ye not that your bodies are the members of Christ? shall I then take the members of Christ, and make them the members of an harlot? God forbid.

6:16   What? know ye not that he which is joined to an harlot is one body? for two, saith he, shall be one flesh.

6:17   But he that is joined unto the Lord is one spirit.

6:18   Flee fornication. Every sin that a man doeth is without the body; but he that committeth fornication sinneth against his own body.

And Proverbs 22:24–25 tells us also, "Make no friendship with an angry man; and with a furious man thou shall not go: Lest thou learn his ways, and get a snare to thy soul."

We should be aware that there are many ways that could develop into ungodly soul ties which can cause us trouble: traumatic and abusive relationships, bad friends, peer pressure, sex outside of marriage, abortion, idolatry, and hypnosis all can develop ungodly soul ties. Word and generational curses, unbelief, and hardness of heart are the precursors to many spiritual maladies, but in my case, I believe they all resulted in my own physical ailments. I thank Jehovah God for His Son, Jesus Christ, and His Holy Spirit for calling me, teaching me, and giving me the privilege of teaching the good news of salvation and restoration through these difficult end times. The ministry of the Lord Jesus while here for three and a half years and His appearance after the resurrection gives a clear picture of that plan.

Luke

4:40   Now when the sun was setting, all they that had any sick with divers diseases brought them unto him; and he laid his hands on every one of them, and healed them.

4:41   And devils also came out of many, crying out, and saying, Thou art Christ the Son of God. And he rebuking them suffered them not to speak: for they knew that he was Christ.

4:42   And when it was day, he departed and went into a desert place: and the people sought him, and came unto him, and stayed him, that he should not depart from them.

4:43   And he said unto them, I must preach the kingdom of God to other cities also: for therefore am I sent.

4:44   And he preached in the synagogues of Galilee. (Luke 4:40–44)

Not only does Jesus reaffirm His purpose as Messiah, but then He explains the consequences of apathy and indifference as well as the power and function of the Comforter in the believer's life. Matthew 16:13-20

When Jesus came into the coasts of Caesarea Philippi, he asked his disciples, saying, Whom do men say that I the Son of man am? And they said, Some say that thou art John the Baptist: some, Elias; and others, Jeremiah, or one of the prophets. He saith unto them, But whom say ye that I am? And Simon Peter answered and said, Thou art the Christ, the Son of the living God. And Jesus answered and said unto him, Blessed art thou, Simon Barjona: for flesh and blood hath not revealed it unto thee, but my Father which is in heaven. And I say also unto thee, That thou art Peter, and upon this rock I will build my church; and the gates of hell shall not prevail against it. And I will give unto thee the keys of the kingdom of heaven: and whatsoever thou shalt bind on earth shall be bound in heaven: and whatsoever thou shalt loose on earth shall be loosed in heaven. Then charged he his disciples that they should tell no man that he was Jesus the Christ.

The example of Jesus' power and authority here in Matthew and later in Luke is available to all believers of the resurrection. Nowhere in the New Testament is there an expiration date to the power given to a believer. The purpose of this section of this book is to teach us all how to receive the baptism of the Holy Spirit, self-restore, self-deliver, and self-heal the damaged areas of our soul and become mighty warriors for the kingdom of our Lord Jesus Christ of Nazareth. There are seventeen areas that influence the foundation of our nine gates. These diversions hinder our ability to reach our fullest potential in Christlikeness. Remember, the fruit of the Spirit are the nine gates that lead to our spirit, and they each are influenced by the work of the flesh and the seventeen spirit-world realities. These points of contention can come from the curse of the law, generational curses, or self-curses, and only the Word of the living God can restore you. These *spirit-world realities* help form the seventeen areas of influence that are un-forgiveness, resentment, retaliation, anger, hatred, violence, murder, bitterness, accusation, envy, jealousy, addiction, occultism, rejection, unloving spirit, and fear. They in turn are then influencing the works of the flesh, which together work to destroy the born-again believer. Ephesians tells us in 6:12,

For we wrestle not against flesh and blood, but against principalities, against powers, against the rulers of the darkness of this world, against spiritual wickedness in high places.

These principalities, powers, and rulers of darkness are the minions of demonic influences sprinkled with worldly spiritual wickedness in high places that are what James (the half-brother of Jesus) was talking about in his epistle.

1:13   Let no man say when he is tempted, I am tempted of God: for God cannot be tempted with evil, neither tempteth he any man:

1:14   But every man is tempted, when he is drawn away of his own lust, and enticed.

1:15   Then when lust hath conceived, it bringeth forth sin: and sin, when it is finished, bringeth forth death. (James 1:13-15 KJV)

Lust conceived brings sin, and sin brings death. So all the works of the flesh begin in your mind and must be conceived before we act. Remember what we discussed in Deuteronomy 27–28: all the curses that are imputed upon us are self-imposed and premeditated. Proverbs 14:30–31 tells us to beware of jealousy and envy of other people and their circumstances or their possessions.

A sound heart is the life of the flesh: but envy the rottenness of the bones. He that oppresseth the poor reproacheth his Maker: but he that honoureth him hath mercy on the poor.

The truth of the matter is that the way we think of a person's financial status, physical appearance, nationality, and race has been planted deep in our minds at a very young age. Depending on how it was nurtured in your life, the resulting heart root is determined and your reactions are the result of that nurturing—whether through loving, biblical understanding with compassion or the deep-seated hatred, anger, and prejudice that cause most of the pain and anguish in this world. The real intent of the heart is the determining factor with God, and the building blocks of the fruit of the Spirit walls of your soul are what God sees in forming your eternal rewards.

To blame God for issues in this life, whatever they may be, is nothing short of cowardice and only tries to shed oneself of personal responsibility. It's not the lot you've been dealt in this life that determines your eternity it's your reaction to them and the choices that you make formulating them that we're judged on. Every one of the fruit is influenced by either love or fear. The first on Paul's list of the fruit of the Spirit is love. Love can and does touch on a myriad of potentially volatile areas that lead to worry, depression, and anxiety. Depending on the issue, fear leads to unforgiveness, resentment, anger, hate, rejection, accusation, strife, physical abuse, depression, suicide, murder, shame, slander, and verbal and sexual abuse. These will form the roots of fear in your soul that not only affect you but can be the reason for racial and ethnic problems for generations.

Satan has a field day playing with the feelings and sensibilities of many professing believers, and he uses our fears, along with our natural responses to act in a fight-or-flight response, to deceive us. His desire is to destroy us, and because he is as old as the creation of other angels, he knows our human nature tendencies. The circumstances to which he is tempting us are the most severe imaginable, and there is no possibility of our facing any greater test of what we could endure in our physical bodies than the ones we face in life here on this earth. From the very beginning of His ministry, Jesus warned us that sin begins in the heart: "But I say unto you, That whosoever looketh on a woman to lust after her hath committed adultery with her already in his heart" (Matthew 5:28).

If we endure and pass this test by choosing God's rescue plan through Christ, then the way is opened for God to deliver us eternally from all sin, death, suffering, and evil without taking away our free will. The test is not too difficult when we remember what Galatians says,

> Be not deceived; God is not mocked: *for whatsoever a man soweth, that shall he also reap.* For he that soweth to his flesh shall of the flesh reap corruption; but he that soweth to the Spirit shall of the Spirit reap life everlasting. And let us not be weary in well doing: for in due season we shall reap, if we faint not. As we have therefore opportunity, *let us do good unto all men, especially unto them who are of the household of faith.* (Galatians 6:7–10, emphasis added)

That means to do good to all believers in Christ and by extension all believers in Jehovah God. God's Word says that He wants none to perish but all to come to the knowledge of Jesus Christ, and that includes every race of human—red, yellow, black, brown, and white they are all equal in God's eyes and precious in His sight.

> But to us there is but one God, the Father, of whom are all things, and we in him; and one Lord Jesus Christ, by whom are all things, and we by him. (1 Corinthians 8:6)

> And to know the love of Christ, which passeth knowledge, that ye might be filled with all the fullness of God. ... Till we all come in the unity of the faith, and of the knowledge of the Son of God, unto a perfect man, unto the measure of the stature of the fulness of Christ. (Ephesians 3:19; 4:13)

Love is the foundation and basis of all the nine fruit of the Spirit gates which are along with *Joy, Peace, Longsuffering, Gentleness, Goodness, Faith, Meekness, and Temperance.*

> The way of the wicked is an abomination unto the LORD: but he loveth him that followeth after righteousness. (Proverbs 15:9)

Love is the basis for your *joy*; it must be the basis for your being at *peace* with all men as well as your actions that must be based in love.

> For our heart shall rejoice (full of joy) in him, because we
> have trusted in his holy name. (Psalm 33:21)

God loves us all individually and has given us the perfect example of His Son Jesus Christ to model ourselves after. John 16:27–28 says,

> For the Father himself loveth you, because ye have loved me,
> and have believed that I came out from God. I came forth
> from the Father, and am come into the world: again, I leave
> the world, and go to the Father.

Not only was Jesus *longsuffering* with the apostles and their human natures, but He showed a *gentleness* and compassion that God exemplified through His Son's life and suffering, and He showed *faith* and *goodness* in patience with them through their failures in the spiritual growing process that we all experience once saved.

> I have given them thy word; and the world hath hated them,
> because they are not of the world, even as I am not of the
> world. I pray not that thou should take them out of the
> world, but that thou should keep them from the evil. They
> are not of the world, even as I am not of the world. Sanctify
> them through thy truth: thy word is truth. As thou hast
> sent me into the world, even so have I also sent them into
> the world. (John 17:14–18)

Like I said earlier, each one of these nine spiritual fruit can and will be influenced by the seventeen works of the flesh, the lusts of the heart and the seventeen spirit-world realities if you allow them to. Remember the words that Jesus said in Matthew 5:13–14.

> *Ye are the salt of the earth*: but if the salt have lost his savor,
> wherewith shall it be salted? It is thenceforth good for
> nothing, but to be cast out, and to be trodden under foot of

men. *Ye are the light of the world.* A city that is set on an hill cannot be hid. (emphasis added)

The meaning of the life and actions we make are immeasurable and not without eternal consequences. By our actions, we can cause traumatic and painful circumstances to occur intentionally or even unintentionally to the people all around us that we know and love. The ramifications of these actions can affect people for as many as four to ten generations if not dealt with specifically and properly. Unfortunately, the majority of the human race and most professing Christians don't even know what the Word of God says on how to defeat the Enemy or how to begin rebuilding the walls of our souls and develop a godly character. Most believe that the Old Testament is irrelevant to them today and that the weapons afforded all believers in the New Testament have ceased and are no longer available.

The misconception that we are powerless and that we have to just make the best of our situation and wait on God to heal our circumstances is exactly where Satan wants us to stay—mentally and spiritually ignorant. The significance of Jesus' birth, life, death, and resurrection outside of Jewish tradition makes absolutely no sense at all if read in the New Testament alone. Until we explain the Bible in the full context of both Old and New Testaments together, the Jewish traditions and laws of our faith seem incomplete and meaningless. Our Christian faith has so many loose ends and indefensible customs outside of Jewish history that it seems ridiculous and the fodder for secular "intelligencia" to claim as mythological or just old wives' tales. When you look at the whole Bible from Genesis to Revelation and read it in the context of Jewish tradition and history with the understanding that its whole purpose was and is to restore man spiritually, morally, and ethically to the place where man was prior to his fall from grace, then you can see why Satan is trying so vehemently to turn the hearts of man from the truth and let him die in ignorance of what sin is without Jesus. If you only knew the power and authority you have in Jesus, we would understand why walking in the Spirit is so critical to victorious Christian living and the development of a godly character. The truth is that we must acknowledge who creator God is, know who the Messiah is, and who the Holy Spirit is. Only the complete Word of God—both Old and New Testaments together—explains man's relationship to the Trinity. How we are to be restored in spirit, soul, and body through the shed blood of Jesus Christ of Nazareth on the cross.

At this point we as believers need to pray the T.R.U.S.T. prayer to identify and rebuke the specific spiritual enemies to our soul that are influencing our thoughts and actions. Listed below are the spirits names of the tormenters to be identified. As you pray to Jesus ask the Holy Spirit to reveal the areas of concern troubling you in the specific situation you are in. Circle the word or words that best describe the issue revealed to you by the Holy Spirit. Renounce it and repent for each spirit that you have entertained with the following prayer.

Heavenly Father God in Jesus name I repent for embracing the spirit of _____ and I renounce it. I ask forgiveness for my thoughts and actions and ask forgiveness and that the curse of _____ be broken in Jesus name by the power of the Holy Spirit over the spirit of _____.

Un-forgiveness Resentment Retaliation Anger Hatred Violence Murder Separation Bitterness Accusation Envy Jealousy Addiction Occultism Rejection Unloving Fear Adultery Fornication Uncleanness Lasciviousness Idolatry Witchcraft Variance Emulations Wrath Strife Seditions Heresies Drunkenness Revelings Gossip Lust Lying Shame Guilt Worry Thefts Deceits Effeminate Abusers of themselves An evil eye Blasphemy Pride Covetousness Depression Wickedness

Chapter 11

OUR SPIRIT'S PROTECTION

he vision I had of Jesus and His soul walls were a perfect example and perfect model for each one of us as we try to attain Christ-likeness to protect our born again spirits. This is what this book is written for, to show us how much God loves all of us by showing us how to reclaim our spirits as well as restore and rebuild our damaged soul walls with the man Jesus Christ and His perfect fruit of the Spirit as our template for reconstruction. God the Father gave His only begotten Son, slain from the foundation of the earth, for you and me to be reconstructed through His shed blood and the baptism of the third person of the Trinity, the Holy Spirit. As a new creature in Spirit at salvation, our soul needs to catch up in Christlikeness to His perfect soul so we as believers can rule and reign with Him forever as kings and priests unto God (Revelation 1:6). Know that many of the actions and lifestyles accepted by society today will not enter into the presence of a Holy God, for God's Word says,

> "For my thoughts are not your thoughts, neither are your
> ways my ways, saith the LORD" (Isaiah 55:8).

It seems very clear to me that through these verses that not only did I need to change my ways (actions) but I had to take control of my thoughts and change my attitude towards fellow believers as well. I remember that every one of Jesus' gates were labeled as one of the fruit of the Spirit, and each wall was built on the foundation of love. As each wall got closer to the gates, they took on that gate's color hue which reverberates God's love throughout His whole spirit temple and soul walls. I could feel the sound and color come together as one. Every newly born-again believing spirit is now newly regenerated but is still protected by our old-world-influenced soul walls, regardless of how damaged they are in this life. God forgives you through the blood of Jesus, but you must stop sinning, repent, and change your mind. Because when you get saved; only your spirit is renewed, not your soul and your personhood remains unless specifically dealt with and restored. Your soul retains all the fleshly desires and habits that caused a myriad of contradictory and hypocritical thoughts and actions that are in opposition to the Word of God, and that is what the process of sanctification is all about. Contrary to the "once saved, always saved" crowd, if you don't start thinking and living differently to your fleshly sinful nature, then your eternal destination is not assured.

> And if thy right eye offend thee, pluck it out, and cast it from
> thee: for it is profitable for thee that one of thy members
> should perish, and not that thy whole body should be cast
> into hell. (Matthew 5:29)

Not only does God's Word warn us as believers to not participate in any of the works of the flesh, the spirit-world realities, or the lusts of the heart—all of which can and will be forgiven—but you can't do them anymore and expect to enter the presence of a Holy God. Sanctification is the procedure and development we all as believers in Christ must "grow" through in order to begin to fulfill the purpose we each were designed for by God. These issues or open doors remain with us until we specifically address, close, and remove them with our newly acquired spiritual weapons of warfare. The depth in color and clearness of our gates and walls are directly influenced by the proximity to the pureness of the fruit label on the gate and the depth of the foundation in Christ-like love below them.

This is exactly how our unrepentant actions hinder the fruit of the Spirit from growing and instead weave their way through our lives and families for generations. These distorted root-shoots constantly influence and damage the walls of our souls with manifestations and emotional strongholds formed by the works of the flesh and the spirit-world realities we've permitted through experimentation, habit or tradition into our lives even after we were saved. The opinions we've formulated towards denominations of fellow believers in the risen Christ, people groups and family members will remain with us until we ask and allow the Holy Spirit to reveal our soul wounds that caused the racism, prejudice and hatred. Only then can the Holy Spirit begin helping us to rebuild our walls and remove that root damaging our walls. But first we have to have an open heart to all believers of different denominations that have a full understanding of what Jesus did at the cross and what was accomplished with His resurrection.

To identify a recurring hurtful issue that has remained in your born-again life, you must first thank the Holy Spirit for calling you into the kingdom, then ask Him in prayer to reveal the source or cause of it. Ask Him then to make you usable in this issue to the glory of God by asking Him to strengthen your character in the face of this issue, and finally, ask Him to teach you from His Word how to begin correcting that specific issue in your damaged soul's wall. I don't personally believe your thoughts alone will keep you out of the kingdom, but I do believe that you will not be permitted to participate or enter into the areas where bitterness, un-forgiveness, jealousy, resentment, anger, rejection and hatred are present. In comparison, the colors of Jesus' gates and walls remained perfectly proportioned and independent but seemed to come together and flow together as if collaborating with each other in a perfect eternal purpose that added strength and depth of integrity and character to each fruit of the spirit temple.

As we go through each of the nine fruit of the Spirit gates, I will show you how the works of the flesh, the lusts of the heart and the spirit-world realities can hinder the Holy Spirit from working in our lives even after you've been born again or are a believer from a different Christian denomination. Once you entertain any of the seven main emotional strongholds in your mind you then give the Devil legal authority to enter your lives by one of these open door's to destroy your soul's walls in the fruit of the Spirit. In each of the nine gates, these seven main strongholds of emotions can combine with any of the seventeen works of the flesh, the lusts of the heart or with the seventeen spirit-world realities and begin to tear down the fortifications we've constructed for your spirit's protection. Only God's Word identifies these seven emotions and feelings that can begin to form strongholds that will manifest into areas that destroy our fruit foundations and then our walls.

Anger

An angry man stirs up strife, and a furious man abounds in transgression. … He that is slow to anger is better than the mighty; and he that ruleth his spirit than he that takes a city. (Proverbs 29:22; 16:32)

Cease from anger, and forsake wrath: fret not thyself in any wise to do evil. Psalms 37:8

But I say unto you, That whosoever is angry with his brother without a cause shall be in danger of the judgment: and whosoever shall say to his brother, Raca, shall be in danger of the council: but whosoever shall say, Thou fool, shall be in danger of hell fire. Matthew 5:22

Let all bitterness, and wrath, and anger, and clamor, and evil speaking, be put away from you, with all malice: And be ye kind one to another, tenderhearted, forgiving one another, even as God for Christ's sake hath forgiven you. (Ephesians 4:31–32)

Envy

Neither shalt thou desire thy neighbor's wife, neither shalt thou covet thy neighbor's house, his field, or his manservant, or his maidservant, his ox, or his ass, or anything that is thy neighbor's. (Deuteronomy 5:21)

Wrath is cruel, and anger is outrageous; but who is able to stand before envy? (Proverbs 27:4)

But if ye have bitter envying and strife in your hearts, glory not, and lie not against the truth. (James 3:14)

Gossip

Thou shalt not go up and down as a talebearer among thy people: neither shalt thou stand against the blood of thy neighbor: I am the LORD. (Leviticus 19:16)

A man of twisted purposes is a cause of fighting everywhere: and he who says evil secretly makes trouble between friends.

The words of a talebearer are as wounds, and they go down into the innermost parts of the belly. (Proverbs 18:8)

Keep thy tongue from evil, and thy lips from speaking guile. Psalms 34:13

Lust

Lust not after her beauty in thine heart; neither let her take thee with her eyelids.

For by means of a whorish woman a man is brought to a piece of bread: and the adulteress will hunt for the precious life.

Can a man take fire in his bosom, and his clothes not be burned?

Can one go upon hot coals, and his feet not be burned?

So he that goes in to his neighbor's wife; whosoever touches her shall not be innocent. (Proverbs 6:25–29)

For all that is in the world, the lust of the flesh, and the lust of the eyes, and the pride of life, is not of the Father, but is of the world. And the world passes away, and the lust thereof: but he that doeth the will of God abides forever. (1 John 2:16–17)

Lying

Your word is your bond with your reputation as a person of integrity and honesty, all we really have as our testimony and that is our reputation. Two things I told my boys as they were growing up don't be a thief and don't lie always say what you mean and mean what you say. Nobody likes a thief or a liar and I know that God doesn't either. And have put on the new man, which is renewed in knowledge after the image of him that created him. (Colossians 3:9–10)

Thou shalt not raise a false report: put not thine hand with the wicked to be an unrighteous witness. Exodus 23:1

But if ye have bitter envying and strife in your hearts, glory not, and lie not against the truth. James 3:14

The lip of truth shall be established for ever: but a lying tongue is but for a moment. Proverbs 12:19

Shame

And hope maketh not ashamed; because the love of God is shed abroad in our hearts by the Holy Ghost which is given unto us. Romans 5:5

As far as the east is from the west, so far hath he removed our transgressions from us. Psalms 103:12

Study to show thyself approved unto God, a workman that needeth not to be ashamed, rightly dividing the word of truth. 2 Timothy 2:15

Yet if any man suffer as a Christian, let him not be ashamed; but let him glorify God on this behalf.......For the time is come that judgment must begin at the house of God: and if it first begin at us, what shall the end be of them that obey not the gospel of God? 1 Peter 4:16-17

If we confess our sins, he is faithful and just to forgive us our sins, and to cleanse us from all unrighteousness. 1 John 1:9

Worry

Be careful for nothing; but in every thing by prayer and supplication with thanksgiving let your requests be made known unto God. And the peace of God, which passeth all understanding, shall keep your hearts and minds through Christ Jesus. ... But my God shall supply all your need according to his riches in glory by Christ Jesus. (Philippians 4:6–7, 19)

The LORD also will be a refuge for the oppressed, a refuge in times of trouble. And they that know thy name will put their trust in thee: for thou, LORD, hast not forsaken them that seek thee. ... He shall call upon me, and I will answer him: I will be with him in trouble; I will deliver him, and honor him. (Psalms 9:9–10; 91:15)

And we know that all things work together for good to them that love God, to them who are the called according to his purpose. For whom he did foreknow, he also did predestinate to be conformed to the image of his Son, that he might be the firstborn among many brethren. (Romans 8:28–29)

These are the warnings and promises of God to the whole of humanity: Jew and Gentile, believer and nonbeliever alike. God wants none to perish but all to come to the knowledge of Jesus the Christ, and He has given us a perfect example to emulate in His Son. After we accept and believe in the Father God of the Old Testament we can acknowledge and receive Jesus Christ as Messiah and Lord of our lives. Now as we continue on in the New Testament we can now Receive the fullness of the Holy Spirit

Acts 19:2

19:2   He said unto them, Have ye received the Holy Ghost since ye believed? And they said unto him, We have not so much as heard whether there be any Holy Ghost.

Here is a prayer that you can pray out loud (you have been given the authority to pray in Jesus' name) to renounce and repent for each emotional spiritual stronghold you have entertained or kept a door open to corrupt your thoughts.

Pray this out loud.

"Dear Heavenly Father God in heaven, I come to you believing that Jesus Christ died on the cross for my sins. I open my heart and invite Jesus to come in and be my personal Lord and Savior. Jesus forgive me for all of my sins and cleanse me from

all unrighteousness. Teach me God's Word and fill me with the power of the Holy Spirit. Give me knowledge, wisdom and the ability to heal my soul. Show me how to live a victorious life that brings glory to only You. Thank you Jesus because I am born again and saved through Your shed blood on the cross of Calvary".

"Heavenly Father I now ask You to fill with your Holy Spirit. I receive Him by faith in the name of Jesus Christ of Nazareth. I thank You Father, for filling me with the power and anointing of the Holy Spirit. Now, I can and will speak in other tongues as the Spirit gives me the language in Jesus name to repent for anger, envy, gossip, lust, lying, shame or worry, " Heavenly Father God in Jesus name I repent for embracing the spirit of _____ and I renounce it. I ask forgiveness and that the curse of _____ be broken in Jesus name by the power of the Holy Spirit over the spirit of _____ I am free, Amen!.

You may think you've not done anything that bad or wrong to deserve the pain or suffering that you're currently going through, but you have to understand that every action taken or word said in vain, anger or jest has a consequence. It doesn't sound fair, but the Devil doesn't play fair, and he wants your spirit and your progenies' spirits if he can get them. He will use any and every opportunity to deceive and destroy your soul walls, and he will use any open door he can find open to do it. Satan will only enter a person's life if he has a legal right to enter, and that right is only given by your active rebellion and sinning. The greatest tools that Satan uses are the ignorance-based theories of God, creation, life, and the afterlife. Ignorance is not an excuse with God, as His Word says in the Old Testament in Hosea 4:6:

> My people are destroyed for lack of knowledge: because thou hast rejected knowledge, I will also reject thee, that thou shall be no priest to me: seeing thou hast forgotten the law of thy God, I will also forget thy children.

To believe there is no Devil plays right into Satan's plans of taking as many souls to hell as he can. Again, this is the purpose of showing you how the lust of the flesh and the strongholds that you've allowed into your life can develop into one of the PPRS's. The New Testament epistles are for you to be aware of Satan's plots, plans and ploys used to deceive you. These strongholds can influence the nine fruit of the Spirit that will in turn inhibit your spiritual growth and ultimately stop you from receiving your eternal rewards that God has prepared for all those that believe. Even after receiving salvation through Jesus Christ, there is more that is expected of us to do and grow in character, integrity, and righteousness. God's goal was and is for us as believers to have a relationship with each one of us personally here in this life and for eternity. Jesus paid the ultimate price for us all by His death, burial, and resurrection on the cross. Through the cross, we have access to the Father, but He still would like to see us at our fullest potential. To defeat the flesh and to walk and live our existence on earth in the spirit we must submit to the authority of Jesus Christ. Know that you can stop sinning and can now utilize all the gifts afforded every believer in the risen Christ. It only took +/- 175 years for man to completely forget about God after the flood and lose his spirituality to where Abraham heard from God. It took another 500 years to the call of Moses and the receiving of the Law, and another 1,500 more years to usher in the Messiah. Now it has taken another 2,000 plus years for us to understand the Holy Spirit and the gifts of the Spirit. So it took a total of 6,000 years to return to the spiritual place that Adam and Eve were at prior to the fall.

As we read Genesis 1–12 in the Word, we can see that it explains the first two thousand years of God's attempts to call man back into fellowship with Him. Jehovah God separated unto Himself a people through Abraham; He then gave us the Law through Moses. Through Jesus our High Priest, after the order of Melchizedek and King in the lineage David "He" has defeated all sin. Jesus after His ascension sent us the Comforter (the Holy Spirit) to be in us and to fall upon us at our baptism of the Holy Spirit. I know that this oversimplification of six thousand years of human history doesn't come close to explaining the importance or theological details of each of these three two-thousand-year increments, but suffice it to say that creator God wants us all to come to a place of righteousness so we can have fellowship with Him again. All God wants is what He wanted in the beginning when He created Adam—fellowship and a personal relationship with His creation.

I have always questioned how a loving God could punish a man for eternity for his choices or the lack of them, but as I read more and more of the Word of God, I discovered that in order to give man the ability to choose, it required that a consequence for those choices be made or else it's really not "free will."

As I thought on the state of humanity without an eternal purpose, I felt the utter hopelessness of the secular world's theories that claim everyone goes to heaven and they are not really lost after death. Then the Lord brought to mind what a dear friend of mine had repeated to me many times of what Jesus said in Matthew.

Enter ye in at the strait gate: for wide is the gate, and broad is the way, that leads to destruction, and many there be which go in there at: Because strait is the gate, and narrow is the way, which leads unto life, and few there be that find it. (Matthew 7:13–14)

What this means is that in this life we live, we have many paths to choose from (broad is the way), many of which lead to destruction. Jesus says that wide and broad is the road that leads to destruction, which is repeated here in Matthew and in Luke 13:24.

The choices we make in this short life are eternally important; none more than to those around us who witness this life that we live and we are a testimony to. Each one of us was created with the ability to choose to do good or evil, love or hate, and most of all believe that God can use you or not. We must believe that we were specifically created for this time in history to be used for His eternal purpose. Salvation requires not only entering into a state of a humble and contrite mind, but it also requires your behavior and character to change as well. This means to take control of the fleshly desires you have with your thoughts, body, and the words you speak.

> I beseech you therefore, brethren, by the mercies of God,
> that ye present your bodies a living sacrifice, holy, acceptable
> unto God, which is your reasonable service. (Romans 12:1)

You have to believe that Jehovah is God, Jesus is the Messiah, and that the Holy Spirit is the third person of the Trinity. Believe that He is creator God and is the God of all you see, hear, taste, smell and touch. Just saying the words to pacify those you've hurt or those who care about you isn't enough; it really only destroys your credibility and your truly heartfelt remorse falls on deaf ears. What you have to do is put those thoughts into action with your daily walk and not let hypocrisy destroy your testimony. Only the Word of the

Living God talks of how the world came to be, only the Word tells us how to live in this world, and only the Word of God tells us the way to get to God: "Jesus said unto him, I am the way, the truth, and the life: no man cometh unto the Father, but by me" (John 14:6).

What God? ... the God of Adam, Enoch, Noah, Moses, David—the Hebrew God Jehovah. Then you have to believe that this God raised His only begotten virgin-born Son, Jesus the Christ, raised Him from the dead as prophesied in the Old Testament in Jeremiah, Isaiah, Psalms, and Proverbs, and written of in the Gospels: Matthew 28:2; Mark 16:1–8; Luke 24:1–12; and John 20:1–10. This is the progression of our faith: to first believe in the Hebrew God of Abraham, Isaac, and Jacob, and then to believe in the Christian Messiah, Jesus Christ of Nazareth is the Son of the Hebrew God. Once these two major hurdles are crossed, then the real work begins to change your character into Christlikeness through the Holy Spirit. Remember, they are not exclusive of each other but necessary so you can begin to believe that the Jesus Christ you profess as Lord is the Son of the Jewish God, Jehovah. That all believers have been given the third person of the Trinity, the Holy Spirit, and He is available and accessible to all believers yesterday, today and forever.

Up until this point, everything was relocated to your belief in either *the God of Israel Jehovah* (Jewish faith) or in *the crucified risen Son* of God Jesus (Christian faith). Many Jews profess that Jehovah is God, and many Christians profess that Jesus is the Christ. This "God" of the Jews raised Jesus on the third day, and He is seated at "Jehovah God's" right hand. They're both correct, but they ain't right with God because they both don't connect the dots with each other's partial acceptance of the same Scripture because of replacement Theology, anti-Semitism and distrust of Christians.

Any of the legalistic traditions that so many of us as believers have accepted and participated in as unquestionable truths have lulled us into a false sense of security. Your prejudice and feeling of superiority over a segment of fellow believers solely on ethnicity, race, or Church traditions alone without accepting all Scripture equally, disqualifies and nullifies your religiosity. Don't be offended with this. My intent in writing this book is not to offend you but rather to open your eyes to the fullness and complete restoration of the spirit and soul of every person that believes in Jesus Christ regardless of race, ethnicity or orthodox Christian denomination. God has outlined His purpose for us and His remedy for sin in Scripture to resolve all our issues in this life that we face as a result of it, and to prepare us while alive to become the sons of God as the bride of Christ.

> And I say unto you, Ask, and it shall be given you; seek, and ye shall find; knock, and it shall be opened unto you. For every one that asketh receiveth; and he that seeketh findeth; and to him that knocketh it shall be opened. (Luke 11:9–10)

Through our intercessor Jesus Christ, we now have the ability to enter into the Holy of Holies that only the high priest was permitted to enter into once a year, but because of Jesus' crucifixion and death, the veil of the temple has been rent in half (Matthew 27:45–56; Mark 15:33–41; Luke 33:44–49; John 19:28–30). We can now petition our requests to God the Father through prayer to Jesus, our perfect sinless High Priest, to enter and intercede on our behalf directly.

> Who is he that condemneth? It is Christ that died, yea rather, that is risen again, who is even at the right hand of God, who also maketh intercession for us. (Romans 8:34)

> Looking unto Jesus the author and finisher of our faith; who for the joy that was set before him endured the cross, despising the shame, and is set down at the right hand of the throne of God. (Hebrews 12:2)

> For every one that asketh receiveth; and he that seeketh findeth; and to him that knocketh it shall be opened. (Matthew 7:8)

Many believers are deceived to think that once you become a church member or get saved and say the prayer of salvation everything is okay you will go to heaven when you die or that nothing bad will ever happen to them again—*not true*. This false sense of eternal security only leaves you vulnerable to attack and destruction from Satan and his minions. Remember that every door, curse, and stronghold that you had previously received intentionally or not into your soul is still there and open to your soul wounds even after you get saved. Not until you specifically counterattack these strongholds, shut the open door points to your mind and bolster the walls of your soul will you be able to be healed, restored, and begin to prune your vine in Christlikeness. It is very much a war as Joyce Meyer's book clearly explains in *Battlefield of the Mind*.

Your mind, soul, and body are the battlefields where the battles are fought, and you must understand that your spirit is the eternal prize. Satan seeks to destroy us, and he entices us all through offering something desirable to our mind (soul) to meet perceived fleshly desires. These open door points initially have no power to influence your newly born-again spirit, but if not addressed specifically and dealt with, your resolve is weakened and destruction or the loss of your rewards is inevitable.

> For all that is in the world, the lust of the flesh, and the lust of the eyes, and the pride of life, is not of the Father, but is of the world. (1 John 2:16)

You give Satan legal right and authority to enter your life by your thoughts and actions, and he will attack you physically, emotionally, or psychologically if you let him. It doesn't matter to him if you're saved or not; Satan is patient, subtle, and resourceful and will finagle his way into your thought life at the slightest provocation, indiscretion, or opportunity that you allow yourself to be overtaken in. Look what Jesus says in Matthew 7:20–23.

> Wherefore by their fruits ye shall know them. Not everyone that saith unto me, Lord, Lord, shall enter into the kingdom of heaven; but he that doeth the will of my Father which is in heaven. Many will say to me in that day, Lord, Lord, have we not prophesied in thy name? and in thy name have cast out devils? And in thy name done many wonderful works? And then will I profess unto them, *I never knew you: depart from me, ye that work iniquity.* (emphasis added)

Again, for wide is the gate and broad is the way that leads to destruction, and many there be which go in there: because straight is the gate and *narrow is the way*, which leads unto life, and *few* there be that find it. How come? ... There are many fleshly influenced things that we do that we think are normal and our family's nature or traditions that we've acquired and have assumed to be ordinary for our ethnicity or culture. Many actions and thoughts we do are done subconsciously but are still diametrically opposed to God and His ways. Wide is the gate and narrow is the way. The gate is wide, meaning that any and all people *can* receive Jesus, "for God is not a respecter of persons," but the way is narrow meaning that there are many temptations that can veer us from the straight path.

Many today take for granted that because you are a believer, all is well, and nothing you do will keep you from the Father until you realize your need for Jesus to forgive you for sins committed and sins omitted deliberately or by accident daily. It is no longer convenient to compromise the sin you are in by the words you use to the attitudes and jokes you portray with the phony countenance and moods you show everyone who sees you. Christlikeness requires that your character needs to conform to His character and take captive every thought you think that is keeping you in bondage. Righteousness is tainted by the flesh, and thoughts bathed in sin are our downfall if we're not seeking after Christ.

> (For the weapons of our warfare are not carnal, but mighty through God to the pulling down of strongholds ;) Casting down *imaginations*, and every high thing that exalts itself against the *knowledge* of God, and bringing into captivity every *thought* to the obedience of Christ. (2 Corinthians 10:4–5, emphasis added)

The weapons of our warfare are not carnal but spiritual that influences our flesh. We need to have our thoughts saturated in the Word of God with the knowledge of the baptism of the Holy Spirit, the third person of the Trinity. The method used by Jesus when tempted by Satan is the same method you and I must use to defeat every temptation Satan throws at us—the Word of God. Compromise and tolerance are the baits used by Satan, and he uses them on a Bible-ignorant people to sin in word, deed, and thoughts. Even worse yet, he tries to convince a Jesus-believing person that is so wrapped up in their narrow-minded denominationalism and legalism to exclude anyone from a different church, tradition, or nationality but still profess allegiance to Jesus while persecuting them. We should understand the differences between truly biblical religious principles and the doctrines laid out by these narrow-minded church elders with their self-imposed legalistic traditions.

The instructions to a righteous and a Holy Spirit–filled person must live according to the Word of God alone. The Holy Bible is for all of us individually Old and New Testaments together and its promises are repeated throughout Scriptures for all believers to practice and grow spiritually.

> Study to show thyself approved unto God, a workman that needs not to be ashamed, *rightly dividing the word of truth.* (2 Timothy 2:15, emphasis added)

> For I reckon that the sufferings of this present time are not worthy to be compared with the glory which shall be revealed in us. For the earnest expectation of the creature *waits for the manifestation of the sons of God.* (Romans 8:18–19, emphasis added)

> Now I beseech you, brethren, mark them which cause divisions and offences contrary to the doctrine which ye have learned; and *avoid them.* (Romans 16:17, emphasis added)

> In all things showing thyself a pattern of good works: in doctrine showing incorruptness, gravity, sincerity, Sound speech, that cannot be condemned; that he that is of the contrary part may be ashamed, *having no evil* thing to say of you. (Titus 2:7–8, emphasis added)

> *Let no man therefore judge you* in meat, or in drink, or in respect of an holyday, or of the new moon, or of the Sabbath days. (Colossians 2:16, emphasis added)

But in vain they do worship me, teaching for doctrines the commandments of men. (Matthew 15:9, emphasis added)

Chapter 12

LOOK WHO JESUS LOVES

There are no secret rules or undisclosed instructions that only a few of the "enlightened" ones can receive. The Word of God is very plain, and all that it requires to understand it is to take your denominational prejudiced blinders off and read it—meditate on the Word and let the Holy Spirit teach you. Ask the third person of the Trinity to give you revelation; make you usable, strengthen your mind, and then to teach you His will and His way through His Holy Word (TRUST). Trust Him to reveal His Word to you so that you can show yourself approved a workman rightly dividing the Word of truth. We are without excuse, and God wants a personal relationship with you. He died on the cross for you, and He sent the Holy Spirit to you with earnest expectation for us to become sons of God (Romans 8:19). His Word is not a secret; it was written over 3,500 years ago for you and me for today. It all fits together, and it makes perfect sense if you take the whole Bible—the Old and New Testaments together, from Genesis to Revelation—and connect the dots and absorb it all.

The God of the Bible wants us spirit, soul, and body, in that order of significance—not body, soul, and spirit, which is the order that the current world society would teach you. Satan teaches people to live with their bodies sensual and sexual desires first, overruling the spirit and putting the spirit last and least in importance. I do believe that Satan has deceived and relocated man's spirit to being insignificant and all references to the spirit are existential, abstract, or of no real value. Satan's goal is to confuse and annul every reference to a biblical God and an eternal spirit with science, evolution, and academia. This validates the point in the Word of God that says the flesh corrupts the soul and the soul is the pathway to the spirit, so Satan makes the soul and spirit not important or something we cannot change.

The spirit can only go to God when you die if you have a personal relationship with Jesus Christ and make Him Lord and Savior of your life. Once there, we will be given new bodies to contain our eternal spirits. What we do once we get to heaven is determined by our soul's walls (character) which surround, identify, and protect our eternal spirit.

Satan's only desire is to destroy the walls of our soul originally conceived at birth with the natural fruit of the spirit and then rebuild them as strongholds through traditions, pride, lusts of the heart, emotional soul wounds and traumatic experiences that dictate our actions and attitudes throughout this life, saved or not. Many times they manifest their destructive ways in families for generations, trying to destroy you and your reputation or at the very least to keep you impudent here and ignorant of your eternal rewards once you get to heaven. This is not new in the Word. It's been written of for thousands of years, and many godly men and women have revealed these nuggets of truth over the centuries, but only in bits and pieces.

I do believe that denominationalism, racism, and anti-Semitism have blinded men from the truth of who God is and the way to Him. God is all-inclusive and wants none to perish but all to come to the knowledge of Jesus Christ and to have an eternal life with Him. The potential of every person is to be one who knows and loves the Lord Jesus Christ and to become a son or daughter of God. Unfortunately, without knowing Jehovah God, His only begotten Son Jesus, and the Holy Spirit, this inherently depraved nature of all humanity gravitates to the works of the flesh and keeps us away from a holy, righteous God. The law was necessary to separate and sanctify a people from the corrupt world to reestablish a relationship with Creator God. Even with the Law and later with Jesus Christ, man has a propensity for other defiling, fleshly works that proceed from the lust of the heart and the pride of life for sensual desires and momentary gratification.

> But those things which proceed out of the mouth come forth *from the heart*; and they defile the man. For out of the heart proceed evil thoughts, murders, adulteries, fornications, thefts, false witness, blasphemies: These are the things which defile a man. (Matthew 15:18–20, emphasis added)

> For from within, *out of the heart of men*, proceed evil thoughts, adulteries, fornications, murders, Thefts, covetousness, wickedness, deceit, lasciviousness, an evil eye, blasphemy, pride, foolishness: All these evil things come from within, and defile the man. (Mark 7:21–23, emphasis added)

And Paul adds in 1 Corinthians:

> I wrote unto you in an epistle not to company with fornicators. ... Know ye not that the unrighteous shall not inherit the kingdom of God? Be not deceived: neither fornicators, nor idolaters, nor adulterers, nor effeminate, nor abusers of themselves with mankind, Nor thieves, nor covetous, nor drunkards, nor revilers, nor extortioners, shall inherit the kingdom of God. (1 Corinthians 5:9; 6:9–10, emphasis added)

My first reaction to these warnings is concern and a fear of God for my having committed a number of these actions even after being saved. Oh, dear God, who is able to measure up to Your standards? Who is able to stand? Fortunately these Scriptures are not to be taken as condemning words but rather as warnings of love from a devoted, caring Father to His believing children for the healing of their wounded soul. God explains the consequences of these human actions and gives reasons for their results through the lives of people in the Old Testament. He then warns us to not participate in them again in the New Testament. We are able to choose not to act, and we are able to not think or act on any of these things if we choose not to.

> For we wrestle not against flesh and blood, but against principalities, against powers, against the rulers of the darkness of this world, against spiritual wickedness in high places. (Ephesians 6:12)

Paul warns us here in Ephesians how these four high-level demonic enemies and their hoards of imps will war against our souls to torment and inflict emotional and psychological pain in order to try to claim our eternal spirits as the prize. Only the Bible warns of these methods, and later in the next verses it reveals to us the protection and weapons to combat them given to every believer at conversion and confession of faith in Jesus Christ of Nazareth.

> Wherefore take unto you the whole armor of God, that ye may be able to withstand in the evil day, and having done all, to stand. Stand therefore, having your *loins girt about with truth*, and having on the *breastplate of righteousness*; And your *feet shod with the preparation of the gospel of peace*; Above all, taking the *shield of faith*, wherewith ye shall be able to quench all the fiery darts of the wicked. And take the *helmet of salvation*, and the *sword of the Spirit*, which is the word of God: *Praying always with all prayer and supplication in the Spirit*, and watching thereunto with all perseverance and supplication for all saints. (Ephesians 6:13–18, emphasis added)

Armor of God

+ **"loins girt about with truth"**: area below the waist, includes refraining from sexual indiscretions

+ **"breastplate of righteousness"**: This armor is to protect the vital organs during battle. Used to protect the chest especially our heart from the love wounds that affect the way we act and react from un-forgiveness, bitterness and rejection.

+ **"feet shod with the preparation of the gospel of peace"**: these signify covering our feet giving protection for where we walk and go. To protect us anywhere we can jeopardize our godly and Christian resolve; we are to place all things beneath and below the gospel of peace and are used to tread softly or to be careful of potential spiritual hazards.

+ **"shield of faith"**: used to protect against projectiles (fiery darts); used for protection and defense against all manner of mental and visual enticements; used to drown out all doubt and unbelief

+ **"helmet of salvation"**: thoughts deflected with the good news of Jesus Christ and Him crucified; reminding us of our position in Christ

+ **"sword of the Spirit"**: Holy Spirit empowered Word of God used to defeat satanic plots, plans, and ploys. "Rhema" is the revealed word of God, as an utterance from God to the heart of the reader via the Holy Spirit, as in John with the "rhema" Word of the living God when uttered signifies the simultaneous action taken.

+ **"Praying always with all prayer and supplication in the Spirit"**: with understanding and in the Spirit, with the baptism of the Holy Spirit, using your private prayer language (tongues).

This armor is given to all believers once they receive Jesus as Lord and Savior to protect and do battle with the revealed spiritual enemies of our spirit, soul, and body. Ephesians 6:12, James 4:1-4, Galatians 6:19 and 1 Cor. 6:9-10.

Then after true repentance we are warned once again that if you refuse to stop acting out your sin and continue regardless of your original repentance then the Holy Spirit tells us our fate.

> For if we sin willfully after that we have received the knowledge of the truth, there *remains no more sacrifice for sins*. (Hebrews 10:26, emphasis added)

There is no forgiveness of sin if you willingly and knowingly sin.

Jesus Christ has borne our sins—past, present, and future; all of them. His requirement is to sin no more. That's it: simply stop sinning. There is not one of the seventeen works of the flesh, seventeen spirit-world realities, or seventeen lusts of the heart that you can't stop from doing. When you confess Jesus as your personal Savior, all your sins are forgiven, and through true repentance, you're given a clean slate in the spirit. However, there really isn't any room for compromising His Word or your character. Our job is to try to catch our souls up to our spirits. I know what His Word says, but I can't do it without His help. So I looked again at the Word in the Gospels, and I read what Jesus said. He used two metaphors to explain what we should do. The first was to be like a tree that brings forth good fruit through the fruit of the Spirit in our life.

> Ye shall know them by their fruits. Do men gather grapes of
> thorns, or figs of thistles? ... A good tree cannot bring forth
> evil fruit, neither can a corrupt tree bring forth good fruit.
> (Matthew 7:16, 18)

And the second verse tells us to abide on the vine to bring forth much spiritual fruit as a by-product of our relationship with Jesus.

> Abide in me, and I in you. As the branch cannot bear fruit
> of itself, except it abide in the vine; no more can ye, except
> ye abide in me. (John 15:4)

As you read these passages, it becomes very clear that Jesus expects us as believers to bountifully bear good fruit, and more importantly, abide in Jesus planting new spiritual seeds to grow more trees and vines. The true believer in Christ is a tree or vine with the corresponding fruit and relationship with Jesus to prove their identity. This fruit must be evidenced by a life with the proper virtues, attributes, and visible works that exemplify these types of spiritual characteristics of Jesus so that the Holy Spirit can manifest His spiritual gifts in us.

> Either make the tree good, and his fruit good; or else make
> the tree corrupt, and his fruit corrupt: for the tree is known
> by his fruit. (Matthew 12:33)

It is our choice if the type of fruit our tree or vine shall produce, bringing glory to His name. The fruit of the Spirit is made up of nine elements that define who we are in Christ, and each one of these fruit must be evident in your life.

> But the fruit of the Spirit is love, joy, peace, longsuffering,
> gentleness, goodness, faith, Meekness, temperance: against
> such there is no law. (Galatians 5:22–23)

No tree can bear good fruit without favorable nourishment and positive conditions. The conditions are the environment around the tree or vine that allow for adequate nourishment and healthy growth for the proper development of the tree to bring it to maturity and bear fruit that later also produces more fruit-bearing trees. This comparison also applies to the individual bricks of the wall supporting the gates that surround your saved spirit temple. As each brick or block becomes thicker, stronger and taller through your walking in the Spirit the enemy can't burrow under, break through or climb over our protective walls. The comparisons to a fruit-bearing tree or vine and a load-bearing wall that both supports and protects the temple of your spirit are only similar in that they both represent you as an individual believer who is influenced by and feeds off of the environment around you.

In the parables of the Gospels, Jesus gave us an example that the people would understand in that time. He compared the type of water and nourishment that a tree receives directly to the health and goodness of the fruit it produced. He inferred that the influences in a person's life drive that person's character traits, and that they are known by their actions and the people they associate with as to whether they have good or bad fruit. Understand that these character flaws will not be able to enter into the presence of a holy God.

The good news is that while you are still alive, you can still change these flaws. Similarly, the walls and gates that protect and support your saved spirit are either being destroyed or are being built up by the influences of your surroundings and the people you associate with. These nine attributes are all components of each fruit and are not competitive or isolated from each other, but complementary to each other, forming a well-rounded individual. Legitimate compassion and love would never belittle or emotionally be cruel to another family member or fellow believer in Christ.

As Jesus is our perfect example of a good tree bearing good fruit, we too must allow these attributes to be exemplified in our lives. The greatest influence we can have is with our own families; mates, children, and coworkers as a Christ-like, motivated life illustration. If we are not careful, they can also be our greatest critics. Remember that our families are with us when we get up in the morning; they're with us when we go to and leave church; and they're with us to see our bad moods, our frustrations, our aggravations. They see our hypocrisies with our cursing and yelling—even under our breath. Our families are our greatest advocates as well as our cruelest critics, and our actions, words, and witness of Jesus are sometimes all they need to see to nullify our walk. Your daily walk is your testimony, and mistakes are normal, but repetitious and constant failure is hypocritical and harmful to the name of Jesus. My own hypocrisy has been called out several times while writing this book when my intolerance, aggravation, and annoyances have been pointed out by the Holy Spirit, my wife, or my kids. I've had to recant and humbly apologize for my actions, especially after meditating on a particular Scripture and immediately afterward, I'm tested on that exact fruit principle and have failed in word or deed.

Chapter 13

THE THIRD PERSON
OF THE TRINITY

All of Christ's authority comes from the Father, and Jesus says that He has given His authority to us after we choose Him. The Holy Spirit as the Comforter or "Helper" and is given to us for the purpose of giving all believers the power to overcome the issues we face daily in this life, but more importantly, the Holy Spirit gives us the power to live for God victoriously. It gives us the power to testify, to witness with boldness, and to walk in all nine of the fruit of the Spirit daily with Kingdom Authority.

> But ye shall receive power, after that the Holy Ghost is come upon you: and ye shall be witnesses unto me both in Jerusalem, and in all Judaea, and in Samaria, and unto the uttermost part of the earth. (Acts 1:8)

Revelations 2:7, 13;9

He that hath an ear, let him hear what the Spirit saith unto the churches; To him that overcometh will I give to eat of the tree of life, which is in the midst of the paradise of God.

If any man have an ear, let him hear.

In all four Gospels, John the Baptist is quoted as testifying about how Jesus would empower us after He comes.

> I indeed baptize you with water unto repentance: but he that cometh after me is mightier than I, whose shoes I am not worthy to bear: he shall baptize you with the Holy Ghost, and with fire. (Matthew 3:11)

> I indeed have baptized you with water: but he shall baptize you with the Holy Ghost. (Mark 1:8)

These are quotes from Jesus Himself:

> He that believeth on me, as the scripture hath said, out of his belly shall flow rivers of living water. (John 7:38)

> If ye then, being evil, know how to give good gifts unto your children: how much more shall your heavenly Father give the Holy Spirit to them that ask him? (Luke 11:13)

> Blessed are they which do hunger and thirst after righteousness: for they shall be filled. (Matthew 5:6)

After the ascension of Jesus, the Holy Spirit was given to us to help us walk daily in the Spirit of God to identify our spiritual failures and to begin rebuilding our walls and gates so that we could be a living testimony in Christlikeness. Jesus introduced the Holy Spirit in John 15:26.

> But when the Comforter is come, whom I will send unto you from the Father, even the Spirit of truth, which proceeds from the Father, he shall testify of me. (John 15:26)

DIMITRI YANULI

The Holy Ghost will not speak of Himself but will glorify Christ by receiving the truth from Christ and showing it to you for our betterment and growth in Christlikeness.

> In the beginning was the Word, and the Word was with God, and the Word was God. The same was in the beginning with God. All things were made by him; and without him was not anything made that was made. In him was life; and the life was the light of men. And the light shines in darkness; and the darkness comprehended it not. (John 1:1–5)

"Darkness" in this Scripture is referring to the Pharisees and the rest of the unbelieving world that didn't (and still doesn't) recognize Jesus today as the God of Israel or the Savior of the world. Too many Christ-believing Christians don't believe that the God of Israel is the God of all Christendom, and too many Jewish believers of Jehovah don't believe that Jesus is the promised Messiah of Israel.

This misunderstanding and demonically provoked prejudice has retarded any spiritual growth for all God-fearing children of the living God, both of the natural tree (Jews)and of those grafted (gentiles) into that natural tree. The church has been deceived to believe that their particular denomination's interpretation of the Bible is the only one, and that all others are deceived. Don't just listen to what one person says, study the Bible to show yourself approved. The gifts of the Spirit that were available to the new Christian converts in the book of Acts are the same gifts that are available to you and me today. Why else are the promises of the Spirit so prevalent in the gospels and epistles? Not only is Jehovah the God of the Jews, but He is also the God of the Gentiles as well; and Jesus is not only the Messiah of the Gentiles, He is the Messiah to the Jews also.

If you believe that the Bible is the inspired Word of the living God, then you must believe that the whole Bible, both the Old and New Testaments, are true. You either believe the whole Bible or you don't; you can't cherry-pick what you like or don't like because it conflicts with your lifestyle or learned denominationalism. Finally, the Holy Spirit of 1 Corinthians 12 is the same Holy Spirit who moved upon the face of the waters in Genesis 1. The Bible tells us how God called a peculiar people out of this corrupt world (the Hebrews), and He reconciled them unto Himself through His Law and later through His Son, Jesus the Christ. He sent the third person of the Trinity, the Holy Spirit, to help all of us to grow individually. This is His plan for humanity to grow and be independent individuals with free wills and with the ability to believe in Jehovah God and His Son Jesus Christ through His Holy Spirit.

We need to have fellowship with the Father through the Son in the Holy Spirit, growing daily. We can do this only by the rebuilding of our soul's walls and gates with the help of the Holy Spirit as we become more Christ-like in our thoughts and actions. We all have nine walls and gates that are represented by the nine fruit of the Spirit in Galatians 5:22–23. These walls and gates are to protect the temple of our believing spirits by capturing these worldly thoughts (spirit-world realities) that influence the mind and heart, taking them captive, and expelling them through prayer and fasting. We can either rebuild our damaged walls and gates from deep soul wounds and traumas in this life through godly love and compassion, or we can suffer with these emotional strongholds, succumbing to them completely as they arise.

Many Christians think that they don't have to worry anymore because they're believers now and are saved. But we must understand that the consequence of an unprotected spirit for years has damaged us somewhere in our love foundation or one of our fruit of the Spirit. Jesus has given us nine spiritual gifts to rebuild our nine gates and walls through the Holy Spirit baptism that every born-again believer can receive to help do this work. Along with our spiritual language and the Word of God, we can commune again with the Creator of everything seen and unseen, but we need to humble ourselves and learn from His Word. Why else would Jesus and the apostles repeat the coming of the Holy Spirit and His gifts if they weren't for His children in this life to use, especially for those of us believers who are alive in these last days?

Remember the acronym TRUST that we spoke of earlier. I used this for every individual fruit of the Spirit, and what I have learned is humbling and very revealing. The Holy Spirit has been very instructive with His admonishments and corrections of my attitudes and false prejudgments in each fruit. What

I've been learning is that my ways are not His ways and that I needed Jesus and the Holy Spirit to help me grow and be an ambassador for Christ. He teaches me daily through small instances and everyday situations that assess my spiritual growth in Christlikeness. Through these small tests I learn that I can become victorious and overcome issues that I thought I had no control over in the past. This is the battle we all face, and only God's Word calls out the Enemies plans, plots, and devices to detour us from God or destroy us completely if possible. Even small, insignificant issues that alone are mostly ignored and overlooked can begin to snowball and cause family strife or lay dormant, rearing their ugly head at the seemingly slightest provocation which could damage or destroy our testimonies with family, friends, and coworkers.

Not knowing what provoked my own attitudes and actions, I asked the Holy Spirit to make me fully aware, knowing that I wouldn't like the answers He was to show me. While mulling over some of my own failings and falling countenance during family functions and work, I came to see the battleground was me and my spirit, and my soul's rewards were the prize. My spirit is with Jesus, and everything else about me was free for the taking unless I took drastic measures to bar the doors and protect my spirit. Like I said earlier, every human who ever lived or is alive today is surrounded by nine gates and walls. These gates are represented by the nine fruit of the Spirit; these fruit are influenced by the Word of God or the spirit-world realities and the works of the flesh. We have free will so we can choose our eternal destination. I will show you the playing field with all the pieces that will either assist us to enter eternity at our greatest godly spiritual potential, or you will be impotent and completely powerless in this life and limited in the Kingdom. The alternative is to live a seemingly powerless and tormented life completely ignorant of His spiritual gifts that are available to all believers the second they verbally confess Jesus as Lord and believe in their heart that God raised Jesus from the dead. Romans 10:9,10

God has given us every tool needed to rebuild and grow our souls and also to battle against principalities, against powers, against the rulers of the darkness of this world, and against spiritual wickedness in high places. The trophy is our spirits; the battlefield is our soul and minds with our eternal destination and duties to be determined by the depth of our character in this brief life we have been given here on earth. Many academics and philosophers scoff at the notion of a God who judges each individual human being on their life's decisions and actions, but the fact remains that no other teaching speaks of a person's existence from the instant of conception to all of their choices in this life to the afterlife for eternity but the Bible. This knowledge of the Word of the living God Jehovah, Jesus Christ of Nazareth, and the Holy Spirit is all that we need to defeat every trial, torment, or temptation we could ever face in this life. The rewards of succeeding are unfathomable to our intellect, and only the Word of God can bring this guarantee. The guarantee is in Romans 10:9–10.

> That if thou shall confess with thy mouth the Lord Jesus, and shall believe in thine heart that God hath raised him from the dead, *thou shalt be saved.* For with the heart man believeth unto righteousness; and with the mouth confession is made unto salvation. (emphasis added)

Once confession is made, we're saved regardless of denomination, ethnicity, race or gender. We can then begin repairing our soul walls so we can begin cultivating and nourishing the fruit of the Spirit and we can bear good fruit in the lives of people we love and meet around us.

The choice is yours if you choose Jesus there can be no compromising the Word of God; His Word is clear and your choice must be definite—your eternity depends on it. We are not graded on a curve with God; you either are or you aren't a Christian, a believer or not. Your speech and your corresponding actions are your fruit, and God will reward you accordingly. Without the complete acceptance of the entire Bible from Genesis to Revelations, the whole assertion of a benevolent God, a Redeemer, and an abiding Spirit who leads and guides us through this life seems fantastical and confusing.

If the Bible isn't taken literally, it makes no sense at all. The whole teaching of replacement theology and the exclusion of Jewish traditions only confuses New Testament Scripture and is proof of human and demonic interference with a judgmental prejudice that only defuses the power and splendor of His Word. The Book of Acts tells us that when a person accepts Jesus as Lord and Savior, the next gift from God after Jesus' sacrifice is the Comforter who dwells in their heart.

> And when they had prayed, the place was shaken where they were assembled together; and they were *all filled with the Holy Ghost*, and they spoke the word of God with boldness. (Acts 4:31, emphasis added)

The assertion that this gift from God ceased when the last apostle died reduces the power of the risen Christ to any other fable or fairy tale. Jesus is the risen Christ, and He did not leave us comfortless.

And many other signs truly did Jesus in the presence of his disciples, which are not written in this book: "But these are written, that ye might believe that Jesus is the Christ, the Son of God; and that believing ye might have life through his name" (John 20:30–31).

The risen Christ proclaimed His undying love for Israel, and everything prior to Acts focused primarily on the hypocrisy of the legalistic religious priesthood that followed the letter of the law but didn't adhere to God's ways. Matthew, Mark, Luke, and John were all written to the Jews because they were all practicing Jews, and only after the death, burial, and resurrection of the king of the Jews, Jesus Christ of Nazareth did they understand the significance of what just happened.

Only after the conversion of the Jewish Pharisee Saul (Paul) were the Gentiles targeted. After Acts, we see the power and authority given to all converts to Christianity whether Jew or Gentile, free or slave, male or female, white, black, brown, or yellow.

> For John truly baptized with water; but ye shall be baptized with the Holy Ghost not many days hence. But ye shall receive power, after that the Holy Ghost is come upon you: and ye shall be witnesses unto me both in Jerusalem, and in all Judaea, and in Samaria, and unto the uttermost part of the earth. (Acts 1:5, 8)

This command was for all Jews or pagan Gentiles to be converted to Christianity by repenting of their sins, being baptized in water by choice, then being baptized with the Holy Ghost. Once baptized with the Holy Spirit, we then are given a prayer language that every believer has been given at conversion with all the gifts of the Spirit. The Word says in Acts 2:4, "And they were *all* filled with the Holy Ghost, and began to speak with other tongues, as the Spirit gave them utterance."

Not just the apostles were filled with the Holy Ghost, everyone was filled with the Holy Spirit, and everyone is to be filled today. You either believe what the Word of God says to be true or you don't; you can't cherry-pick only the parts you understand or like with your tolerating liberal mind-set that the world teaches. Replacement theology is doing just that replacing the Jewish promises with Christianity, which in a sense is only partially correct. Many Christian denominations ignore parts or all of the Old Testament and just read past the references to the Old Testaments of commonly understood Jewish traditions and generally held requirements of the Hebrew believer. You can't just accept the parts of scripture that you understand by replacing the promises to the Jews with your denominations prejudgments and biases. To ignore the parts that admonish the believer and only accept the good parts is what we need to fully grasp and accept in these last days. When you receive Jesus at salvation, the Holy Spirit comes to dwell in the heart and life of the individual and you are a believer.

> Even the Spirit of truth; whom the world cannot receive, because it seeth him not, neither knoweth him: but ye know him; for he dwelleth with you, and shall *be in you.* (John 14:17, emphasis added)

The initial physical evidence of the baptism of the Holy Spirit is the speaking with other tongues as the Spirit gives utterance. Naturally there are other evidences that should and will manifest themselves, such as increased power, charity, love for Christ, faith, boldness, strength, and a deepened prayer life. But speaking in tongues is the biblical unmistakable evidence of the baptism in its fullness

(H. Courtney & V. Courtney). One year after Pentecost in Samaria, "Then laid they their hands on them, and they received the Holy Ghost" (Acts 8:17). And eight years after Pentecost, the Gentiles were heard speaking in tongues and magnifying God.

> While Peter yet spake these words, the Holy Ghost fell on all them which heard the word. And they of the circumcision which believed were astonished, as many as came with Peter, because that on the Gentiles also was poured out the gift of the Holy Ghost. For they heard them speak with tongues, and magnify God. (Acts 10:44–46)

And twenty-three years later in Ephesus, Paul prayed for new Gentile believers, and we read in Acts 19:6, "And when Paul had laid his hands upon them, *the Holy Ghost* came on them; and *they* spoke with tongues, and prophesied" (emphasis added).

To assume that the gifts of the Spirit ceased with the death of the last apostle would mean that all nine spiritual gifts ceased as well and that assumption is just not biblically or factually true. We either believe all the Word Jesus preached or we don't. In order to bring clarity to the warnings that He and the Apostles gave in the epistles and the book of Revelation we need to accept it all to make sense.

With the baptism of the spirit know that there are two types of tongues that you have access to. The first is tongues, given to all believers, and is your personal prayer language that is private for your personal use in prayer as your heart cries out to God and the second is given corporately for the edification of the church.

> Likewise the Spirit also helpeth our infirmities: for we know not what we should pray for as we ought: but the Spirit itself maketh intercession for us with groanings which cannot be uttered. (private tomgues) And he that searcheth the hearts knoweth what is the mind of the Spirit, because he maketh intercession for the saints according to the will of

God. (corporate tongues with interpretation) (Romans 8:26–27)

If the gifts of the Spirit are no longer available to believers today, then the healing of the excruciating pain I had been healed from by an evangelist to my legs in Florida was and isn't real. These spiritual gifts are given specifically to meet a need. Like my pastor said at church in one of his Sunday sermons, the gifts of the Spirit in 1 Corinthians 12 are like appliances in the home, and you only use them when you need them. The gift of the Holy Spirit in the baptism of the Spirit is primarily in your private prayer language and is separate from the other nine gifts of the spirit of 1st Cor. 12. Your personal prayer language is vitally important to all believers because of the need to hear from God and for God to hear from you in prayer. By the way, the Devil can't understand tongues, so it's your private communication line to the throne room of God with Jesus at His right side, intervening on our behalf. Do you think this is why Satan doesn't want us to speak in tongues, and why Paul said, "Now concerning spiritual gifts, brethren, I would not have you ignorant" (1 Corinthians 12:1)? This is the power Jesus promised in Acts 1:8:

> But ye shall receive power, after that the Holy Ghost is come upon you: and ye shall be witnesses unto me both in Jerusalem, and in all Judaea, and in Samaria, and unto the uttermost part of the earth.

The one and only requirement to receiving these gifts is that you must be saved and a born-again believer.

Jesus answered and said unto him, Verily, verily, I say unto thee, Except a man be born again, he cannot see the kingdom of God. (John 3:3)

You may never speak corporately but we all need to pray in the spirit privately to hear from God and to trust that He hears from us. The second requirement is the willingness to forsake control of the sharpest and most dangerous member of our bodies—the tongue. James said that the tongue is a fire; it is the power of evil placed in our bodies, making all the body unclean, putting the wheel of life on fire, and getting its fire from hell. But the tongue may not be controlled by man completely. It is an un-resting evil, full of the poison of death and influenced by the hurts and pains of this life. With it, we give praise to our Lord and Father; and with it, we put a curse on men who are made in God's image.

Praying in the Spirit is to believe that the heartfelt thoughts and prayers you're having come out in moans, groans, and feelings—in sigh's and sounds similar to words in a foreign language. To pray with a repentant heart is to pray with the willingness to be taught to change your mind and control your thoughts. To speak in tongues is to relinquish control of your tongue. Speaking diverse kinds of tongues as defined in Scripture is to speak more than one language or with a combination of various types foreign to the individual's natural knowledge. This spoken language is not understood as the individual's native language but must be accepted by the believer in faith and the Word of the living God that these sounds mean something to God from their heart.

By losing control of the words that you think and habitually speak, it gives the Holy Spirit access to the heart and soul of the person speaking them. These sounds are the words of our heart that are actually the sounds of our soul speaking to God about our troubles, even if it sounds like gibberish to your mind's ear.

True repentance is to change your mind and change the way you act or react in any situation and allow Jesus, with the Holy Spirit, to take control of your body and soul. There is not one of the seventeen works of the flesh or the seventeen spirit-world realities or the seventeen lusts or emotional strongholds of the heart that you can't choose not to do or act upon. You have been given the ability to choose not to open a door to your spirit or port of your hard drive (brain) to corrupt it with sin as a virus to your personal computer. True praying in the Spirit is meditating on the written Word of God and being in prayer when the Holy Spirit speaks to you individually that will help close those doors (ports) of your soul with (conviction) and not condemnation. He edifies us personally and teaches us something that improves our character as a child of the living God. Through this private prayer in the Spirit, He speaks to us specifically to meet the needs of healing, correction, and restoration in our soul walls and fruit of the Spirit gates that have been corrupted in this life.

Again, understand that our thoughts are influenced by the things we hear and see, and the Holy Spirit has been given to us to help us identify the corruption, evict it, and then restore our fruit walls and gates. The second form of tongues is the gift of the Holy Spirit spoken of in 1 Corinthians 12 and is given in a public setting for the edification of the whole congregation or a specific person dealing with an issue and names are never used. This second form of speaking in tongues is public and is different in that these tongues are one of the nine gifts of the Spirit which include knowledge, wisdom, faith, prophecy, healing, miracles, discerning of spirits, tongues, and interpretation of tongues (1 Corinthians 12–14). These nine gifts are all done publically and are visible manifestations of the power of God as a witness and testimony of the Holy Spirit working in the life of a believer submitted to the authority of Jesus Christ and Him alone.

Only this type of public tongues requires an interpretation that should be given immediately after the word is given and your private prayer language does not need interpretation. Don't confuse the two; the Holy Spirit will impress upon your heart the direction and correction needed for you and you alone. This type of public corporate tongues is not always interpreted by the same person giving the word and can be given by a different person. This only adds to its validity and further proves its authenticity. This experience of the baptism of the Holy Spirit is the gateway for a new intimacy, a new nearness, and a new oneness in fellowship with a new walk with God in the Spirit: "This I say then, Walk in the Spirit, and ye shall not fulfill the lust of the flesh" (Galatians 5:16) (Prince).

What I believe God desires is for us to commune with Him in the Spirit. To do this, we need to re-establish our thoughts and begin to rebuild the walls of our soul. This re-establishment begins with a reassessment of our senses and the inputs of the things we smell, hear, taste, touch, and see. To reboot our computer or brain and get rid of all the viruses, we need to be saved and change our minds (repent). Viruses that limit access to our programs on the computer are very similar to our thoughts and the works of the flesh in that they can prevent us from doing or being the kind of person we were designed to be. When our five senses are entertained by these works of the flesh with these lustful indulgences they then become an open door point that then is used to access our hard drives (brains). Once they have access to our thoughts Satan will then try to influence our actions or distract us with fantasies or delusions of grandeur. Like our computers, once accessed, any and all viruses (malware, spyware, adware, etc.) will try to open our computer to corrupt, prevent, and steal information for later use or shut it down completely. Our souls are exactly the same, and Satan will try to access one or more of the open doors that we have legally opened with our seemingly harmless but still sinful indulgences. To limit these visual and audible indulgences we need to set boundaries for ungodly things that entice the flesh. We then need to allow the Holy Spirit to warn and assist us by not being tempted or provoked to lust after things unbecoming to the Lord especially when emotionally driven.

The Word of God clearly points to the works of the flesh and the tongue needing to be kept completely under our control, with the consequences of them being explained in Biblical Scripture alone. We can and should be in complete command of the things we see and hear that influence the thoughts that we have and the words that we speak. Know that every idle word spoken comes from the heart of a man or woman and the saying by computer-savvy people—"garbage in, garbage out"—is very applicable to all believers. The things we allow in our thoughts through our eyes and ears plant corrupt seeds that are then nurtured with every seemingly innocent superficial dip into sin.

> A man shall eat good by the fruit of his mouth: but the soul of the transgressors shall eat violence. He that keeps his mouth keeps his life: but he that opens wide his lips shall have destruction. … A wholesome tongue is a tree of life: but perverseness therein is a breach in the spirit. … Death and life are in the power of the tongue: and they that love it shall eat the fruit thereof. (Proverbs 13:2–3; 15:4; 18:21)

> But those things which proceed out of the mouth come forth from the heart; and they defile the man. (Matthew 15:18)

> But above all things, my brethren, swear not, neither by heaven, neither by the earth, neither by any other oath:

but let your yea be yea; and your nay, nay; lest ye fall into condemnation. (James 5:12)

These verses are so vitally important to your walk with Jesus in that the more control you have of your thoughts, the more control you will have of your tongue; and the more control you have over your tongue, the more control you will have over your life. Both your thoughts and your mouth can inhibit your spiritual growth. This is why I believe people have such a hard time with the manifestation of the nine gifts of the Spirit. Lack of a personal prayer language and especially your lack of the fruit of love will inhibit your spiritual growth even more.

You need to submit to the authority of Jesus Christ in love and to the power of the Holy Spirit in obedience for you to be used by a Holy God. You also need to understand that with your prideful denominational countenance and perverted conditional foundation of love, every relationship you have is adversely affected and stunted, producing no fruit. These are the same reasons the walls of our souls are damaged, having such destructive and hurtful consequences to our actions in this life that we never move beyond the salvation experience.

This is also the reason that communing with the Holy God in the Spirit is so difficult for some people. Difficulty in receiving the baptism in the Holy Spirit occurs when believers allow the pride of this life, the lust of the flesh and their wounded soul to dominate every thought and action they have. Today many denominations believe that these gifts of the Spirit were for saints long dead and not for us today. This is only a shallow excuse for not facing the truth of your sinful thoughts and uncontrollable tongues. Not only do we as believers have our personal prayer language that only God can understand we have the nine gifts of the Spirit as part of our arsenal (1 Corinthians12), the armor of God (Ephesians 6:10–18) we have the Fruit of the Spirit that we walk in daily. (Gal.5:22-23)

The Devil can only try to anticipate our common human nature reactions from observing humanity for thousands of years responding the same way over and over again. Only God in His omniscience, knowing all things from what we think to the motives of everything we do—even in secret can. Identifying our motives and intentions can be used to help us grow into Christlikeness and only if we identify these issues and learn to control them. This is the purpose of our personal prayer language.

Listen all blood bought children of God; once saved we all have praying in the Spirit in our personal prayer language, the armor of God, the nine Fruit of the Spirit, the nine gifts of the Spirit and the Word of the living God, along with the blood of Jesus which is the most powerful weapon in our armory to use in battle and defeat any attack from Satan or his minions. To me and my limited theological knowledge, what I read in Scripture I believe…. And what it tells me is that we win! It has taken six thousand years of biblical history to bring man to this point, which brings him back to where Adam and Eve were before the fall.

I don't understand how some people can cherry-pick only the parts they can explain or understand in Scripture with the natural senses and completely ignore the supernatural. To think that God doesn't work with man today like He did in early Scripture only shows a lack of faith in the creator God. Jehovah God, Jesus Christ the Messiah and the Holy Spirit as outlined in the Old and New Testaments are the same yesterday, today and forever. I repeat again that I can't find anywhere in Scripture where there is an expiration date on any of the gifts of the Spirit, our prayer language, or any of God's armor that is given to us the second we believe in the risen Savior. In the natural, I can't explain why some people are called and some are not, but I do believe that as you relinquish control of those fleshly natural aspects of your being to Jesus, the Spirit of God will begin to grow in His love and you will learn to walk in the Spirit daily.

Jesus said,

> And I say unto you, Ask, and it shall be given you; seek, and ye shall find; knock, and it shall be opened unto you. (Luke 11:9)

If we don't seek, we are without excuse, and the consequences of choosing to ignore His Word will be eternal—there are no "do-overs." Still, a loving God has provided a way to salvation through His beloved Son, Jesus Christ of

Nazareth. God has called *all mankind* to come to Him through a Pharisee of Pharisees, Saul of Tarsus, who spoke to the non-Jews. After his conversion, his name was changed from Saul to Paul.

> For I speak to you Gentiles, inasmuch as I am the apostle of the Gentiles, I magnify mine office. … For I will not dare to speak of any of those things which Christ hath not wrought by me, to make the Gentiles obedient, by word and deed, Through mighty signs and wonders, *by the power of the Spirit of God*; so that from Jerusalem, and round about unto Illyricum, I have fully preached the gospel of Christ. (Romans 11:13; 15:18–19)

The good news is for everyone because there are two kinds of branches (Romans 11:16–17), and both of these branches will be saved: the Messianic Jews when they receive Jesus as Messiah; and all the Gentiles, regardless of race, gender, nationality, or Christian denomination. As long as they confess Jesus as Lord and believe God raised Him from the dead, they're in.

> That if thou shalt confess with thy mouth the Lord Jesus, and shalt believe in thine heart that God hath raised him from the dead, thou shalt be saved. … And so *all Israel shall be saved*: as it is written, There shall come out of Zion the Deliverer, and shall turn away ungodliness from Jacob: For this is my covenant unto them, when I shall take away their sins. (Romans 10:9; 11:26–28, emphasis added)

What the Holy Spirit is calling us to do is present our bodies a living sacrifice, holy, acceptable unto God, which is your reasonable service. And be not conformed to this world, but be transformed by the renewing of your mind, that you may prove what is that good, and acceptable, and perfect will of God.

> Let every soul be subject unto the higher powers. For there is no power but of God: the powers that be are ordained of God. Whosoever therefore resists the power resists

the ordinance of God: and they that resist shall receive to themselves damnation. (Romans 13:1–2)

You must choose to believe the Old and New Testaments together, not just the parts you like and accept by a particular denomination, for it to make sense to your traditional way of thinking. Jehovah is God, Jesus Christ is the Messiah, and the Holy Spirit is the third person of the Trinity spoken of in both Old and New Testaments. This is who God is, and we as His ultimate creation are to praise and worship Him as such. You must believe that the whole Word of God from Genesis to Revelation is true and believe that the Holy Spirit inspired believers to write it in its entirety. Only the Bible explains and resolves these mostly ignored eternal issues that we face daily and can only be conquered through repenting and changing our minds, habits and actions. The Bible alone places meaning and value to all human life and gives every life purpose and significance.

I will praise thee; for I am fearfully and wonderfully made: marvelous are thy works; and that my soul knoweth right well. (Psalm 139:14)

You must take your worldly, religious, and denominationally influenced blinders off and look at what this book (the Bible) is telling you.

Knowing this first, that no prophecy of the scripture is of any private interpretation. For the prophecy came not in old time by the will of man: but holy men of God spake as they were moved by the Holy Ghost. (2 Peter 1:20–21)

It's not a secret or a mystery that only a select few are able to be enlightened to receive but rather an open invitation to *all* who believe in the triune God— Father, Son, and Holy Spirit. You're not going to be a type of Jesus on your own planet (Mormons) so you don't need to marry as many wives as you can (polygamy) to have as many children as you can to populate your own planet. You're not going to have seventy-two virgins if you blow yourself up killing infidels, nonbelievers, and Jews, and live eternity as the center of your own narcissistic sex orgy for eternity (Islam). You don't become one with the universe or part of God at your death (Universalists) or worse yet, just stop being (academics and evolutionists). You're not one of the special 144,000 to get into heaven (that number was reached 1934), while the rest of humanity are earth dwellers, separated from the first special 144,000 (Jehovah Witnesses). You don't get a second chance to try again with reincarnation (Hindus) to get a do-over, and lastly, you will never reach perfect eternal peace in the state of nirvana and deathlessness as claimed by Buddhists.

You are a human being made in the image of the living God (spirit, soul, and body), and this life we live determines our eternal destiny and our eternal rewards. It is never too late to change your mind (repent) and there's nothing that you could have done that Jesus won't forgive you for. Jesus hung on the cross for everyone to pay the price for our sins. (Atonement)

Christ hath redeemed us from the curse of the law, being made a curse for us: for it is written, Cursed is every one that hangeth on a tree: (Galatians 3:13

Chapter 14

REBOOT YOUR BRAIN

The fruit of the Spirit in Christlikeness are the principle standards and attributes we must try to emulate to attain our complete array of eternal rewards. These same attributes individually are the methods with which we can defeat Satan and his influences as we grow in sanctification and walk in the Spirit daily. We as His church are to be presented to Him not having spot or wrinkle, and we must be holy and without blemish as His bride to receive our eternal rewards. God's Word alone explains what we will do for eternity in that we will worship and serve Him daily. We will enjoy God's presence and fellowship, and we will rule and reign with Jesus as we help administer His kingdom in the New Jerusalem for the millennium and all of eternity.

> The Spirit itself beareth witness with our spirit, that we are
> the children of God: And if children, then heirs; heirs of God,
> and joint-heirs with Christ; if so be that we suffer with him,
> that we may be also glorified together. (Romans 8:16–17)

We as the children of the living God must remove as many spots and wrinkles as possible while we are alive or they will be removed (burned) away from us as we enter into His presence. This includes every snide, sarcastic, prideful, nasty, mean, spiteful, ugly attitude of superiority that can be seen in our soul's fruit. Because of them, we can never enter into the presence of a Holy God.

> But the day of the Lord will come as a thief in the night; in the which the heavens shall pass away with a great noise, and the elements shall melt with fervent heat, the earth also and *the works* that are therein shall be burned up. (2 Peter 3:10, emphasis added)

Any and every self-seeking or fleshly motivated action done in this life will be exposed and not permitted into the kingdom. This is where many self-professing, legalistic, and doctrinally rigid believers shun and turn away from anyone who doesn't fit the "religious" mold of their specific denomination's traditional rules. This is also where you can be right about an issue *scripturally* (nugget of truth), but you aren't right with God *spiritually* (heart), and your inflexible unloving rejection of a fellow Christian and believer in the risen Christ will keep you as a believer from entering into the presence of a holy God. If you call yourself a Christian and there is a person whom you love in Christ that is still in a sin issue and they refuse to stop with their sinful lifestyle decisions, then you must do as the father did with the Prodigal Son and let them go (Luke 15:12). Continue to show the love of Christ but set Godly parameters and do not relent. If they come back, praise God. If not, you may end up compromising God's Word, hoping they will change and conform to God's Word, and in reality all you're only doing is fooling yourself and allowing sin in Jesus' presence to appease your conscience.

Yes, this attitude toward the people we love seems cruel and seems to show very little love, but allowing their sin, whatever it may be, into your home or presence only weakens the Holy Spirit's conviction in that person's life and opens the door for your possible compromising of your Christian resolve. We need to understand that with heartfelt inspired hope for someone we love, hitting rock bottom is sometimes the only thing that will work with them.

Having hate, judgment, or prejudice with their lifestyle of sin will only drive them further away, and the walk you walk is a very fine line. God hates the sin, not the person.

I guess that line of demarcation needs to be made abundantly clear and the division greater between fleshly living and your godly walk, because you have to separate yourself from the world we live in. Your hateful, murderous rejection of someone of a different race, ethnicity, or denomination is not the same as a person living a sinful lifestyle by choice. Works of the flesh and lusts of the heart are choices and not a necessity to live. You don't have to act on them to live—honestly, you won't die physically but you will lose spiritually if you participate in any of them. The people you deem unworthy to live by or associate with you regardless of all the good things that you've done in the past are irrelevant to God if you have hate for a particular race or the denomination of a fellow Christian. Compromise and potential conciliation of godly standards with sin will only weaken and distort that godly line of demarcation and should not be confused with race, ethnicity or Christian denominations. Your narrow-minded justification of racial prejudice and ethnic cleansing over past indiscretions has no validity with a loving God and the only hate with a Holy God claimed by man stems from the motivations and intents for their sinful lifestyles and ignorance of the Word of God.

Compromising your faith with unrepentant people will cause you the spiritual loss of your rewards—if not your salvation altogether. If you're not careful all your good works will be burned away (2 Peter 3:11) tolerance and compromising God's Word even a little opens doors to your mind. There are sometimes a fine line between the qualities of love, mercy, and grace and those of tolerance and compromising Gods Word. This is where real confusion and hypocrisy tarnishes the Christian name with fleshly tolerance and worldly compromise that will not enter into the presence of a Holy God. A definite line of separation needs to be made.

> Submit yourselves therefore to God. Resist the devil, and he will flee from you. Draw nigh to God, and he will draw nigh to you. Cleanse your hands, ye sinners; and purify your hearts, ye double minded. (James 4:7–8)

These Scriptures reflect God's ultimate purpose for creating mankind, especially with the book of Revelation and it's revealing the culmination of this life on earth as we know it.

> **We will worship Him**—Isaiah 6:1–6; Revelation 4:8–11; 5:11–14; 7:9–12
> **We will serve Him**—Revelation 2:26; 5:10; 20:6; 22:3
> **We will enjoy God's presence and fellowship**—Revelation 21:3–7; 21:27
> **We will rule and reign with Him forever**—Daniel 7:27; Romans 8:16–17; 2 Timothy 2:12; Revelation 2:26; 3:21; 5:10; 20:4–6; 22:3–17

God's desire is for all of repentant mankind to take part and enjoy His creation forever. The spiritual attacks to every person with the works of the flesh, the lusts of the heart, the spirit world realities and the emotional strongholds in our life are to keep us from attaining this destiny. God's Word alone tells us all how to remove strongholds (spots, wrinkles, and blemishes) and maintain it even after we're saved. The Baptism of the Holy Spirit is given for all believers to restore and rebuild the walls of our soul that protect our spirit and then to ultimately rule and reign with Jesus our Lord and King in the presence of a Holy God.

> But the fruit of the Spirit is love, joy, peace, longsuffering, gentleness, goodness, faith, Meekness, temperance: against such there is no law. (Galatians 5:22–23)

The fact that God never gave up on us in spite of all our failings proves His love for us. We as individuals are guilty of failing in any one of these basic fruit principles by word or deed, and as we go through the fruit of the Spirit, we will see how only the Word of the living God shows us how to deal with these issues and conquer them. Only on the cross of Christ was sin's penalty paid for and the eternal remedy was given for all of mankind. God's holy wrath against sin is immeasurable and incomprehensible to the liberally minded, so-called educated people of today. God's Word tells us that "the fear of the LORD is the beginning of knowledge: but fools despise wisdom and instruction"

(Proverbs 1:7). The atheists of today have their own holiday to rival Christmas and Easter, and that would be April 1 (April Fools' Day).

> The fool hath said in his heart, There is no God. They are corrupt, they have done abominable works, there is none that doeth good. (Psalm 14:1)

I have to reiterate that God offers to "whosoever will" to repent and come to the Lord. Romans 5:5 tells us: "And hope maketh not ashamed; because the love of God is shed abroad in our hearts by the Holy Ghost which is given unto us."

The Spirit of God who called you to repentance bears His fruit in the heart that is submissive to Him. The Holy Spirit is the third person of the Trinity and is in harmony with God the Father and His Son Jesus. First John 4:8 says that God is love and that Jesus and the Father are one, and later in 1 John 5:7—"There are three that bear record in heaven, the Father, the Word, and the Holy Ghost: and these three are one." The Holy Spirit is our intermediary with all our acquaintances and contacts in this world, and He brings glory to Jesus through us. The Holy Ghost is the one who leads us, guides us, and helps us to navigate our way through every thought and action we have or do in this life. Jesus is our perfect advocate with the Father and our perfect example of how to live and how to die, how to love, how to live in joy, and how to be at peace. He exemplifies how we're to be longsuffering with gentleness and goodness, full of faith, meekness, and temperance for all those we come in contact with. Jesus' soul was perfect and as we look to Him for guidance, He has not left us comfortless but rather has given us His Word and the Holy Spirit to direct us through this life.

It is up to you to decide on who you will follow: either to walk after the Spirit, living off the fruit and gifts of the Spirit, or to live after the works and lusts of the flesh, fulfilling their eternally empty desires.

> That he would grant you, according to the riches of his glory, to be strengthened with might by his Spirit in the inner man; That Christ may dwell in your hearts by faith; that ye, being rooted and grounded in love, May be able to comprehend

with all saints what is the breadth, and length, and depth, and height; And to know the love of Christ, which passeth knowledge, that ye might be filled with all the fullness of God. (Ephesians 3:16–19)

The Holy Spirit is working with the Father and the Son to strengthen our soul so that we can understand and develop the love of God in every fruit and supporting wall structure. Once that love emanates from the walls and gates of our soul's fruit foundation, we can then be filled with all the fullness of God and fulfill our purpose as sons of God. So great a love God has for us that it surpasses human understanding: "But God commended his love toward us, in that, while we were yet sinners, Christ died for us" (Romans 5:8). God knew from the foundation of the world that man would sin and would need redemption.

Forasmuch as ye know that ye were not redeemed with corruptible things, as silver and gold, from your vain conversation received by tradition from your fathers; But with the precious blood of Christ, as of a lamb without blemish and without spot: Who verily was foreordained before the foundation of the world, but was manifest in these last times for you, Who by him do believe in God that raised him up from the dead, and gave him glory; that your faith and hope might be in God. (1 Peter 1:18–21)

We've heard it so often that we forget the price paid for our salvation by the sacrifice of Jesus. "That God so loved the world that He gave His only begotten Son" has become a bumper sticker or a sign at a football game, but the deeper meaning of His death, burial, and resurrection is that God Himself would become the sacrifice in the person of His Son Jesus Christ who is the glorious reconciliation between a sinful trespassing and depraved mankind, and a loving and holy, but offended God. God is holy, and man in his own mind has elevated himself above reproach, thinking of himself as worthy of eternal life and rewards despite his rotten fruit and evil works by ignoring God's holy principals.

Who hath saved us, and called us with an holy calling, not according to our works, but according to his own purpose and grace, which was given us in Christ Jesus before the world began. (2 Timothy 1:9)

Now our Lord Jesus Christ himself, and God, even our Father, which hath loved us, and hath given us everlasting consolation and good hope through grace, Comfort your hearts, and establish you in every good word and work. (2 Thessalonians 2:16–17)

Beloved, if God so loved us, we ought also to love one another. (1 John 4:11)

If for no other reason than for God's love toward us, we should demonstrate His love through all nine fruit of the Spirit to the rest of the world through our life's testimony: "Beloved, if God so loved us, we ought also to love one another".

This Scripture and others like it are the most misunderstood and misrepresented principles about godly love perpetrated by the unbelieving population today that worldly lusts and love have become synonymous. Not only has the intent of the Word of God been perverted and distorted, but it doesn't even take into account the basics of the Ten Commandments that have never really been replaced with better precepts to live by today.

Chapter 15

CLOSE THE PORTS TO OUR HARD DRIVES

W e as believers are to bear fruit in every situation and circumstance
we find ourselves in. Each situation is an opportunity to bring
glory to the Lord Jesus Christ and our God of righteousness,
regardless of how small or insignificant we may initially think that it may be.
If we're annoyed and quick to yell and get angry when things don't go the way
we think that they should, remember that we wrestle or grapple not against
flesh and blood but rather against principalities, powers, rulers of darkness,
and spirits of wickedness in high places that all can comes at us as thoughts
from the situations we find ourselves in. Not only are we dealing with the
situation that annoyed us in the first place but with all of the secondary issues
surrounding them as well. From interruptions and annoyances to everything
that leads up to the issue including our impatience with mates, children and
co-workers that only add to our false sense of justification of your aggravation
or your quick sharp tongue in frustration. These cracks in our foundation
are actually unmet lusts and expectations that leave us unprotected and
vulnerable to their entry by provoking, prodding and enticing our hearts that

war against our members (James 4:1–4) and we lash out and wreak havoc and cause strife to all those around us. Our testimony and witness are tarnished by our short fuse and our walk in the spirit is detoured by our hypocrisy to those we lashed out at.

For from within, out of the heart of men, proceed evil thoughts, adulteries, fornications, murders, thefts, covetousness, wickedness, deceit, lasciviousness, an evil eye, blasphemy, pride, foolishness: All these evil things come from within, and defile the man. (Mark 7:21–23)

Know ye not that the unrighteous shall not inherit the kingdom of God? Be not deceived: neither fornicators, nor idolaters, nor adulterers, nor effeminate, nor abusers of themselves with mankind, Nor thieves, nor covetous, nor drunkards, nor revilers, nor extortioners, shall inherit the kingdom of God. (1 Corinthians 6:9–10)

I know it seems a little one-sided against us, but it really isn't. It is the result of a loving God giving us the free will to choose, and the consequences of these choices can result in a penalty or a prize with God. These choices that we make are always evident in our fruit, producing good or rotten fruit. We must choose between belief in the grace and mercy of the Messiah Jesus Christ or the sinful worldly choices as outlined repeatedly in Scripture as the works of the flesh and the lusts of the heart.

It is your choice, especially after you're saved and believe in the resurrected Jesus Christ. To choose to believe in the God of the Bible—Jehovah, Jesus, and the Holy Spirit—between His ways or the carnal world in which we live must be made. Believing in Jesus isn't the end; it is actually only the beginning of a blessed eternity as the bride of the living Christ.

Having to choose between continually opposing the natural world views of society with Jesus or succumbing to your natural fleshly instincts in this life is hard, but it is a choice we must continually make. To live and think by the words and example of Jesus Christ in every thought, decision, word, and action is ultimately your choice, but it must be made. Know this, that what your eternity and eternal rewards will all rest upon is your daily walk, your every thought, and every word you speak whether saved or not. Every choice we make in this life is a reaction or result of another previous action taken or thought made which in turn causes us to react in a certain way. The way we act or think always seems to return back to us when done with evil intentions. Hate and fear are the only emotions that reverberate and affect generations upon generations of people and their children's children if not removed. They are the exact opposite of the fruit of love and joy. Once planted into an article of faith toward a different denominations or group of people it is easy to accept and to allow their festering disease of hate to grow into un-forgiveness, retaliation, bitterness, anger, and rage. The complex aspects of love and hate are not only that they can be the foundation of all works of the flesh, but they can easily become the lust of the heart and the pride of life that through biblical ignorance have killed millions in the name of their God.

You Might Be Right but … You Ain't Right With the Word of God

We are linked together either with a godly love or a worldly prejudice that binds us all together. You have to *want to* show His love to overcome hate and really mean it, because it's hard. This collaboration of all nine fruit of the spirit work together, not only to produce the productive fruit of our lives but to define us as believers in the risen Christ. If not, then we as fallen sinful men and women will produce nothing but rotten, perverted fruit. If unproductive and left stagnant or apathetic to our faith, then each one of these nine fruit will be influenced by the seventeen spirit-world realities, by the seventeen works of the flesh or the lust of the heart that when combined together with emotional strongholds adversely affect our spiritual walk and lead us to destruction and produce rotten fruit. Each one can be individually influenced by the desires and lusts of the heart (James 4:1–4). Without Jesus, these will first lead us into futility and confusion then ultimately into a self-destructive, miserable lifestyle.

> For God hath not given us the spirit of fear; but of power, and of love, and of a *sound mind*. (2 Timothy 1:7, emphasis added)

These seventeen spirit-world realities of un-forgiveness, resentment, retaliation, anger, violence, separation, bitterness, accusation, envy, jealousy, addictions, occultism, rejection, unloving, shame, guilt, and fear can lead us into an even deeper depression or foul mood if not controlled and ignored. These are the lower-level demonic influences that are commissioned by Satan to destroy us by first entering our inactive minds through television, movies, music, video games, and any medium of the senses or they come at you by a spouse, child or co-worker that strikes a nerve that rubs you the wrong way and your "off" . They're like kamikazes that strafe our minds causing enticements, temptations and suggestions to lure you to think and then act on them. You don't have to believe me or accept these warnings, but the Bible is warning us as believers to mend our fences and bolster our walls to protect our eternal spirit from these attacks.

If you say you believe in Jesus, then believe His words ... your eternity depends on them. Know that our brains are like a computer main frame and that it retains all the information it receives, whether good or bad, whether from your childhood, high school or last week your brains hard drive retains them all as outlined in the Word of God. 2 Peter 1:4-9, 2 Timothy 3:10-15, Col.2:6-10, Phil. 2:3-5, James 3:1-6.

Any one of these spirit-world realities will latch on to a thought like attachments to your computer's hard drive and provoke us to act or speak and sow rotten seeds of discord. Know that wherever it is legally permitted to enter in to pervert and corrupt your thoughts is where it will begin building an emotional stronghold. Anywhere and at any time, these sin viruses can begin slowing you down and distracting you from God's original plans for your life and run you on rabbit trails to self-justify your actions. These bits of information either edify the foundation of love or they infect it by perverting any one of the nine fruit with a virus of sinful thoughts. Love's foundation builds up all the walls of our soul's walls, and on them hang all the gates of our fruit of the Spirit that protect our born-again believing spirits. These seventeen spirit-world realities are only the beginning thoughts for the construction of emotional strongholds manifesting on our soul walls and in our personality traits. There is any number of combinations of ways or possible entry points through your emotions by way of the mind, producing sense overload that causes you to react. These resulting strongholds and manifestations can occur through self-perceived unmet expectations, soul wounds or with imagining our obtaining these visual lusts and physical enticements in our mind's eye. These fantasies obscure reality and cause dissatisfaction with our current lot in life, our job, our church or our spouse and children. Satan has a field day posing "what if's" and "you should have's" to justify your fantasies and actions to complete the deception, choosing to divide and conquer as his modus operandi.

Past traumas and emotional pains are revisited with accusations and un-forgiveness, with depression or anger resulting when the memories of what happened to us then sets in and these spirit-world realities begin dominating our thoughts that affect our personality. These strongholds are areas of our soul that are unwilling to submit to the authority of Jesus Christ because of fear of past pains or the reality of unmet desires. In Jesus we have the perfect example of God's Son who substituted Himself for all sinners as a sacrifice, taking our pains and emotional hurts by becoming the curse for us as we begin to overcome by the blood of the Lamb.

> Even as the Son of man came not to be ministered unto, but to minister, and to give his life a ransom for many. (Matthew 20:28)

> Christ hath redeemed us from the curse of the law, being made a curse for us: for it is written, Cursed is every one that hangeth on a tree. (Galatians 3:13)

> For the grace of God that bringeth salvation hath appeared to all men, Teaching us that, denying ungodliness and worldly lusts, we should live soberly, righteously, and godly, in this present world; Looking for that blessed hope, and the glorious appearing of the great God and our Savior Jesus Christ. (Titus 2:11–13)

Christ made himself an offering for us; it was His own act and His decision to pay the price in our place with His blood shed on the cross.

Being every bit God, He became every bit a man in every sense—spirit, soul, and body.

> And when Jesus had cried with a loud voice, he said, Father, into thy hands I commend *my spirit*: and having said thus, he gave up the ghost. (Luke 23:46, emphasis added)

> Then saith he unto them, *My soul* is exceeding sorrowful, even unto death: tarry ye here, and watch with me. (Matthew 26:38, emphasis added)

> This man went unto Pilate, and begged *the body of Jesus*. And he took it down, and wrapped it in linen, and laid it in a sepulcher that was hewn in stone, wherein never man before was laid. (Luke 23:52–53, emphasis added)

The Son of God became the son of men so that the sons of men could become the sons of God.

> The Spirit itself beareth witness with our spirit, that *we are the children of God*: And if children, then heirs; heirs of God, and *joint-heirs with Christ*; if so be that we suffer with him, that we may be also glorified together. For I reckon that the sufferings of this present time are not worthy to be compared with the glory which shall be revealed in us. For the earnest expectation of the creature *waits for the manifestation of the sons of God*. (Romans 8:16–19, emphasis added)

Because of this, Jesus is able to understand every lie and temptation that we can be confronted with. These low-level demons (thoughts) can cause continual confusion, aggravation, frustration, impatience, and a spirit of being just plain mean to the saved and the unsaved persons alike. This results in recurrent hostility and annoyance toward our mates, siblings, friends, and children. These abnormal emotions and feelings of pressure, anxiety, and fear lead many people—including born-again believers—to act impulsively and do things they wouldn't normally want to do or say. Negativity, gloom and doom, the constant fear of personal loss, and frequent mood swings make normal relationships extremely difficult if not impossible to flourish, and that fruit withers.

When these things occur, some newly born-again believers find it much easier to go back to the way they were living before they made a commitment to follow Jesus rather than deal with the satanic oppression that they now encounter. In fact, most devout, organized denominational Christians are ignorant of the spiritual power and authority they've been given once they invite Jesus into their hearts and Satan is evicted. This response is exactly what Satan's end games are all about: to keep believers in Jesus Christ powerless and preoccupied in their church's traditions and ceremonies, impotent and ignorant of who they really are in Jesus Christ.

> Beware lest any man spoil you through philosophy and vain
> deceit, after the tradition of men, after the rudiments of
> the world, and not after Christ. For in him dwelleth all the
> fulness of the Godhead bodily. And ye are complete in him,
> which is the head of all principality and power. (Colossians
> 2:8–10)

Many of these visually ornate and opulent ceremonies appease and pacify the lusts of the flesh with grandiose traditions, but they have very little or nothing at all to do with your individual salvation or spiritual growth as a child of the living God.

> For we wrestle not against flesh and blood, but against
> principalities, against powers, against the rulers of the
> darkness of this world and against spiritual wickedness in
> high places. (Ephesians 6:12)

Principalities, powers, rulers of the darkness of this world, and spiritual wickedness in high places (PPRSs) are all the upper levels of demons or generals (so to speak) that we or our ancestors have given legal right to stay in and on the family tree. Many Christians are offended at the thought of being tormented or under spiritual attack by demons assigned to a particular sin or temptation in our life or our children's lives after our salvation.

But these demons are very real and crave to return to be fed by a particular action or desire explained to us as works of the flesh in Galatians 5:19–21. These works of the flesh have a myriad of subgroup demons that try to tempt and persuade us to act in any of the fleshly inspired desires which are sins that have returned by our legal permission into our thought life. These mentally programmed attachments are the foot-soldier demons (viruses) that are assigned to us, and unless we destroy these strongholds and mend the gaps (firewall) in our souls, we are susceptible to their enticements. If not specifically addressed, we will continue to struggle in these areas even after we have been saved. To begin the restoration process and be healed spiritually, you must first be born again.

> That if thou shalt confess with thy mouth the Lord Jesus,
> and shalt believe in thine heart that God hath raised him
> from the dead, thou shalt be saved. For with the heart man
> believeth unto righteousness; and with the mouth confession
> is made unto salvation. (Romans 10:9–10)

I believe this prayer can also be used as the greatest deception and false sense of security ever perpetrated on a believing people. That is to think that once you're saved or are a member of a particular Christian church denomination you are immune to demonic attack and the consequences of your past or your families past can't affect you. Not that the judgment of their sin is passed on to you and your children (i.e., Cain; John 9:2–3), but the same demons that tormented you and your ancestors before you were saved are the same demons that will try to torment you after you are saved. These demons know your address, your family, your e-mail (so to speak), and your habits, and unless you close the gaps and heal your soul-wounded wall openings, you and your family are susceptible to recurring and habitual issues as well as demonic attack. They will prick and prod you until you open the doors of your soul by entertaining these works of the flesh, spirit-world realities, or the lusts of the heart—whether you believe they're real or not. That is why as a believing parent, pleading the blood of Jesus over your children for protection is so important.

Last year, my oldest son Chris came home on leave from the Air Force and after his first night's sleep back in his old bedroom, he woke up in the morning to tell us that he had had a dream. He said that he was standing in the front yard and could see demons standing across the street, complaining to each other that they couldn't come across because of the holy hedge of protection of the blood of Jesus that wouldn't let them cross.

When a hedge of protection is placed around your family and home with your blessings that are given as a believer over your spouse and children, then the Holy Spirit is able to warn you and protect your family and the home. I pray over my home the blood of Jesus above, below, and around my house, and I call holy warring angels to be posted at the perimeter of our property line. I have prayed blessings over my sleeping wife and young children as they slept and have prayed blessings over my children's friends as well when they stayed over.

Deep wounds of the soul are long lasting and are a means of access to the torment of your spirit, soul, and body. Only the Word of the living God (the Judeo-Christian Bible) speaks of this and gives a remedy for spiritual damage done to us. Jesus calls us all to put off all the retaliations and protective responses to defend our deep soul wounds from being injured again and to be renewed in the love of Jesus and forgive. Never forget but forgive in Jesus name and then ask the Holy Spirit to help you.

> But now ye also put off all these; anger, wrath, malice, blasphemy, filthy communication out of your mouth. Lie not one to another, seeing that ye have put off the old man with his deeds; And have put on the new man, which is renewed in knowledge after the image of him that created him: (*Jesus the Christ*). (Colossians 3:8–10, emphasis added)

The Holy Spirit can identify the strongholds and soul wounds in your life that need repair, and He will help you to dislodge them. Only God's Word of truth and deliverance can destroy these strongholds to begin the healing process and restoration of the deep soul wounds that we've been dealt through this life.

Let me reiterate what we have discussed thus far: We are all triune beings created in the image of Jehovah God with a spirit, soul, and body. The spirit never dies and is who we really are. It is what is saved and is washed by the redeeming blood of Jesus Christ at confession, and our names are written in the Lamb's Book of Life.

> He that overcomes, the same shall be clothed in white raiment; and *I will not blot out his name out of the book of life,* but I will confess his name before my Father, and before his angels. (Revelations 3:5, emphasis added)

Our souls are our mind, thoughts, intellect, emotions, feelings, and character traits and are what constitute the walls of our being (soul), and the gates are the fruit of the Spirit as the Bible states.

> But the fruit of the Spirit is love, joy, peace, longsuffering, gentleness, goodness, faith, Meekness, temperance: against such there is no law. (Galatians 5:22–23)

Finally, our body is where the spirit and soul both reside until we die, and our beliefs determine our eternal destination. This is true of believers and unbelievers alike. If we believe in the theory of evolution and science, then when you die, according to this "theory" we cease to exist consciously and we then become fertilizer, reverting back to the dust we were created from. Not a very significant purpose for one of the only mammals to ever live on this planet that dwells on the past memories and contemplate the future planning for it. We can choose to not believe in a creator God who designed every living thing seen and unseen in this universe and that when we die, our existence ends except in the memories of people who knew us. Or we can believe that the Creator of this universe created man as a living spirit with free will that, coupled with a soul, would live in a body that at its deadline would return to Him in eternal bliss or because of their arrogant rebellious lifestyle would be sent to a hell of torment in outer darkness never to have communication with Him again. Know that Jesus spoke more of the torment of hell than He did of heaven in the Gospels, and the Epistles continually warn believers to avoid the lures and lusts of the pride of life and the works of the flesh. While the person lives, they are given free will and the ability to choose to live in righteousness and follow Jehovah God or not. The God of the Bible; the Messiah Jesus Christ; His laws and precepts; and the third person of the Trinity, the Holy Ghost, is the path the Bible says all believers must follow in order to enter heaven. I personally believe that there really is no difference between the non-believer and the Jews in that they both don't except Jesus as Messiah and the express image of Jehovah God. Philippians 2:5,6

> Let this mind be in you, which was also in Christ Jesus:
> *Who, being in the form of God, thought it not robbery to be equal*
> *with God*: But made himself of no reputation, and took upon
> him the form of a servant,

But like we said earlier I do believe God has a special place in heaven for the practicing Jew for their obedience and faith in Jehovah God. When you as a believer are saved, sanctified, and filled with the Holy Spirit, you are then able to commune with the Father in the way man was designed to commune with the Creator before the fall of Adam and Eve in the garden in spirit. Each person at salvation is then seated with the Son in His kingdom for eternity and has their name written in the book of life. We then can begin to accumulate the rewards spoken of in scripture. These rewards are determined by **the heart's motives** and **your hearts intents** for each of the believer's thoughts, words spoken, and action taken while alive and not from works, tithes or offerings given out of obligation.

It is vitally important that as believers, we repent daily for the sins we commit daily whether sins of commission (known sins) or sins of omission (unknown sins). Each believer must stand before Christ to be judged for their life's work; not that your salvation depends on them, but rather to receive your rewards that are again only outlined in the Judeo-Christian Scriptures. These rewards are given to us because of the outpouring of the love of Christ in us after salvation and not in trying to gain salvation through works. These acts of love shall then be laid at the foot of the cross of our Lord and Savior Jesus Christ as an offering of homage, reverence, and honor to our Lord and King.

For we must all appear before the judgment seat of Christ; that every one may receive the things done in his body, according to that he hath done, whether it be good or bad. Knowing therefore the terror of the Lord, we persuade men; but we are made manifest unto God; and I trust also are made manifest in your consciences. (2 Corinthians 5:10–11)

Chapter 16

OUR ETERNAL REWARDS

Romans 14:10–12 tells us again that each one of us will stand personally before the judgment seat of the Lord Jesus Christ at the "bema" seat.

> But why dost thou judge thy brother? Or why dost thou set at naught thy brother? *For we shall all stand before the judgment seat of Christ.* For it is written, As I live, saith the Lord, every knee shall bow to me, and every tongue shall confess to God. (emphasis added)

You alone shall stand in judgment before the Lord and are without excuse; but this is not the judgment seat for salvation, this judgment seat is for the believer's rewards. Our rewards shall be given or lost depending on how the believer spent his or her life for the Lord. There are five crowns that every believer can receive, the first being the "crown of righteousness."

> Henceforth there is laid up for me a *crown of righteousness,* which the Lord, the righteous judge, shall give me at that

day: and not to me only, but unto *all* them also that love his appearing. (2 Timothy 4:8, emphasis added)

And, behold, I come quickly; and my reward is with me, to give every man (woman) according as his work shall be. This crown is for all believers who were ready and waiting for the return of Jesus and all those who had loved His appearing. (Revelation 22:12)

The next is the "crown incorruptible."

Know ye not that they which run in a race run all, but one receives the prize? So run, that ye may obtain. And every man that strives for the mastery is temperate in all things. Now they do it to obtain a corruptible crown; but *we an incorruptible [crown]*. (1 Corinthians 9:24–25, emphasis added)

This crown is received for those exercising self-control in all disciplined training of body and mind. This crown is exemplified in Chris-likeness in longsuffering and temperance. It is followed by the "crown of life" which is found in James 1:12.

Blessed is the man that endures temptation: for when he is tried, he shall receive the *crown of life*, which the Lord hath promised to them that love him. (emphasis added)

This is received for those who are faithful unto death and those who endure testing's, temptations and trials mentally, physically and emotionally. The next is the "crown of glory" and is made available to all leaders, pastors, elders, and teachers who were godly examples to the flock of believers.

Feed the flock of God which is among you, taking the oversight thereof, not by constraint, but willingly; not for filthy lucre, but of a ready mind; Neither as being lords over God's heritage, but being examples to the flock. And when the chief Shepherd shall appear, ye shall receive a *crown of glory* that fades not away. (1 Peter 5:2–4, emphasis added)

The "crown of rejoicing" is in 1 Thessalonians 2:19–20.

> For what is our hope, or joy, or *crown of rejoicing?* Are not even ye in the presence of our Lord Jesus Christ at his coming? For ye are our glory and joy. (emphasis added)

The soul winner's crown is received by those winning people to the Lord Jesus Christ after they had rightly divided the Word of God and helped expand the kingdom by telling them about Jesus. The soul of each person is then compared to the soul of the perfect man, Jesus Christ, which is the standard their life is measured to. Jesus' walk in the Spirit through the fruit of the Spirit needs to be exemplified in your life. These spirit fruit are love, joy, peace, longsuffering (a quiet patient mind), gentleness (kind acts), goodness (well-doing), faith, meekness (gentle behavior), and temperance (control over desires, angers) and are the gates and walls of our soul protecting the newly redeemed spirit that confessed Jesus as Lord. Remember, each one of these fruit can be replicated by Satan as good works, but the fruit is rotten and unproductive. He is a liar and the father of lies; know that the best lies are the closest to the truth but never reaches it. Jesus said of the Devil in John as He spoke of the religious leaders of the temple and who their real master was and is today.

> Ye are of your father the devil, and the lusts of your father ye will do. He was a murderer from the beginning, and abode not in the truth, because there is no truth in him. When he speaks a lie, he speaks of his own: for he is a liar, and the father of it. (John 8:44)

How is he a murderer? He is first the murderer of the souls of Adam and Eve, and he introduced sin by way of the works of the flesh to all humanity's minds. Once washed in the blood of the Lamb, we must remember that we are then given the whole armor of God (Ephesians 6:14–17). As a child of the living God, you may now be able to stand against the wiles of the Devil and withstand his attacks. There is no difference if a person is saved or lost; whether you believe or not, everyone gets attacked by the same PPRSs, works of the flesh, spirit world realities and the lusts of the heart tied with emotional strongholds. The difference is that those who are saved have access to God's nine gifts in the Spirit, your personal prayer language and the armor of God to identify battle and defend their eternal spirits.

Again, this armor consists of your loins or procreative parts girt with constraint and controlled with truth, and then having the breastplate of righteousness which is to act with equity of character and integrity. Your feet shod means to place all things beneath and below as inferior to the gospel of peace, and above all to take on the shield of faith to quench or to drown out all doubt and unbelief with the spiritual gifts and testimonies of our victories in this life building up our faith. Taking then the helmet of salvation to remind us constantly of our position with Christ, and finally the sword of the Spirit, which is the Word of the living God or *rhema* spoken words, it is responding to temptation as Jesus did when He was tempted in the garden and He defeated Satan with the written and spoken Word of God.

When we make the decision for Christ, we not only receive eternal life, but we also receive a sort of outward protection that needs our assistance to build and grow in faith into Christlikeness. At this foundational level, we find ourselves dealing primarily with the root of the sin that affects and torments us. They are the sensory or worldly temptations that deal with the visual, tasting, touching, smelling, and hearing senses and initially have nothing to do with us spiritually. These tend to please only for the moment, giving temporary physical gratification that seemingly gives control to the person but ultimately destroys them.

This first level of attack is the battles we face daily between the fleshly desires of the world over spiritual control spoken of only in the Word of God (the Judeo-Christian Bible). A very good enticement will lean more heavily in the physical direction than the spiritual but will always lead to gratification of your fleshly desires. When a choice needs to be made, the flesh usually overrides the spiritual with things that you can see and touch over the feelings or warnings that you might feel spiritually from the Holy Ghost. This is where I believe our salvation walk can be detoured and the unction's of the Holy

Spirit are usually ignored because we don't know His voice. The lie of "once saved, always saved" deceives many believers because the spiritual desires a person has in their mind can't control the fleshly desires they have in their heart and the flesh desires to continue sinning until they submit control to the Holy Spirit and learn to listen to Him. This is another one of the nine Gifts of the Spirit 1 Cor. 12:10 (discerning of spirits) and is one of the appliances given to us with the Baptism of the Holy Spirit. Again, you are known by your fruit, good or rotten, and you need to dress and prune your life daily through the Word of God as it teaches you in study, meditation, prayer and fasting.

> Wherefore by their fruits ye shall know them. Not everyone that says unto me, Lord, Lord, shall enter into the kingdom of heaven; but he that doeth the will of my Father which is in heaven. Many will say to me in that day, Lord, Lord, have we not prophesied in thy name? and in thy name have cast out devils? And in thy name done many wonderful works? And then will *I profess unto them, I never knew you: depart from me, ye that work iniquity.* (Matthew 7:20–23, emphasis added)

Many converts who don't completely change their life's actions "backslide" or live in a deceived sense of security and will be very surprised at death's door. Dr. James Kennedy once said, "I wouldn't want to be handcuffed to some so-called Christians when they die." Compromise only leads to spiritual deception and ultimately spiritual death. Political correctness is compromising God's Word with the lusts of the flesh that leads to separation from a Holy God.

The next level of attack is again on a spiritual faith level over the control of the flesh. As we spoke of earlier, it is by giving up control of the tongue to the Holy Spirit in faith which deals with our prayer language and that the gifts of the Spirit become available to *all born-again believers at salvation.* The baptism of the Holy Spirit is probably the most important thing we can get after making the decision to receive Jesus as Lord and Savior of our life. It is critically important as we prepare for these spiritual battles that we grow in the Lord with the Holy Spirit.

Once you ask and receive the baptism of the Holy Ghost, He falls *on* you (Acts 1:8) and you now are given power and authority spiritually through the name of Jesus, the Son of the living God Jehovah. The gifts of the Spirit are given to all (1 Corinthians 12:8–10), and they are wisdom, knowledge, faith, healing, working of miracles, prophecy, discerning of spirits, divers kinds of tongues (given corporately), and interpretation of tongues (which is required when tongues are given corporately), which the Spirit is "dividing [when needed] to every man severally as he wills" (verse 11). These gifts are needed by every born-again believer to battle with evil spirits, we will explain further later in chapter twenty.

So when we get saved and baptized in the Spirit ,we not only have our name written in the Lamb's Book of Life (Revelation 3:5; 13:8; 20:12) to enter eternity in the kingdom, but we are given the keys to the kingdom to bind and loose (Matthew 16:18), the armor of God (Ephesians 6:10–17), the gifts of the Spirit (1 Corinthians 12:7-11), the fruit of the Spirit (Galatians 5:22–23), and our prayer language with power (Acts 1:8) to do battle with Satan and his minions. God's Word tells us,

> My people are destroyed for lack of knowledge: because thou hast rejected knowledge. (Hosea 4:6)

> Now concerning spiritual gifts, brethren, I would not have you ignorant. (1 Corinthians 12:1)

Jesus did not leave us comfortless at His death, resurrection, and ascension. He sent us the Holy Spirit to abide in us and on us. We as believers are to use all of these gifts of the Spirit, the fruit of the Spirit, and the armor of God to mend our walls and rehang our gates in our quest to become more Christ-like in every area of our life before we die and can no longer change our eternal destiny or gain rewards. Once we die, there's no coming back to fix past failures. God has given us all we need to defeat every principality, power, ruler of darkness of this world, and every spirit of wickedness that are in high places that have been assigned to oppress, suppress, depress, and ultimately to try to destroy us.

The Holy Ghost will water, till, and cultivate our trees and dress our vines to defeat the works of the flesh and bear good fruit to increase the kingdom, but you have to ask Him. The Holy Spirit is a gentleman and will never force Himself on anyone. He will only act if you have asked Him to help you in the name of Jesus. This is our destiny to serve, cultivate, and increase the kingdom for the glory of the Father.

Of course, God can use you in any condition you're in. Unfortunately, even after we've been saved and assured of our salvation, we can still be damaged goods suffering from deep soul wounds and traumatic emotional pains. Only the Holy Spirit can help you identify the breaches in your soul's walls, and only Jesus can heal them at the cross with His shed blood.

You should try to receive all the medical and scientific protocols that have proven results. This is not a lack of faith to receive medical attention. I do believe God has given many men and women brilliant knowledge and wisdom to treat many maladies and ailments—maintaining or curing many of them. I am not inferring or condoning any refusal or denial of medical attention that just doesn't make sense. What I am saying is that what God's Word calls "infirmities" are caused many times because of curses and works of the flesh that are the results of sin, trauma, and ungodly soul ties that need to be addressed spiritually as well as seeking medical help.

Satan has to be given a legal right by you to gain entry into your life, and ignorance is not an excuse for allowing him access. When you allow or come into agreement with an evil act that is outlined in Galatians 5:19–21 as the works of the flesh, you then open the door for him and his minions to enter in. If this act is in any way related to a traumatic experience, ungodly soul tie, curses, generational or self-imposed, it can then introduce a myriad of related demonic principalities, powers, rulers of darkness, and spiritual wickedness (PPRSs). They will then legally have permission by *you* to enter into your mind and try to subvert and challenge Jesus' influence to your soul and spirit.

Soul ties have the most far-reaching influence to our decision making and the thought processes we might have; they actually influence the way we think. Godly soul ties reinforce spiritual truth with love in our mind, will, and emotions. Ungodly soul ties reinforce deception and lies in our life through unhealthy and unstable influences that produce spirit-world realities and emotional strongholds which can destroy and pervert any and every godly relationship. These ungodly soul ties, lusts of the heart, and spirit-world realities can be caused by any combination of authority figures, desires, aspirations, and issues (real or imaginary) that can cause situations with family, friends, and enemies that will cause you to race through imaginary situations with imaginary results and unfortunately very real consequences. Ungodly soul ties can be created with family members (dead or alive), ethnicity, cultures, other Christians and Christian leaders, sexual partners outside of marriage, coworkers, wayward friends, famous people infatuations, and judgments that are completely self-imposed, self-contrived, and self-manufactured. These ungodly soul ties (PPRSs), lusts of the heart, works of the flesh, spirit-world realities and emotional strongholds are real and are closely related to each other, resulting in fear and depression destroying everything they come in contact with.

I saw how the walls of Jesus' soul were built. They were virtually seamless, with one block on top of another, connected and influenced by the blocks directly above, under, and all around them; the mortar that connected them was righteousness and love. Now the PPRSs, works of the flesh, lusts of the heart, and the spirit-world realities with emotional strongholds are connected together very similarly as my fruit of the Spirit, but its mortar was hate, anger, bitterness and fear, causing distorted manifestations that grow and become bridges corrupting other gates by opening doors to more spiritual attacks. These manifestations are the foundation, or what the Word of God calls our countenance, attitude, and intents of the heart.

Just as Cain's countenance fell creating a visible mark in his spirit and countenance, so too is it with us: "But unto Cain and to his offering he had not respect. And Cain was very wroth, and his countenance fell" (Genesis 4:5). His ruthless, cold, murdering black heart was evident for all to see with what are principalities, powers, rulers of darkness, and spirits of wickedness influenced by the works of the flesh, the spirit-world realities, and the lusts of the heart with emotional strongholds that are implied throughout Scripture.

Cain had no chance without God, just like we don't have a chance today without Jesus. All of these human emotions are the same emotions and temptations that cause us aggravation, irritation, and stresses that we end up taking out on those closest to us. Again, the difference is *Jesus!* The same Jesus who was prophesized some 740 years before His birth by Isaiah (Isaiah 53) and the chosen one outlined in Psalm 2 by David three-hundred years before him. Jesus' perfect soul—or better, His perfect fruit of the Spirit—is our sinless and perfect model of how we're to act and live in this life. Jesus is not only the perfect sinless High Priest ordained as the only begotten Son of the most High Jehovah, but He is the perfect sinless Lamb of God, slain from the foundation of the earth as the perfect sacrifice for all of mankind.

> For we have not an high priest which cannot be touched with the feeling of our infirmities; but was in all points tempted like as we are, *yet without sin.* Let us therefore come boldly unto the throne of grace, that we may obtain mercy, and find grace to help in time of need. (Hebrews 4:15–16, emphasis added)

Jesus is the only High Priest not to be called after the order of Aaron.

> For it is evident that our Lord sprang out of Juda; of which tribe Moses spake nothing concerning priesthood. And it is yet far more evident: for that after the similitude of Melchisedec there ariseth another priest, *Who is made, not after the law of a carnal commandment, but after the power of an endless life.* For he testifieth, Thou art a priest for ever after the order of Melchisedec. (Hebrews 7:14–17, emphasis added)

Jesus became the innocent sacrifice to atone for the sins of all men and women, bearing their iniquities on the cross. But He is also the perfect, sinless High Priest.

> Wherefore he is able also to save them to the uttermost that come unto God by him, seeing he ever liveth to make

intercession for them. For such an high priest became us, who
is holy, harmless, undefiled, separate from sinners, and made
higher than the heavens; Who needeth not daily, as those
high priests, to offer up sacrifice, first for his own sins, and
then for the people's: for this he did once, when he offered
up himself. For the law maketh men high priests which have
infirmity; but the word of the oath, which was since the law,
maketh the Son, who is consecrated for evermore. (Hebrews
7:25–28)

He shall see of the travail of his soul, and shall be satisfied:
by his knowledge shall my righteous servant justify many;
for he shall bear their iniquities. (Isaiah 53:11)

If we allow the Holy Spirit to show us all the breaches in our soul walls and
allow Him to help us identify all the combinations and root causes of the
PPRSs which are based in the works of the flesh, the lusts of the heart, and all
the spirit-world realities that tempt and torment us in racial, denominational,
and ethnic hatred in this life, we then can begin to restore the foundation of
love through the atonement of our perfect High Priest, Jesus. The walls of
denominational prejudices that we have toward fellow believers in Christ
would stop. Once these are identified, we can then mend the breaches of our
self-righteous, putrid souls. If we understood what the Word of God says
about what is expected of us, we would all act differently. Defeating these
issues of sinful thoughts and attitudes would no longer ensnare us if only
we took into account all the weapons we have as believers at our disposal to
completely destroy them. If we could capture the thoughts of the flesh that
come from Satan's enticements and dispel them from our hearts, we would
not act the way we do.

Before the Messiah Jesus came, Moses and the subsequent high priests were
the only mediators between man and a Holy God. Each year, the appointed
high priest as the firstborn son of the current high priest had to make a
sacrifice for himself as a sinner and then for the people's accumulated sins.
The high priest had to make a sacrifice of a young lamb by the shedding of
its innocent blood on the temple altar for the remission of his sins and all the

nation's sins. Then he had to ask for forgiveness and sacrifice another innocent animal all over again the next year.

At Jesus' incarnation, death, and resurrection, He became mankind's definitive mediator seated at God's right hand, and He is our advocate who allows us to have access to Jehovah God in the Holy of Holies. Through Jesus, we can now once and for all be redeemed, and mankind never needs a sacrifice for sin again for the past sins committed are all washed white as snow by the innocent blood of Jesus. Jesus tasted death for all men on the cross and shed His innocent blood for the remission of all sin. There is nothing we could have done in this life that is not covered by the blood of Jesus—past, present, and future sins are all remitted. Then Jesus died and gave up the ghost (John 19:30) and ascended to the right hand of Jehovah God for us.

The veil in the temple was rent in half, giving all believers access to the Holy of Holies and the mercy seat of the living God with Jesus as our intercessor: "And the sun was darkened, and the veil of the temple was rent in the midst" (Luke 23:45). Through King Jesus, we can now deal with every single issue that troubles us; we can now come boldly with all our issues of temptations and lusts of the heart emotional strongholds, holding fast in perilous times to come: "For there is one God, and one mediator between God and men, the man Christ Jesus" (1 Timothy 2:5).

Jesus, who is not only our King and High Priest after the order of Melchizedek, He is our sinless Lamb sacrificed on the altar of God where He will help us through each and every area of need.

> For verily he took not on him the nature of angels; but *he took on him the seed of Abraham*. Wherefore in all things it behoved him to be made like unto his brethren, that he might be a merciful and faithful high priest in things pertaining to God, to make reconciliation for the sins of the people. For in that he himself hath suffered being tempted, *he is able to succour them that are tempted* ["succour" (succor) means to give help to someone in serious need]. (Hebrews 2:16–18, emphasis added)

Jesus can empathize with us through our infirmities because He was tempted as we are tempted and He won. The man Jesus knows how we feel, and in Hebrews 4:15–16 Paul tells us,

> For we have not an high priest which cannot be touched with the feeling of our infirmities; but was in all points tempted like as we are, yet *without sin*. Let us therefore come boldly unto the throne of grace, that we may obtain mercy, and find grace to help in time of need. (emphasis added)

Let me re-emphasize once more that unless specifically dealt with and eradicated from our soul's foundation, then the seeds of lusts of the heart or seeds of hatred, un-forgiveness, jealousy, and bitterness will manifest in a false sense of self-righteousness again and again. Unfortunately this occurs at the most unexpected and inopportune times and the rebuilding of the strongholds of hate, pain, and anger begin again. These spirit-world realities and emotional strongholds can attach themselves to any one of the nine fruit of the Spirit, corrupting and perverting the perfect will of God in our life.

It seems to me that these PPRSs, works of the flesh, lusts of the heart, and spirit-world realities are so subtle at times that we take them for granted or ignore them all together as no big deal. Even worse yet, we accept them as family traits by saying such things as, "You act just like your mother (or father)," etc., and accept them as normal and natural reactions that lead us to fall right back into the sin that hurt us in the first place. These commonly accepted actions and comments from friends and family can actually be word curses and seeds of sin that are placed on us that seem like compliments or normal life. In fact, if we acknowledge and accept them, we open the doors to Satan and his minions to attack and manifest.

We need to be aware of these dangerous self-imposed word curses and tolerated actions that on the surface seem insignificant, but if they are continually tolerated with friends and families, these issues will snowball into major personal problems. Words of honor that esteem and treat us as very important are a form of judgment, and judgment is the first of the spirit-world realities that can be good or bad when obtained through superficial worldly lusts. Genuine approval, praise, and thankfulness can lift a child's or person's self-esteem to levels of honor and respect but is shallow without godly love. Actions speak so much louder than hollow words and can shatter a person's self-esteem with no real value or worth being evident. Judgment is an issue of honor and dishonor, and the Bible speaks expressly about honor or the lack thereof throughout Scripture, showing respect and admiration for others, fellow believers, mates, family and especially parents.

> *Honor thy father and thy mother*, as the LORD thy God hath commanded thee; that thy days may be prolonged, and that it may go well with thee, in the land which the LORD thy God giveth thee. (Deuteronomy 5:16, emphasis added)

> Be kindly affectionate one to another with brotherly love; *in honor* preferring one another. (Romans 12:10, emphasis added)

> *Honor all men. Love the brotherhood (fellow believers).* Fear God. Honor the king. (1 Peter 2:17, emphasis added)

> Likewise, ye husbands, dwell with them according to knowledge, *giving honor unto thy wife*, as unto the weaker vessel, and as being heirs together of the grace of life; that your prayers be not hindered. (1 Peter 3:7, emphasis added)

Conversely, when we dishonor God's creation by judging and ridiculing other people because of race, sex, age, physical and mental abnormalities, socioeconomic status, or demographics, we open doors of resentment, bitterness, un-forgiveness, jealousy, envy, accusation, fear, and depending on the level of racism and prejudice, murder, eugenics, or genocide can result. Many times these actions are claimed to be done in the name of God and tradition (albeit not the God of heaven), but they are deceived by their biblical ignorance of the Word in Scripture and in reality it's done in the name of the god of this world. You can be right about some things (nuggets of truth), but you ain't right with God in your attitudes and actions to fellow believers and even nonbelievers. By having any of these forms of judgment and hatred, we give Satan the legal right to torment us and our families, using us to carry out his plots and plans of death by word or deed. By relinquishing our God-given authority, we then sow seeds of discord in our own lives and reap judgment from family and friends.

> Judge not, that ye be not judged. For with what judgment ye judge, ye shall be judged: and with what measure ye mete, it shall be measured to you again. (Matthew 7:1–2)

> Be not deceived; God is not mocked: for whatsoever a man sows, that shall he also reap. For he that sows to his flesh shall of the flesh reap corruption; but he that sows to the Spirit shall of the Spirit reap life everlasting. (Galatians 6:7)

> Therefore thou art inexcusable, O man, whosoever thou art that judges: for wherein thou judges another, thou condemns thyself; for thou that judges does the same things. (Romans 2:1)

> Wherefore, as by one man sin entered into the world, and death by sin; and so death passed upon all men, for that all have sinned. (Romans 5:12)

Remember, if we are to allow the nature of Jesus Christ to grow in us, we need to allow God's ways to be filtered through the Holy Spirit in our life by our witness and testimony as we exemplify Him daily. In the Old Testament, God called men to build a temple for His people where they could worship Him, but now in the New Testament, God calls His people through Jesus Christ to build the temple of God within themselves to worship Him daily by our walking in the Spirit.

> Know ye not that ye are the temple of God, and that the Spirit of God dwells in you? If any man defile the temple of God, him shall God destroy; for the temple of God is holy, which temple are you. (1 Corinthians 3:16–17)

> There is therefore now no condemnation to them which are
> in Christ Jesus, *who walk not after the flesh, but after the Spirit.*
> (Romans 8:1, emphasis added)

God's plan for us is more than for us to be in the place where Adam and Eve were after the fall in the garden. His plan is to bring all of us as believers into sonship with the Father so that our relationship is on the same relationship level as Jesus (Christ-likeness). The relationship of the Father and His Son, Jesus Christ, is ultimately His desire for us today. To be sons and daughters of the living God through our daily walk in the Spirit and as we grow to show Jesus everywhere we go. We must do this not only in our conforming to Christlikeness after repenting for our sins, but also in our preemptive responses in spite of our failures and weaknesses by showing grace, mercy, and forgiveness in the face of offences. Conforming to Christlikeness is to learn to understand your own human nature (lust of the heart and works of the flesh) and to allow the Holy Spirit to show Christ in you. It takes practice, which means failures. Not that we're to be taken advantage of, but we are to show Christ's spiritual superiority over our natural abrasive, worldly and carnal responses. We're also not to avoid contact or interaction with the world but instead be a light in this world of darkness and show the love of Jesus where ever you go.

The hardest thing I personally had to learn with my wife, kids, and family was to not be so mean and judgmental all the time when offended and I had to learn to apologize when I offended them. Keeping quiet is nearly impossible, even to this day, when "my standards" aren't met. I would lash out in my self-righteous indignation to try to prove a point that, in most instances, everyone agreed with in principle, but I had to learn to *just shut up.* I still have to learn to listen before I talk, and I need to get my facts straight and show mercy and grace at all times because we are a representatives of the Lord, King Jesus Christ. Honestly it gets easier to apologize the quicker you recognize your offence and the faster you ask for forgiveness.

> And we know that all things work together for good to
> them that love God, to them who are the called according
> to his purpose. For whom he did foreknow, he also did

predestinate to be *conformed to the image of his Son*, that he might be the firstborn among many brethren. Who is he that condemneth? It is Christ that died, yea rather, that is risen again, who is even at the right hand of God, who also makes intercession for us. (Romans 8:28–29, 34; emphasis added)

Chapter 17

THE POWER OF GOD

It would be so much easier to believe that when we die, we just cease to exist and that for millions and millions of men and women's existence of the past all just ended when they died. How senseless and hopeless our existence and our purpose would be if that were the case. To believe anything less solely to pacify our eclectic sense of fairness and what you believe is justice rather than what the Word of God states in Torah and the Bible puts us all into this category of what the apostle Paul calls "foolish": "For the preaching of the cross is to them that perish foolishness; but unto us which are saved *it is the power of God*" (1 Corinthians 1:18, emphasis added). And in 1 Corinthians 1:27: "But God hath chosen the foolish things of the world to confound the wise; and God hath chosen the weak things of the world to confound the things which are mighty." I guess that explains me! Thank You, Jesus!

In the Judeo-Christian Bible alone is God's wisdom spoken of to us in a mystery hidden and ordained from before the world began. We as converted believers in the resurrect Messiah must believe that Jesus is the great I AM THAT I AM of Exodus 3:14, and that He is the Word spoken of in John 1:1 and Romans 1:16, and that the Holy Spirit is available to all believers after salvation as stated in Proverbs 1:23; Ezekiel 36:27; and Galatians 3:14. The Word of God is plain and easy to understand once you take the prejudicial worldly dominated blinders off and get off your self-elevated intellectual high horse of religiously pious superiority and "love" like Jesus commanded us to. Then you may be able to see the simplicity of God's Word and the necessity of the body of believers to accept the whole Judeo-Christian Bible completely and work together in these last days as one.

I don't like or want to think of what happened to previous generations in times past or what will happen to the rebellious, unbelieving populations of today, but there can only be one of two answers: either the God of the Bible is true and every man a liar; or man's theories are true and there is no God, and it all doesn't matter what we do. Anarchy, chaos, and lawlessness are of no consequence; we can rape, molest, murder, and steal, because we all end up as a pile of dung anyways. So who cares? It doesn't matter, does it? I choose to believe my life means something for eternity, and I choose the God of the Bible to help me through this life.

God's Word alone tells us that there is a God and He judges men on their life's thoughts and actions and that we have an opportunity to correct every issue we face in this life as long as we're still breathing. To try to judge God, His decisions, and His processes only confuses and detracts us from what the real purpose for this existence is for. It only does what Adam and Eve did when they questioned God's motives for the forbidden fruit and they fell from grace. What we can do now is make sure our spirit, soul, and body reach their fullest godly eternal potential possible. That means that all the racism, prejudice, and hatred that professing Christians have towards non-believers and especially other believers from different races, nations, or orthodox Christian denominations needs to stop. These actions only bring into question their true faith in a loving God. Only the Bible affirms the purpose and reason for our existence, and it alone determines our eternal destination. The Judeo-Christian Bible alone shows how to heal our wounded souls so we can receive our greatest rewards and live for eternity as kings and priests with new duties in the new kingdom of King Jesus' in the new Jerusalem.

Just as Nehemiah provided supplies and instructed the Jews on how to rebuild the walls and gates of Jerusalem after the temple was rebuilt, the New Testament tells us how to acquire spiritual supplies and tools to rebuild our soul's walls to protect our born-again spirit temple. Nehemiah is a picture of the Holy Spirit instructing us as born-again believers after our confession of faith (Romans 10:9–10) to repair our soul's gates and walls.

> This only would I learn of you, *Received ye the Spirit by the works of the law, or by the hearing of faith? Are ye so foolish? having begun in the Spirit, are ye now made perfect by the flesh?* Have ye suffered so many things in vain? if it be yet in vain. He therefore that ministers to you the Spirit, and works miracles among you, does he it by the works of the law, or by the hearing of faith? Even as Abraham believed God, and it was accounted to him for righteousness. Know ye therefore that they which are of faith, the same are the children of Abraham. *And the scripture, foreseeing that God would justify the heathen through faith, preached before the gospel unto Abraham, saying, In thee shall all nations be blessed. So then they which be of faith are blessed with faithful Abraham.* For as many as are of the works of the law are under the curse: for it is written, Cursed is every one that continues not in all things which are written in the book of the law to do them. (Galatians 3:2–10, emphasis added)

The process is virtually the same, with very similar obstacles to our reconstruction processes by God. Just as Nehemiah had trials and tribulations with Sanballat, Tobiah, and Geshem, so too are our efforts obstructed and hindered by Satan and his angels (demons). There is no difference, and regardless if Jesus is in our lives or not, Satan never stops and he only gives up trying when we die or he has succeeded with our return to a sinful lifestyle. He continues to torment and tempt us at every opportunity and chance he gets. Every human is given the same nine fruit spiritually, and through them we act and react naturally until taught differently. These fruit are corrupted by the flesh at birth through the (Adamic nature). Still, everyone is given these potential fruit attributes that need to be fed and watered to grow and produce either good or rotten fruit.

Our soul is natural and worldly, with only our conscience and feelings guiding us in this life unless taught to love in godly righteousness. Intelligence, craftiness, and physical strength are what rule and direct the worldly body, soul, and spirit. I don't understand how God judged or judges the Jewish believer before the incarnation of Jesus or those who never heard of God in times past. We just need to trust God in His wisdom as it states in Romans 1:20 by the Apostle Paul;

" For the invisible things of him from the creation of the world are clearly seen, being understood by the things that are made, even his eternal power and Godhead; so that they are without excuse:"

The fruit of the natural man—love, joy, peace, longsuffering, gentleness, goodness, faith, meekness, and temperance—are the same as those of the saved man, but they are perverted and produce only rotten fruit without Jesus. Producing hateful, rotten fruit and having no lasting love, joy, peace, goodness, gentleness, or faith in everything done. The Word warns us that our works without love becomes nothing but hay and stubble to be burned away as works of the flesh. They diminish in purity and spirituality with age and worldly experiences without God. These rule the fleshly natural-influenced man by the PPRSs, the lusts of the heart, the seventeen spirit-world realities, with the seventeen works of the flesh, completely dominating every thought. They are corrupted and perverted in all intent and desires and justify these actions and attitudes as natural to all mankind is inevitable without God.

Only until the heart of a person seeks repentance and the desire to change their mind will Jesus come in. If Satan can convince a biblically ignorant people that the God they believe in will not punish sin, then he wins. So too is it with the Holy Spirit.

He will not come in or upon you until you personally ask Him to come. The real work begins in rebuilding the walls of your soul to be acceptable to God, but if you don't think His gifts are available to you today … Satan wins again! When you verbally confess Jesus as Lord and believe that God raised Him from the dead, only then can you ask for the baptism of the Holy Spirit, and only then will He come in. But if denominational traditions and church pride keep you ignorant of the third person of the Trinity, then a third of New Testament Scripture is useless to you, and you are left powerless. When you trust Jesus and His Word (the whole Judeo-Christian Bible) you now can begin rebuilding the walls of your soul. Once you get saved and baptized with the Holy Ghost, you can begin praying in the Spirit and begin construction to rehang your gates and protect your eternal spirit.

> Blessed are they which do hunger and thirst after righteousness: for they shall be *filled*. (Matthew 5:6, emphasis added)

Remember the acronym TRUST I told you about earlier; I begin my prayers this way: *Thank* You, Father, for saving me and giving me the Holy Ghost. *Reveal* to me the nine individual fruit areas of my wounded and damaged soul, make me usable and *use* me in these fruit areas, *strengthen* my body and mind to deal with each fruit issue and *teach* me in your Word how to deal with each issue, and teach me your promises in your Word in each area of my life. Amen.

The process begins with the tongue confessing Jesus as Lord of your life, and you invite Him into your heart and are filled with the Holy Spirit. Then you hunger for more and are baptized in the Spirit. Your private prayer language then begins, and the spiritual relationship with Christ starts, which builds your faith and reliance upon Him in everything you do.

I know some will refute and object to the baptism of the Holy Spirit as not being necessary or no longer available to new believers, but again I read nowhere in Scripture where there is an expiration date on the Holy Spirit. The Holy Spirit is the most important aspect of your spiritual walk as a believer since your decision and confession of faith in Jesus Christ. Praying in the Spirit with your own personal prayer language is the only biblical proof and evidence of the baptism of the Holy Spirit, which is precisely why so many professing biblical theologians and organized religious leaders object to it.

> And they were *all* filled with the Holy Ghost, and began to speak with other tongues, as the Spirit gave them utterance.

... And when Paul had laid his hands upon them, the Holy Ghost came *on* them; and they spoke with tongues, and prophesied. (Acts 2:4; 19:6, emphasis added)

The tongue is the last unruly member of the flesh to be yielded over to God, and this experience is the gateway to a new intimacy and oneness in fellowship, correction, and growth with the omniscient, omnipresent, and omnipotent God of all. We have access through Jesus Christ in the Holy Spirit, and only through the Holy Spirit do we have access to the creator of everything seen and unseen. He cares about you and your needs. Know and understand that as long as you're breathing, you can repent and can correct and heal any wounded areas of our soul. As you ask individually on each of the fruit the Spirit, the Holy Spirit will begin to not only edify you in the Spirit, but He will begin to reveal areas of that fruit of the Spirit that you've failed in or need to work on to heal past wounds. He will bring to mind everything hurt in your soul and will also show you everyone who has been damaged or offended by your actions or words.

As we go through each of the fruit of the Spirit, please become aware of areas of the wall damaged by trauma or word curses that caused soul wounds, strongholds, or opened door points to spiritual attack. There will be revelation when asked specifically in prayer for each of the fruit for you to begin self-restoration, self-deliverance, and self-healing of your soul. The Holy Spirit will show you areas and times you have offended and destroyed the walls of people you've come in contact with as well. When trying to heal your fruit, realize that some areas you can correct personally, others you can only pray for, and still others you recognize ahead of time and can avoid recurrences. Yes you should go to preachers and evangelists for prayer, but I believe that the first line of defense is a good offence, and God's Word tells us in Ephesians 6:13 to take unto you the whole armor of God, which includes both offensive and defensive articles of warfare that are needed. There are promises in Scripture for our restoration, deliverance, and healing in every area of our hurts and pains but also to protect against future attacks by Satan.

My people are destroyed for lack of knowledge: because thou hast rejected knowledge. (Hosea 4:6)

Don't be deceived I repeat again and again that Satan is behind every issue and circumstance you face. Maybe not directly, but by his minions' prodding, tempting, insinuating, and coaxing us to act in unison with our Adamic nature, planting seeds of rebellion that bear corrupted fruit later. The God of the Bible has given us power, armor, and weapons for spiritual protection and warfare. They're in His Word, and it's your choice not to see, believe, or utilize them. You have to ask Him specifically, and He will show you specifically. You need to ask the Holy Spirit to reveal to you specifically what it is in each of the nine fruit that you are lacking spiritual strength in. In what part of that fruit tree/vine have you been hurt or damaged in that produces damaged or unproductive fruit? The byproduct of your damaged fruit may not be obvious to you at first, but the effects of them are long lasting. There is a reason why Jesus spoke of love first as a loving God to us, and to then show God's love in us toward other believers, and finally brotherly love toward all others, including nonbelievers too. These three faceted teachings of Love not only are the foundation to all of the nine fruit of your soul, it is where Jesus began to teach the new commandment. This new commandment was diametrically opposed to anything ever seen or taught before anywhere in the world.

> A new commandment I give unto you, That ye love one another; as I have loved you, that ye also love one another. By this shall all men know that ye are my disciples, if ye have love one to another. (John 13:34–35)

> Let love be without dissimulation. Abhor that which is evil; cleave to that which is good. Be kindly affectionate one to another with brotherly love; in honor preferring one another. (Romans 12:9–10)

In the natural, love is usually perceived as a weakness, but true love is not only verbalized, it needs to be proven concretely through our intents and actions regardless what the world might say. These concrete evidences must give satisfactory proofs of selfless love that is pure in intent with trust and faith seeking nothing in return. Sometimes we only have an inward proof that we just know that we're to show Godly love. Other times, we never see any proof that your love or your compassion will be received or reciprocated. Romans

5:1 tells us that when we get saved, we're justified: "Therefore being justified by faith, we have *peace with God* through our Lord Jesus Christ" (emphasis added).

What this means is that when we get saved and receive Jesus as Lord of our lives, we become a new creature in Christ Jesus, with the inward evidence being at peace with God and the outward evidence being our having great joy (the proof being a desire to live a holy life). This holy life is the fruit of love—not from duty or obligation, but as a result of God's love for us we reciprocate with a love that makes you an overcomer of your flesh dominated responses.

> For God so loved the world, that he gave his only begotten Son, that whosoever believeth in him should not perish, but have everlasting life. (John 3:16)

> I love them that love me; and those that seek me early shall find me [says the Lord]. (Proverbs 8:17)

> Herein is love, not that we loved God, but that he loved us, and sent his Son to be the propitiation for our sins. (1 John 4:10)

> Jesus said unto him, Thou shalt love the Lord thy God with all thy heart, and with all thy soul, and with all thy mind. This is the first and great commandment. And the second is like unto it, Thou shall love thy neighbor as thyself. (Matthew 22:37–39)

This is not exclusive to your particular denomination as some might think or have been taught. Jesus is all-inclusive to all those who truly believe and walk after the Spirit. Small nuggets of truth are evident in many of the world's Christian denominations, but like most, they fail to connect the eternal dots of a holy God using a peculiar people (Hebrews) separated from all the masses of humanity to usher in an eternal bride. My purpose in writing this book is not the denunciation of any denominational faith in the risen Christ, but rather in the calling out of multitudes of traditions and customs of men and women who truly love the Lord Jesus but have been led astray by these works, rules, and fleshly inspired standards that have nothing to do with true compassion, repentance or true salvation. These fleshly inspired work requirements only detract us from receiving all our eternal rewards as we enter through the gates into the Holy City.

> Behold, I come quickly: blessed is he that keepeth the sayings of the prophecy of this book. And, behold, I come quickly; and my reward is with me, to give every man according as his work shall be. I am Alpha and Omega, the beginning and the end, the first and the last. Blessed are they that do his commandments, that they may have right to the tree of life, and may enter in through the gates into the city. (Revelation 22:7, 12–14)

Power, money, and positions evident in the pomp, reverence, and beauty of many religious traditions and ceremonies have little or no real spiritual purpose other than to the participants and viewers that relish in them in their futility. The sins of the Old Testament are still the sins of today, and we as believers are just as susceptible to them as past generations were eons ago. We must try to avoid them as much as possible. Yes, we are no longer under the Law, but by grace through our Lord Jesus Christ, we must still flee sin. Whether the pride of life or the lust of the flesh in Moses' day it is still abhorrent three thousand five hundred years later. Adultery, sodomy, lesbianism, and fornication are all still an abomination in the sight of a Holy God no matter how badly we wish it were not so or society disagrees.

> Blessed are they that do his commandments, that they may have right to the tree of life, and may enter in through the gates into the city. For without are dogs, and sorcerers, and whoremongers, and murderers, and idolaters, and whosoever loveth and maketh a lie. I Jesus have sent mine angel to testify unto you these things in the churches. I am the root and the offspring of David, and the bright and morning star. And the Spirit and the bride say, Come. And let him that heareth say,

Come. And let him that is athirst come. And *whosoever* will,
let him take the water of life freely. (Revelation 22:14–17,
emphasis added)

I am convinced that along with the seventeen works of the flesh, there are
seventeen spirit-world realities and seventeen lusts of the heart that all fall
under the headings of principalities, powers, rulers of darkness, and spirits
of wickedness in high places (the PPRSs). Each soul (mind) when saved
(Romans 10:9–10) is eternally different from an unbeliever in that their sins
are forgiven and their spirit is as perfect as it will ever be, but our souls retain
our old lifelong habits and thoughts. Temptations, enticements, and the lusts
of the heart are forever before us, and these are the moment-by-moment, day-
by-day battles that every believer faces. For this reason, it is vitally important
that we use all the weapons afforded every believer after our commitment to
follow Jesus. As we stated previously in these lessons, these battles are real
affecting our attitudes, annoyances, and aggravations that are all too real
too, but they don't have to be permanent and they don't have to stop us from
receiving our eternal rewards. We will be given an opportunity to put a halt
to the torments to each of our nine fruit of the Spirit through the prayer Jesus
gave us to use in Matthew.

And I will give unto thee the keys of the kingdom of heaven:
and whatsoever thou shalt bind on earth shall be bound in
heaven: and whatsoever thou shalt loose on earth shall be
loosed in heaven. ... Verily I say unto you, Whatsoever ye
shall bind on earth shall be bound in heaven: and whatsoever
ye shall loose on earth shall be loosed in heaven. (Matthew
16:19; 18:18)

Unless we stop partaking and abstain from acting out these perversions from
hell, then hell awaits us. You might be right, politically correct and tolerant,
but it still is a conscious act of rebellion by that person against their own
bodies, and you aren't right with Jehovah God, Jesus Christ, or the Holy Spirit
no matter how unfair or archaic you think God's commands are. Honestly,
you don't have to have sex, you don't have to live with your boyfriend or
girlfriend, and your twelve-year-old child will not die if they wait to have sex

or abstain from sex outside of marriage. We are living in the last days spoken of by many in Scripture and we must pray, tell the truth, prepare physically and spiritually for the days we now live in.

> And it shall come to pass in the last days, saith God, I will pour out of my Spirit upon all flesh: and your sons and your daughters shall prophesy, and your young men shall see visions, and your old men shall dream dreams. (Acts 2:17)

> This know also, that in the last days perilous times shall come. (2 Timothy 3:1)

> Hath in these last days spoken unto us by his Son, whom he hath appointed heir of all things, by whom also he made the worlds; Who being the brightness of his glory, and the express image of his person, and upholding all things by the word of his power, when he had by himself purged our sins, sat down on the right hand of the Majesty on high. (Hebrews 1:2–3)

> Be patient therefore, brethren, unto the coming of the Lord. Behold, the husbandman waits for the precious fruit of the earth, and hath long patience for it, until he receive the early and latter rain. Be ye also patient; establish your hearts: for the coming of the Lord draws nigh. (James 5:7–8)

> Knowing this first, that there shall come in the last days scoffers, walking after their own lusts, And saying, Where is the promise of his coming? for since the fathers fell asleep, all things continue as they were from the beginning of the creation. For this they willingly are ignorant of, that by the word of God the heavens were of old, and the earth standing out of the water and in the water. (2 Peter 3:3–5)

Chapter 18

WERE YOU THERE CHARLIE?

*U*nderstand that we are without excuse before a Holy God. Just because it's too hard for people to accept the Bible's explanation of creation, a creator God, or His commands doesn't make evolution and science justify your lifestyle. Only the Holy Ghost's conviction of an individual's heart will be what I believe causes that person to change their perverted, sinful, politically correct minds to repent. If the foundation of your faith is based only on the evidence given by the enlightened academics, then you ain't right with a Holy God.

Your conclusions and assertions of evolution without a designer are as dubious as the believers in bigfoot or the Loch Ness monster. Just as there is no concrete undeniable proof of these animals, there is no proof of a transitional kind of progression between species as outlined in Charles Darwin's book to explain his theory. What many advocates of this theory claim are transitional proofs are what I believe just variations within the same species and not an actual progression from simple to more complex organisms. The fact is that any mutations in nature end in rejection and death by its host or mother. Being not convinced of a designer for the complexities and fine tuning required for the universe or the intricacies in micro-biology shows your unwillingness to be accountable to anyone or anything for your actions and this only proves your self-absorption, narcissism and arrogance.

This is the real reason why our pulpits are filled with actors and entertainers who are truly nonbelievers in the risen Christ and are only in our churches for position, recognition, and money. Their purpose, whether they know it or not, is to deceive as many true believers as possible, filling the parishioners with the doubt and unbelief that they have. Their canned sermons on easy-to-accept subjects only raise more questions than they answer, because their doubt and unbelief is exposed by their condescension to the Word of God. Only by the gift of the indwelling of the Holy Spirit and its promptings to true believers of the Word of God can the fivefold ministry be truly disseminated to a Bible-ignorant people. Confusion reigns in the professing so-called Christian churches, and ignorance. of the Word will not be an excuse on judgment day. Know that for many who do not change their minds or change their lifestyle are doomed. These unrepentant so-called believers are the same ones who will be cursing God in the last days spoken of in the Olivet discourse in Mathew 24–25 and when the four horsemen and seven seals are unleashed on an unprepared group of believers then they will have to come to grips with their failures. (Revelation 6:1–17).

Too many professing Jesus-believing people "once saved, always saved" believers or the two day a year "Christmas and Easter only" church goers will be lulled into a false sense of security about the tribulation, the pre-wrath trials of God and about when and if the rapture of the church is delayed (pre-tribbers). These I believe will be like the five unwise virgins Jesus talked about in Matthew 25—those who are saved yet don't have the power of the Holy Spirit to withstand (overcome) persecution in these last days. Marvin Rosenthal's book *The Pre-Wrath Rapture of the Church* has the best explanation of the culmination of the six-thousand-year time frame written about for man once they reconnect with Elohim (creator God). He poses the question that if God's Word alone says that there is no difference between Jew or Gentile, black or white, male or female, natural or grafted in as a believer, why would He treat people differently in these last days? A believer in Jesus Christ the Messiah is a believer in Jesus Christ the Messiah, and only prideful, arrogant, self-righteous, religious denominationalists and anti-Semites differentiate His believers by race, denomination and nationality.

The Word of God says in Matthew 24, Mark 13, and Luke 21 that in the last days before Christ's return, all believers should take heed that no man deceives them, that all are to prepare for the coming woes, and that these woes are the beginning of sorrows to all of humanity and not just the Jews. Remember earlier when I said that I believe there is no difference between the practicing Jew and the unbeliever for they both don't receive Jesus. Jesus said " No man can come to me, except the Father which hath sent me draw him: and I will raise him up at the last day. It is written in the prophets, And they shall be all taught of God. Every man therefore that hath heard, and hath learned of the Father, cometh unto me. Not that any man hath seen the Father, save he which is of God, he hath seen the Father. Verily, verily, I say unto you, He that believeth on me hath everlasting life." (John 6:44-47)

The importance of the reiteration of Jesus' words in the Gospels is to warn us as believers of these coming woes, and that not only must they come to pass, but we as believers, in these last days are going to have to live through some bad times that we need to prepare for. Pastor Bev Hills, a dear friend of mine before she passed away, told us in her weekly Bible study that the Lord told her three things all believers should do: first, pray for Jesus' coming and for the peace of Jerusalem where He will rule and reign in the millennium; second, always tell the truth about what the Word of God says, no matter what your denomination says; and thirdly, prepare both spiritually and physically for tough times ahead if the Lord tarry.

I know this is not the message most Christians want to hear, but I am convinced that the Holy Spirit is telling me not only to warn "ALL" His children to prepare for tough times ahead but to remove all the hate, pride, and prejudice they have toward fellow believers in Jesus Christ regardless of if you believe in a pre- mid- or post tribulation rapture of the church. Our adherence to a specific Christian denomination is irrelevant if we don't live as committed Christians in the love of Jesus Christ. The Word tells us that we as believers must correct the areas of our soul that are displeasing to Jehovah God. We must stop cherry-picking and misinterpreting the Scriptures to ease our minds and acknowledge His warnings. Know that we have been chosen to live in these "last days" because of our faith and strength in the Spirit. You can't read biblical Scripture and have prejudice toward fellow believers regardless of skin color or denomination, and most of all, you can't be anti-Semitic toward our Jewish brothers and sisters who originated our faith. Like I said earlier, you can't justify your hatred for Jews with a form of replacement theology or believe that blacks are cursed with the mark of Cain, justifying your racism. Religious, self-righteous bigots who still claim to be Christian and lovers of Jesus Christ can't be like this. Matthew 24:29–31 says that Jesus Christ said He was coming back again immediately after the tribulation of those days (this is also in Mark 13:24–27 and in Luke 21:25–28). Only the Judeo-Christian biblical Scripture talks about the future and that we *all* will face troubles if the Lord tarries.

Ask yourself what makes us so special that the first church would have to face persecution but we won't? Life itself is a "tribulation" and our job is to show Christ in whatsoever we do. Do you believe that we are so much better than the first century believers were, or do you live closer to God than the believers of Jesus' day who witnessed His crucifixion and ascension? Were the converts of Peter, Paul, and John who received revelation of these last days less of believers in the risen Christ than we are today? Why would such a Holy God want to save such a perverted, unloving, self-absorbed people who believe they're the King's kids but can't even pray in the promised third person of the Trinity (tongues) to intercede for our persecuted brothers and sisters in foreign lands or our downtrodden neighbors who are struggling and live down the street?

The God of the Bible is real, and He wants none to perish but all to come to the knowledge of Jesus Christ. The Devil is also real, and God has given us everything needed to heal our wounded souls and battle demonic forces with the helper (the Holy Spirit). Not much has changed with people's character since God created man, and we are tormented with the same issues today as they were six thousand years ago. That's why the Old Testament's wisdom is as relevant today as the New Testament is. Each period of time might use different terminology and different technology, but the root issues are the same to all mankind. The same seventeen works of the flesh, seventeen spirit-world realities, and seventeen lusts of the heart have not changed over the eons (Mark 7:21–23; Ephesians 6:12; and James 4:1–4). These demonic forces that tormented Cain and convinced him to kill his brother Abel are the same demons telling you to terminate your unborn child in your womb for convenience sake or to divorce your husband of thirty years because the guy at the office really understands your needs and listens. In either case, you made a choice to act on a thought planted in your head, and you consciously acted on the desire and temptation, and now you will reap its harvest.

Listen to me. The battles we face are not carnal but spiritual, and God has given every believer in Jesus the tools to protect and fight for his soul. If you don't realize the eternal prize of salvation at the cross while you're still alive, you will when you reach your final destination and you've missed it. Many people have clinically died and have either had a heavenly experience as they expired or they have experienced one of separation and excruciating torment in hell. They then all came back to life from this deathbed experience, and many have changed their lifestyles and thoughts completely about this life. Both confessing Christians and those who are nonbelievers have experienced this phenomenon. We can't discount all of these experiences as a figment of their subconscious minds, but I do believe that because of medications given to the dying in hospitals, too many unconscious people aren't aware of their impending doom until after they have expired.

The purpose of humanity is not only to provide an eternal companion for the Son of God, Jesus, as the bride of Christ, but we were designed to worship and serve our God for eternity, freely choosing Him as our Lord and King. After the call of Abram, God separated a people to usher in the Messiah. He called them from a world of people that had not followed and lived by His laws and precepts any longer but lived after the works of the flesh and the lusts of the heart. Man had forgotten who the creator of the world that he lived in was, and the world is doing it again today. With Jesus' death, burial, and resurrection, His church (the bride) was born, and as born-again saved believers in Jesus Christ we have been called according to this purpose to proclaim the good news and expand the kingdom of Jesus. All believers in the risen Christ, regardless of denomination or traditions, must unite and work together to prepare His bride for the soon-coming King.

> And we know that all things work together for good to them that love God, to them who are the called according to his purpose. For whom he did foreknow, he also did predestinate to be conformed to the image of his Son, that he might be the firstborn among many brethren. Moreover whom he did predestinate, them he also called: and whom he called, them he also justified: and whom he justified, them he also glorified. (Romans 8:28–30)

His purpose was and is for us to be a part of His story, to be His church, and to be His bride for eternity. If His Word (the Bible) is just a fable and His life is just a story and you would rather believe science with all it purports as to us just becoming part of a dung heap in this cosmic crapshoot, then I choose to believe in "His story" (the Bible) and live forever as "His bride" (the church) in His kingdom the New Jerusalem.

> Verily, verily, I say unto you, He that believeth on me hath everlasting life. I am that bread of life. Your fathers did eat manna in the wilderness, and are dead. This is the bread which cometh down from heaven, that a man may eat thereof, and not die. I am the living bread which came down from heaven: if any man eat of this bread, he shall live forever: and the bread that I will give is my flesh, which I will give for the life of the world. (John 6:47–51)

The choice is yours. Only the Judeo-Christian Bible speaks of the creation of the heavens and the earth in Genesis 1:1–2 and then records six thousand years of history, talking of you as an individual before your birth (Jeremiah), all the issues we struggle with in life (1 Thessalonians), and how we will live for eternity after our death (Revelation 7:15-17).

Before I formed thee in the belly I knew thee; and before thou came forth out of the womb I sanctified thee, and I ordained thee a prophet (witness) unto the nations. (Jeremiah 1:5)

That every one of you should know how to possess his vessel in sanctification and honor. (1 Thessalonians 4:4)

Therefore are they (believers) before the throne of God, and serve him day and night in his temple: and he that sitteth on the throne shall dwell among them. They shall hunger no more, neither thirst any more; neither shall the sun light on them, nor any heat. For the Lamb (Jesus) which is in the midst of the throne shall feed them, and shall lead them unto living fountains of waters: and God shall wipe away all tears from their eyes. (Revelation 7:15–17)

Only the Bible speaks of the birth, life, death, and the afterlife of a human being and gives us hope for eternity. The Devil—along with his powers, principalities, rulers of darkness, and spirits of wickedness in high places— seeks to destroy us using a perverted interpretation of the Word of God. At the very least, he tries to hinder us from reaching our spiritual potential and receiving our eternal rewards because of rotten attitudes and perverted fruit. Since everything Jesus taught was based on love, Satan and his minions seek to pervert, misrepresent, and distort anything resembling God or His love with his seeds of hate, envy, covetousness, self-righteousness, religion and confusion only to hinder us because of his jealousy of mankind's position before God. This unloving spirit and its accompanying cohorts gain access into our lives very subtly and cleverly, using misdirected affections and psychological ploys to deceive and frustrate us.

The first sign that the foundations of your soul have been wounded and possibly damaged is the inability to really connect emotionally with another person and show love. If there is any love, then the relationships are usually volatile and one-sided. In place of a pure godly love, some perverse, fleshly motivated imitation of love is evident. The brokenhearted soul is full of self-pity, fear, and a lack of confidence, which breeds doubt and unbelief to any real love or their ability to attain it. This lack of self-confidence and double-mindedness leads to a myriad of self-questioning, self-consciousness, and self-deception issues. All of which lead to a poor level of self-esteem, self-worth, and a lack of self-confidence.

Not being able to accept any genuine love with truly loving intentions that are motivated by a selfless, giving heart is what I believe the Holy Spirit showed me causes the other eight fruit walls to be damaged and to produce the bad fruit of fear, stress, depression and anger. Fear, stress, rage, and anger are what I believe contributed to the diagnosis of MS and the autoimmune confusion with my white blood cells. Low self-esteem from not meeting my father's expectations at a very young age, along with his humiliating me in front of my teammates, attributed to my constant quest to try to prove my self-worth and win.

This is why when I asked the Holy Spirit to show me why I'm always so mean, defensive, and angry all the time, He showed me that my Love gate was imperfect and discolored with the guilt and un-forgiveness of my supporting walls. They were damaged by anger, vengeance, and cynicism. Throughout the walls of my fruit of the Spirit were emotional strongholds of self-bitterness, self-rejection, self-hatred, and self-guilt. Each one of these feelings of self-loathing, coupled with the negative cynicism and always questioning the motivation behind any form of love, was always there. The expectation of national pride, racial prejudice, and the ignorance of the true Christian faith make me wonder why my wife ever married me in the first place. As I look back at who I was, I can see why my mother-in-law had the keys and car ready for her daughter just in case she changed her mind and did not want to marry me.

But God in His mercy has allowed me to grow spiritually the right way through His Son, Jesus Christ, and in the baptism of the Holy Spirit for His glory in spite of all these obstacles in my life. The foundation of love in me as a gate to my soul's fruit influenced by the PPRSs, the seventeen spirit-world realities, with the seventeen works of the flesh, with all the deep-seated lusts and emotional pains of my heart, makes my salvation truly a miracle. Jesus Christ and Him crucified alone could have taken this mess of a man that I was, work with him, love him, and mold him into a usable vessel for the

Kingdom of His Son. To Him be all the glory and honor forever and ever, amen.

We spoke earlier about the constant attacks to our soul walls seeking points of weakness to influence the foundation of Love (which is the foundation of all the other eight fruit), but we need to also remember that all nine fruit are dependent upon each other, and that they in unity represent what and who we really are. When these spiritual attacks come at us and we're not aware of the spirit-world realities and lusts of the heart in our lives, then we can come to believe that these dysfunctions are normal and that we are going to just have to deal with all the soul wounds. God never intended for our emotions and psyche to be battered and bruised the way only people who we love can damage us.

It is Marvin Rosenthal's contention (and mine as well) that the Olivet Discourse is Jewish in character, sequential in progression, logical in argument, parallel to the seals of Revelation 6 in nature, covers the seventieth week of Daniel in scope, answers the dual question concerning the Lord's coming and the end of the age posed by the disciples (which was the catalyst for the Lord's teaching), and encompasses both the rapture and the return of Christ within its borders. It will also be demonstrated that the seventieth week of Daniel has three major, distinct, and identifiable periods of time—the "beginning of sorrows," the "Great Tribulation," and the "Day of the Lord"—which are all found in the Olivet Discourse (Rosenthal, 60–61).

Christ is coming again, and the time of His return is unknown to the faithful and the unfaithful alike, but we as believers are not to be as the five unwise virgins who were not prepared. Thinking that the Lord is going to come and take us out of the world of pain, anguish, and tribulations only mocks the torture and trials of those martyred before us and again reveals our perverted sense of unwarranted pride and superiority over our fallen brothers and sisters in Christ. Remember what my friend Bev Hills told us before she passed: first, pray always for Jesus' coming and for the peace of Jerusalem where He will rule and reign in the millennium; second, always tell the truth about what the Word of God says, no matter what your denomination says about the coming trials and tribulations; and thirdly, prepare both spiritually with the Holy Spirit's gifts, your personal prayer language, the armor of God, and fruit of the Spirit as we walk daily in the Spirit of God and physically with food, water, and supplies for tough times ahead if the Lord tarry. Most of all, learn how to become a bold witness of your Lord and Savior Jesus Christ to the lost in your families, your neighbors, and any stranger the Holy Spirit gives you the unction to bring to the Lord. One thing is for certain, if the Lord comes tomorrow, then the Bibles and supplies we leave behind will be well used and maybe save a soul from hell, or if Jesus tarry, these supplies will equally be used wisely.

Maranatha—Come Lord Jesus

Chapter 19

EVIL SPIRITS TORMENT
BELIEVERS TOO

*T*hrough eons of observing human actions and reactions to common issues with all our hurts and pains to mankind, Satan and his minions can virtually predict how we will react. Competition, isolation, guilt, jealousy, accusation, shame, panic, fear, and a lack of confidence bring predictable reactions and results of emotional protectionism to fill the void left by an unloving spirit. The Bible alone tells us that when an issue is addressed or a spirit removed through our own efforts and not refilled with godly fruit then Satan will send seven more destructive spirits to fill the void. You have to understand that we battle not against flesh and blood but against demonic spiritual entities and that if the void is not filled by a godly, inspired fruit of the Spirit based in love, then Satan assigns spirits to fill the empty space and the issue exacerbates.

> When the unclean spirit is gone out of a man, he walks through dry places, seeking rest; and finding none, he says, I will return unto my house whence I came out. And when he

cometh, he finds it swept and garnished [clean but empty].
Then he goes, and takes to him seven other spirits more
wicked than himself; and they enter in, and dwell there:
and the last state of that man is worse than the first. (Luke
11:24–26)

There are two questions that are posed by these verses that need to be asked
and then answered by the Word of God. First, "what" is the unclean spirits that
is gone out of a person, and secondly, are you and I susceptible as believers to
having an unclean spirit to influence us? The answer to both of these questions
is yes. We've already discussed earlier that principalities, powers, rulers of
darkness, and spirits of wickedness will try to monopolize and dominate our
every thought, giving Jesus no other choice but to tell us, "Depart from me,
you worker of iniquity," even after we're saved and have committed our lives
to Jesus but still dabble in sin.

But he shall say, I tell you, I know you not whence ye are;
depart from me, all ye workers of iniquity. (Luke 13:27)

As believers, how could we have opened a spiritual door for an attack on us,
and how could a spirit have taken up residence on one or more of our spiritual
fruit if we're believers? Yes is the answer to both of these questions Yes -Yes
–Yes *very easily*—through the media, political correctness, tolerance of people
partaking in sin around you, ignorance of Scripture, and ignorance of who
you are in Jesus Christ. Thousands and thousands of doors are opened to
Satan's influences daily through any of the areas mentioned, and all he needs
is a small crack to enter in. Jesus told us in John that if you love Him, keep
His commands; that He will give you another Comforter; and that that
Comforter will abide with you forever.

If ye love me, keep my commandments. And I will pray the
Father, and he shall give you another Comforter that he
may abide with you forever; Even the Spirit of truth; whom
the world cannot receive, because it seeth him not, neither
knoweth him: but ye know him; for he dwelleth with you,

and shall be in you. I will not leave you comfortless: I will come to you. (John 14:15–18)

My whole premise and assertion in this section of the book is twofold: one is to show that you as a believer in Jesus Christ of Nazareth can fall or at the very least lose your eternal rewards. If not careful, we could revert back into a life of sin. Secondly, your ignorance of the Word of God and your desire for acceptance and love for a fallen spouse, child, or fellow believer can open doors to sinful thoughts and actions if not careful. The adherence to vain genealogies or repetitious religious traditions avail nothing in the light of Scripture. Seemingly innocent actions like watching regular television with all its soft-porn programming and lurid commercials can allow a myriad of unclean spirits in to do irreparable damage to one or all of your nine spiritual fruit, destroying your marriage through mental adultery, suspicion of infidelity, and verbal murder through accusation and innuendo.

These forms of perversion can influence people so much that they become entangled in a preoccupation with the works of the flesh in their fantasies. Worse yet, a believer can get so wrapped up into fleshly indulgences with jealousy and accusations that the holy, righteous God of all will not even consider their excuses. Entertaining friends and unsaved neighbors and acquaintances conversing in coarse jesting and sexual innuendos between couple's only plants seeds of dissatisfaction and unhappiness. To think mercy covers active conscious sinning that you as a believer knows is wrong is a lie straight from the pits of hell and claiming that your trying to conform the lost only contaminates your Christian walk.

Many self-righteous church leaders steeped in doctrinal traditions become haters of the other denominational Christian brethren instead of embracing the common belief in the Father, Son, and Holy Spirit as they stick to their rigid religious legalism. Their refusal to rightly divide the Word of God and even discuss the possibility of accepting and understanding the Scriptures in their entirety only hinders the Holy Spirit from healing their personal individual fruit as a person. Demonic spirits can also oppress and suppress any human being, saved or not, persuading an entire group of church believers to think that "works" are more important than their daily "walk" in the Spirit. I don't wish to be disrespectful but these same religious spirits will convince an entire group of family and church members to pray for a person who died and spend their precious little time before God praying for the non-repentant dead or praying to long dead so-called saints that can't help themselves or their own standing before a Holy God let alone yours. Jesus said in Luke 16:19-31

*But Abraham said, Son, remember that thou in thy lifetime received thy good things, and likewise Lazarus evil things: but now he is comforted, and thou art tormented. And beside all this, between us and you there is a great gulf fixed: so that they which would pass from hence to you cannot; **neither can they pass to us,** that would come from thence. Luke 16:25-26*

If a demon can convince a believer that they are in complete control of a normally considered sinful act and that they can quit at any time when done in secret, those believers will lose. If they can convince a person that Satan and demons don't exist, then Satan wins and he will persuade, coerce, and manipulate a person's sense of obligation and duty to dedicate their entire life to an eternally irrelevant cause then Satan wins again. This same sense of biblical ignorance of sin and the consequences of sinful lifestyles only validates the importance of my writing this book. Most Jesus-believing Christians outside their particular denomination are quick to condemn any difference to their religious traditions by cherry-picking only the parts of Scripture that applies to their line of thinking. You need to understand that every word in the Scriptures is there for a purpose, and that purpose is for you and me "today." But customs and traditions do not equate with scripture and you personally need to question a traditions origin and corroborate it with the written Word of God to be valid.

If you have made Jesus Christ of Nazareth the Lord of your life by believing that God raised Him from the dead and confessing Him with your mouth, then a demon cannot possess or enter you because you were bought and paid for with Jesus' redeeming blood. What Satan will try to do is convince you through religious traditions and secularly accepted notions that you as a believer are immune from attack or that you have no power or authority because that passed with the last apostle over two thousand years ago. It is my contention that you as a believer can and will be oppressed or suppressed by unclean spirits if you give Satan the legal right to enter your gates by entertaining these perversions of the Word or the perversions of the flesh through religious traditions. If you as a Christian dabble in any of the works of the flesh, have un-forgiveness or bitterness, you will fail and be considered a worker of iniquity. If you entertain any of the spirit-world realities or lust in your heart and don't stop and repent, then you will fail, and the rewards God has prepared for you for eternity shall be given to someone else who *is* bearing fruit and walking in obedience to their individual gifting and calling.

> Thou oughtest therefore to have put my money to the exchangers, and then at my coming I should have received mine own with usury. Take therefore the talent from him, and give it unto him which hath ten talents. For unto every one that hath shall be given, and he shall have abundance: but from him that hath not shall be taken away even that which he hath. (Matthew 25:27–29)

Remember that your spirit is the prize, and if Satan can't get your spirit through the works of the flesh, then he will try to corrupt your mind by perverting your soul's fruit with spirit-world realities, the lusts of the heart, emotional strongholds or the pride of life. Satan will try to destroy your walk and your testimony with your insecurities, inhibiting you from receiving your eternal rewards, even though you're still saved. As a believer, the blood of Jesus Christ at the cross cleans your spirit afresh, rebuilding it as a new temple of God to worship Him as a new creature in Christ. Each one of us is a part of the body regardless of Christian denomination as long as we've made Jesus the Lord of our life (Romans 10:9,10). Jesus and His Word alone are the only determining factors for salvation not church affiliation.

> For as the body is one, and hath many members, and all the members of that one body, being many, are one body: so also is Christ. For by one Spirit are we all baptized into one body, whether we be Jews or Gentiles, whether we be bond or free; and have been all made to drink into one Spirit. *For the body is not one member, but many.* (1 Corinthians 12:12–14, emphasis added)

With your spiritual fruit walls and gates being the only things separating Satan's influences from your spirit, then each one of the nine fruit of the Spirit is your testimony. We as believers should fortify our spiritual resolve and abstain from even the appearance of sin. What all believers who profess Jesus as Lord need to do is unite under the banner of King Jesus and not a particular denomination. Again these fruit of the Spirit are the determining factors of our eternal rewards and our eternal duties in the New Jerusalem, not your salvation, which is determined by your personal relationship with Jesus Christ and your ability to play with other believing kids on this playground called life. It only makes sense that we are then called to prune, water, and weed our vineyard to produce the largest and best harvest possible while here in this life.

Since your salvation was established the millisecond you made the decision to follow and serve Jesus as Lord and Savior, then it is incumbent upon you to walk in obedience to the Word of truth.

Again your soul walls are made up of the nine fruit of the Spirit which are love, joy, peace, longsuffering, gentleness, goodness, faith, meekness, and temperance, and these gates with their supporting walls are all built upon the foundation of love. These fruit are the only things separating Satan from your born-again, believing spirit. The choice is yours each time an issue requires a decision on your part to be made. You can either follow the words of Jesus or follow the works and lusts of the flesh. You can struggle with your believing spirit, battling your lifelong dominant flesh or walk in the Spirit. Whether in thought, word, or deed which involves one of the nine Fruit of the Spirit, we have to make a conscious decision in rebellion or obedience to Jesus. It is my contention also that no matter how long you've been a saved (a blood-bought) believer in Jesus, you are still susceptible to any of the works of the flesh, any of the spirit-world realities, or any of the lusts of the heart. The biggest lie ever perpetrated on a believer is that they can put their guard down and believe that they are immune to demonic attack because they're a saved believer. Hogwash!

If your Love foundation has been perverted (distorted, tainted, rejected, or misrepresented) by a parent, mate or authority figure in your formative years in any way, then your fruit will be perverted and compromised with false expectations, and unfulfilled emptiness occurs. Your opened doors to your soul foundation invite attack by any of these PPRSs, works of the flesh, spirit-world realities, lusts of the heart or emotional strongholds that then will pervert and destroy your ability to show Godly love through any one of your nine spiritual fruit.

Soul wounds are areas of your soul that have been wounded by traumatic, physical, emotional, or psychological hurts and pains that are still there even after you've been saved. Each one of these wounds will manifest an emotional stronghold in your personality that is reflected by your attempts to protect that wounded part of your fruit gate or its supporting walls if not removed specifically. The Word of God alone identifies and specifically calls out these unclean spirits like in Matthew 15:18–20; Mark 7:21–23; 1 Corinthians 6:9–10; Galatians 6:19–21; Ephesians 6:12; and James 4:1–4. All of these identifying Scriptures in God's Word have been given to us (believers in the risen Christ) with warnings that the actions and thoughts we entertain can and will open the doors to our soul for demonic attacks. It is just plain foolishness to assert that because you are a believer, you are immune from all these repeated warnings of unclean spirits by Matthew, Mark, James, and Paul, but because of your confession of faith, I guarantee Satan will try to pervert your fruit.

With this spiritual war waged against *all believers* in Jesus the Christ, Jehovah God then gives *all believers* through the Holy Spirit the tools and methods to protect, prevent, and heal these soul wounds: Matthew 16:19; 18:18–20, 22, 35; 19:9; Acts 10:38–39; Romans 8:26–27; 14:10, 17; Galatians 3:14; Ephesians 6:14–17; 2 Timothy 3:15–17; James 1:21–25; 1 John 2:27. All these Scriptures state that un-forgiveness, resentment, bitterness, jealousy and the rest of these hurtful heartfelt lusts that war against our members can cause deep soul wounds that are affecting every fruit of the Spirit of who we are as people of God. Through these Scriptures and their methods of identifying the fruit walls damaged, we will learn that by entertaining these thoughts of fleshly desires (double-mindedness) we give Satan a legal right to access our soul fruit. We will then learn that these areas of our soul walls that have been damaged by these entertained thoughts of hatred, jealousy, guilt, shame, and fear are causing our frustrations, aggravations, and angers that we feel. Satan then has access to our souls to build strongholds that grow with increased familiarity, intensity, and hostility with the least insignificant indulgences with spirit-world realities.

We as believers in Christ have been given the Comforter to help us by simply asking the Holy Spirit through the TRUST prayer to reveal to us the situation and what is instigating these unclean spirits that are oppressing and suppressing our God-given sense of right and wrong and causing us pain, fear, and offences. Ask Him to reveal to you areas of your soul's walls that need strongholds of sinful oppressive habits, roots of bitterness and un-forgiveness to be removed. Now the walls can begin to be repaired with the love of Jesus for that particular fruit. For instance, the fruit of love may be nonexistent or perverted in your personality. If you are always are in a bad mood and get annoyed and angry when people around you are joking and being silly, you have to ask the question, Why? Who hurt you and made it so difficult for you to show love freely and to show love with no strings attached? When and why was your love rejected? Ask Him in your natural language, and then ask Him in your spiritual language while you talk to God with your thoughts and commune with the God of all creation. Allow your tongue to communicate spirit to spirit and your mind to communicate with Jesus where Satan cannot hear or understand you.

Pray now out loud with me:

Heavenly Father God,

I come to You in the name of Jesus Christ of Nazareth, and I thank You, Holy Spirit, for calling me into Your kingdom. Holy Spirit of God, reveal to me the painful rejection of my love and reveal to me the instances that occurred that damaged all of my fruit in my soul so I can bind the feeling of rejection, self-hate, and shame and remove them out from my soul's fruit foundation. I now loose godly love and I do now plant godly seeds of love in every fruit of my soul to grow and fill the voids and damaged areas in my love that were swept clean and repaired in Jesus' holy name. Amen.

Know that when your Love gate and Love foundations are in disrepair, all nine fruit of the Spirit are affected by that one soul wound. It is so far-reaching that every relationship, acquaintance, and conversation we have reflects that pain as your normal personality. My countenance because of my pain, guilt, and anger was considered an attribute in the business world as I yelled and screamed for results. I was in a spiritual battle between my worldly natural man and my newly born-again spirit. The stress, strain, and constant pressure to succeed and satisfy all my self-imposed financial and social status aspirations robbed me of any love in my joy, peace, longsuffering, gentleness, goodness, faith, meekness, and temperance fruit of my soul as I tried to attain self-imposed expectations. My worldly soul was at odds with my born-again spirit, and I just didn't know how to deal with this type of mental conflict and anguish.

> My brethren, count it all joy when ye fall into divers temptations; Knowing this, that the trying of your faith worketh patience. But let patience have her perfect work, that ye may be perfect and entire, wanting nothing. If any of you lack wisdom, let him ask of God, that gives to all men liberally, and upbraided not; and it shall be given him. But let him ask in faith, nothing wavering. For he that wavers is like a wave of the sea driven with the wind and tossed. (James 1:2–6)

Godly wisdom tells us to "grin and bear it" or "pull yourself up by your bootstraps" and do what you've got to do to get it done and not sit there and feel sorry for yourself (very easy to do). This is so much easier said than done until it happens to you for real and every step, every emotion, and every thought is toward moving your legs forward for one step. Know that when trials and tribulations occur, only the Word of the living God tells us to count it all joy; that as you are tested with your reactions and responses through these trials, they only work patience for the next life trial which Satan will try to attack you with as he turns up the pressure to get you to fail and give up. After all, Satan's mission after you receive Jesus as Lord and Savior is to keep you as a Christian from learning of the power and authority you receive from believing in the death, burial, and resurrection of Jesus Christ the Messiah. If

Satan can get you to blame God for natural calamities, your sickness, and the death of innocent people, he wins. Calling these natural life occurrences an act of God is incorrect for the god of this world is Satan and it's not Jehovah Elohim that causes them. Again, if Satan can convince you that the promises and gifts of the Spirit are no longer available to us today, he wins again and we are left defenseless and vulnerable to his demonic spiritual attacks.

If not dealt with and eradicated from the roots, separation and seclusion then occur within your mind, causing divisions and strife to manifest with family, friends, and coworkers. From this spiritual seclusion starts self-abasement, and an unloving spirit will then begin to manifest. If hurt or damaged by verbal or physical attacks, then this type of unloving torment and mental abuse will be self-induced and self-debasing later in life. The result of your own fabricated personality of reprogramming will then start to destroy you and all your relationships as more and more self-destructive activities increase.

This unloving spirit is the open door that allows strongholds of self-degrading and inferior self-worth to begin to develop in your soul, and it all stems from that single soul wound seed planted as you developed emotionally and were hurt. The rulers of the darkness and spiritual wickedness in high places (your mind) will then enter into your thought life, causing depression and suggesting the desire to self-destruct. Even though you're unaware of the consequences of your actions or the cost to your soul's fruit, these open doors will allow any number of demonic influences to infiltrate your spiritual defenses; even after you are born again. Bitterness, resentment, un-forgiveness, anger, hate, and wrath are all precursors to Satan's ultimate goal which is to cause the spiritual ruin of your fruit as it rots and dies on the vine from them.

I believe that Satan has used the hatred of different denominations and people of color for no other reason than causing division to occur among fellow believers in Jesus Christ. Through misinterpreting Scripture and justifying segregation to all those who look and act differently then you, you are fueling Satan's persecution and mistreatment of believers. Once Satan succeeds in filling your heart full of racism and anti-Semitism, you then give Satan authority to destroy parts of all the fruit of your soul, nullifying your works done in godly love. If you *do* know Jesus, Satan then wants to inhibit you from reaching your fullest potential as a Christian, spiritually using a false sense of security, superiority, and the false safeguard of eternal protection through denominational legalism.

If Satan can keep you as a believer in Christ full of self-righteous hate, spiritually impotent, in doubt about creation and in unbelief questioning God's plan for all nonbelievers to come to Jesus, then he wins again. A religious spirit full of false piety and self-righteous indignation doesn't show Christlikeness to grow the Holy Spirit or the love of God in your fruit, but the hate and jealousy of the god of this world that retards and delays your spiritual growth. What it also shows is the influence of an unloving spirit and any of the other works of the flesh influenced by the spirit-world realities and the lusts of the heart to dominate your thoughts. This gives Satan the right to enter your life.

You don't receive because you don't ask, and you don't ask because you really don't want to give up the controls of your flesh to God—especially your tongue to the Holy Spirit with tongues (Acts 4:2). You then end up limiting God with the stipulations of your heart's lusts and religious doctrines (religiosity). These are the spirit-world realities and the lusts of the heart that Jesus warned us about:

> And he said, That which cometh out of the man, that defileth the man. For from within, out of the heart of men, proceed evil thoughts, adulteries, fornications, murders, Thefts, covetousness, wickedness, deceit, lasciviousness, an evil eye, blasphemy, pride, foolishness: All these evil things come from within, and defile the man. (Mark 7:20–23)

> Ye adulterers and adulteresses, know ye not that the friendship of the world is enmity with God? whosoever therefore will be a friend of the world is the enemy of God. (James 4:4)

> Dearly beloved, I beseech you as strangers and pilgrims, abstain from fleshly lusts, which war against the soul. (1 Peter 2:11)

> Whereby are given unto us exceeding great and precious promises: that by these ye might be partakers of the divine

nature, having escaped the corruption that is in the world through lust. (2 Peter 1:4)

Ye have heard that it was said by them of old time, Thou shall not commit adultery:
But I say unto you, That whosoever looks on a woman to lust after her hath committed adultery with her already in his heart. (Matthew 5:27–28)

Satan brings thoughts of lust, un-forgiveness, resentment, retaliation, anger, hatred, and violence to manifest bitterness in your heart. Once in your heart, Satan helps to provoke you to act upon evil thoughts, adulteries, fornications, murders, thefts, covetousness, wickedness, deceits, lasciviousness, an evil eye, blasphemy, pride, and foolishness. These are all in the plural because of the many simple and subtle ways Satan attacks you and me with them. Once in your souls fruit and not identified and removed, anger, bitterness, jealousy, accusations, and un-forgiveness will develop and cause sickness and disease to begin destroying your body like I believe Satan has tried to in me.

Looking with care to see that no man among you in his behavior comes short of the grace of God; for fear that some *bitter root* may come up to be a trouble to you, and that some of *you* may be *made unclean* by it. (Hebrews 12:15, emphasis added)

The things most of the secular world thinks are normal, just fun, and of no real consequence are exactly what Satan uses to gain access into our lives. Satan's demons launch hundreds of fleshly temptations daily through TV shows, movies, commercials, songs, tastes, feelings, and smells. Satan uses every one of our five senses to entice us to think on and desire these things in the lust of the heart, and to ultimately act on—then he wins again. This has nothing to do with our salvation, but it does affect our daily walk in the Spirit to preserve our salvation and receive all our rewards for eternity.

To be influenced by unclean spirits is what Jesus spoke of in Matthew 8, Mark 5, and Luke 8 when confronted with the demoniac possessed man. When Jesus asked its name, the demon in charge (PPRSs) said "Legion" which means at least two thousand spirits had taken up residence in and on this man. Not that a born-again believer can be possessed by any demons today, but I do think we can be oppressed, suppressed, and influenced by them, causing us to backslide and then live in sin.

The biggest misnomer for believing peoples of the risen Christ is the word *possessed* and the misinterpretation of this word as it relates to our individual walk. In the Greek *possess, possessed,* or better *possessing* is demonized—*daimonizomai*—and is translated "to be possessed or held on to by a demon." This does not mean completely possessed like Linda Blair in the *Exorcist*, but influenced by a dominate spirit. Acts 8:7 and 16:16 show that a person can be coerced or influenced by a demon if given permission. Again, it is my contention that you must choose to open the doors and partake in the thoughts and acts that could entangle anyone, saved or not, to involve yourself in potentially sinful acts of jealousy, pride, bitterness, anger, un-forgiveness, etc. You choose consciously to have a portion of your personality—or more correctly, one of your fruit of the Spirit—to be influenced and under enemy control by one or more of the works of the flesh, spirit-world realities, or the lusts of the heart. You as a saved, sanctified, and filled with the Holy Spirit child of the living God are still tempted and can still potentially sin. Right.…. RIGHT!!!

Honestly, don't we all still sin daily or have you already arrived to perfect Christ-likeness? Do you get angry at your spouse, children, or animals because they just don't listen? Is there still the potential to get jealous and envious of a person who has stolen, lied, or prospered through ill-gotten gains? Can bitterness and hatefulness cause your insides to do summersault's as soon as that certain someone walks into the room or their name is mentioned at the family party, and you say something ugly or hateful? Have you ever thought lustful thoughts of "what-ifs?" if an attractive, nice person shows you special attention? Do you get violently angry when things or jobs don't get completed or done to your standards? Then *wake up*! You have been demonically attacked!

In each of these examples plus millions more in this life, you have choices to make (free will), and these choices all have consequences here in this life and for eternity. You can take any of these thoughts captive, choose not to react, take the high road, and show Christlikeness, or you can succumb to the demon and allow *daimonizomai* to take over and influence your next decision. Satan's attacks on the love fruit and foundation of love for all nine fruit of the Spirit is his first line of attack on us as individuals.

First, quietly and seemingly quite innocently, we compromise our reservations to partake in the thoughts which are his mode of operation. Then he entices us to dabble more and more in these dream fantasies while we are, of course, in complete control, still promising in our minds the potential for riches, status, and true happiness. He starts with separation by causing strife and divisions with family and friends by calling into question your self-worth, and he tries to remind us of all our past failures. If unguarded by the blood of Jesus, he will point out the insignificance of the life you're living or point out all of those hypocrites who try to practice godliness and righteousness and never meeting up to your expectations. He doesn't have to have anyone say a word to you—you do it all by yourself. Then when the thought is introduced into our minds, the Word of the living God tells us in 2 Corinthians what we should do as believers.

> Casting down imaginations, and every high thing that exalts itself against the knowledge of God, and *bringing into captivity every thought* to the obedience of Christ. (2 Corinthians 10:5, emphasis added)

When these notions enter into your thoughts, only God's Word gives us a way to defeat them by bringing into captivity the thoughts being held captive by satanic forces. James 4:7 says, "Submit yourselves therefore to God. Resist the devil, and he will flee from you." Resist the Devil whenever the Holy Spirit convicts you of the impending attack. This principality of separation and its minions of strife, un-forgiveness, and bitterness spirits can prick at you and irritate every last fiber of your being if you let them. As a believer, you don't know where this thought came from until it's too late and you've already damaged your testimony with family and acquaintances because you acted on these thoughts and allowed your countenance to fall or you opened your big fat mouth.

Again, remember you can choose not to partake or indulge in any fleshly inspired thought. You can be right about someone or something, but you ain't right with God because "it" has the power to overtake your sensibilities. Your testimony is all people see, and your self-righteous hypocrisy does more damage than any secular heathen could ever do, especially to children and family members. Bitterness takes root and infiltrates the other walls and gates of love, joy, peace, gentleness, goodness, and without these influenced with the love of Christ, you are unable to show temperance and longsuffering to family and friends.

We as mothers and especially fathers can destroy our children's self-esteem, causing resentment, anger, self-hatred, self-torment, and self-mutilation because they can never reach that unattainable standard placed on them. These demons of isolation, loneliness, and a lack of self-confidence can bring on behavioral issues such as anorexia, bulimia, bingeing, alcoholism, drug abuse, obsessive-compulsive actions, promiscuity or cutting with the ultimate desire by Satan of self-murder of the only creation made in the image of the living God. The first cousins of these actions that are just as damaging and far-reaching in their effects are selfishness, self-exaltation, self-pride, and self-idolatry. These truly insecure behaviors are rooted in loneliness and a lack of self-confidence. This lack of self-confidence rears its ugly head as pride, cynical course jesting, and attention-getting that only increases in severity as the approval increases with our approving laughter.

This selfish attention-getting spirit is rooted in envy, jealousy, and rejection from a mother or father, and it expresses itself as a Luciferian spirit of an "I, I-me,me,me" and "I will or why not me?" rebellion. Excessive talking with the need of constant approval and perfectionism is the telltale indicator that, that person has had their heart broken by a mother or father figure, and these actions are the consequences of self-preservation and protectionism from any future heartbreak from an authority figure. Isolationism causes rejection, and rejection causes accusations which cause envy and jealousy to create even more isolation, loneliness, and self-pity, all of which lead into addictions of alcoholism, drugs, food, sexual perversion, and sexual abuse. ("A More Excellent Way" Henry W. Wright)

Just as love is the foundation of the fruit of the Spirit, fear and hate are the foundation for the works of the flesh with all the spirit-world realities as their offshoots. Not only is fear the basis for the unloving and bitter spirits, but the hateful, accusing, envious, and jealous spirits are all connected and are the result of a broken heart seeking love, affirmation, and attention from a parent or authority figure. They all need to be broken, evicted, and filled again with the love only Jesus can provide. Still others that manifest within the searching soul cause many to fall into occultism and mysticism as they look for answers for their existence, future, and the eternal destination of loved ones that have died.

This is the whole purpose of the Word of God in the Epistles, and I'm writing this book so that you as a believer in these last days can fortify your protective soul walls and defeat these demonic manifestations with godly love and reach your fullest spiritual potential now and for eternity. This godly love permeates every fruit of the Spirit that emanates from your core, and once saved, your fruit bears more fruit sown to bear more fruit in someone else's life. As an ambassador of Jesus Christ showing His mercy and grace, we are equipped with the armor of God, a personal prayer language, the nine gifts of the Spirit, and the nine fruit of the Spirit. This all equips us for spiritual battle to defeat the four PPRSs, the seventeen works of the flesh, the seventeen spirit-world realities, and the myriads of demonically inspired lusts of the heart. Then we can till, sow, and plant more fruit to reap and expand the kingdom of God, spreading the love of Christ as a consequence of the fruit of the Spirit in our lives.

God's Word alone speaks of the spirit-world realities and the effects they have on every person saved or not, and only Scripture gives us the way to heal the wounds they inflict to our soul's walls that protect our spirit. Jesus said in Matthew that He will give us the keys to the kingdom, meaning that after we receive Christ as our Lord and Savior, we have been given the authority to evict any and every unwanted spirit from our soul walls. The real key is to find out where they are entrenched in our soul's wall and evict them.

> And I will give unto thee the keys of the kingdom of heaven: and whatsoever thou shall bind on earth shall be bound in

heaven: and whatsoever thou shall loose on earth shall be
loosed in heaven. (Matthew 16:19)

Again, I think it is foolish to believe that you as a believer are immune from satanic attacks. Your susceptibility to these attacks doesn't just disappear the day you get saved; in fact, it only increases. You were not born an alcoholic, but generations of alcoholics with your relatives only attract the addictive demons to your family line. If enticed by these spirits to partake, then the door is opened legally by you, and that particular indulgence is encouraged and the curse is perpetuated. With the baptism of the Holy Spirit, God's Word tells us that you are not only given your personal prayer language to identify and combat these demons, but you also then have access to the nine gifts of the Spirit and the armor of God as we spoke of earlier to identify, protect, and assist your spiritual healing process.

There are ten references in Scripture that are named unclean spirits these are the PPRSs of Ephesians 6:12. This Scripture tells us that we battle not against flesh and blood but rather powers, principalities, rulers of darkness of this world, and spirits of wickedness in high places. It is imperative for us to acknowledge and identify these PPRSs in our lives to protect our born-again spirits against these attacks as believers. His Word tells us that Jesus would not leave us comfortless. What? Why would we be left comfortless after we've come to the Lord Jesus? Why would we ever need anything more to worry about and need a comforter after we've been converted and are born again and are believers in Jesus Christ as our Lord and Savior? Unless, of course, once we've been saved and try to change our sinful fleshly lives and live in opposition to the Adamic natural habits we've become accustomed to and try to live in Christlikeness, the spiritual attacks will increase in severity from Satan. God has given us the Holy Spirit to protect and help our newly saved spirits heal and fight back. It only makes sense that as we leave worldly Adamic lusts of the flesh, that the god of this world would use every weapon at his disposal to make us fail—and he never stops.

As we read Scripture from Genesis to Revelation, we can see the progression that God has taken man through to commune with Him in the spirit again. From believing in one God (monotheism) and His laws and precepts with the Ten Commandments to believing in a separated people (Israel), He could then keep a priestly, kingly bloodline pure for His only begotten Son Jesus to be incarnated into this world for the redemption of all mankind. Finally, through His saving grace and the baptism of the Holy Spirit (the third person of the Trinity) we can commune again with our Creator in spirit. We can then maintain and expand the kingdom as Jesus' bride in preparation of the thousand-year reign of Jesus as High Priest and King of Kings.

That is why all believers in Jesus must come together under one common edict and dispense with unscriptural denominationalism in these last days. As believers in the Father, Son, and Holy Spirit, we all shall rule and reign with Him forever and there can be no hatred or prejudice toward fellow believers in Jesus or the true God of Israel, Jehovah. Anti-Semitism, racism, and cultural biases have no place in a true Bible-believer's heart. Like I said earlier the Jew is to be looked at as equal to all non-believers in Jesus as the Messiah but is still the apple of God's eye for acknowledging Jehovah as creator God for thousands of years. I do believe that God will honor them for their faith and they will be permitted into the outer courts of the kingdom. This is why He is God and we're not and He makes the rules.

To spiritually heal and protect our believing souls, we then are given the keys to the kingdom to bind and loose these unclean spirits that can oppress and suppress any born-again believer spoken of here in Matthew 16:19 and 18:18.

I do believe that Satan wants us to believe that we as believers in Jesus Christ don't ever have to worry about these unclean spirits after we are saved, which I believe is setting us up for future failure if not addressed and avoided. Why else would the Word of God continue to warn us through parables and direct quotes from Jesus to avoid circumstances and conditions that we could find ourselves in? There are *the unclean spirits* spoken of in Matthew 10:1, *foul spirits* (Mark 9:25), *the spirit of fear* (2 Timothy 1:7), *the seducing spirit* (1 Timothy 4:1), *the spirit of infirmity* (Luke 13:11), *the spirit of divination* (Acts 16:16), *the spirit of bondage* (Romans 8:5), *the spirit of slumber* (Romans 11:8), *the spirit of this world* (1 Corinthians 2:12), and finally *the spirit of antichrist* (1 John 4:3). These all can work independently but usually work in combination like the pack of wild dogs that they are, feeding off each other's gains to weaken our resolve and will to live as a believer.

This information is not only important to every unsaved person, but is more critical to believers who think that because they're saved, they are okay and they don't ever have to be concerned with these PPRSs, the works of the flesh, any of the spirit-world realities, or the lusts of the heart. Ignorance is not bliss in this case, but it is your eternal spiritual loss. There is no reason for us to suffer and to continue to spread our misery and bitterness in this life on our families, our progenies' lives, or on anyone else we come in contact with again. There is only one reason why the Holy Spirit inspired these writers of the Word to repeat these warnings over and over again—that is because God loves us and wants to protect His children from the pains and hurts of this life. No matter what the god of this world hurls at us to inhibit and deter us from receiving Jesus as our Lord or our rewards for eternity, His Word alone reassures us of our eternal victory if we choose Jesus as our Lord and Savior.

Chapter 20

RECEIVE THE HOLY SPIRIT

emember that just as the gifts of the Holy Spirit and the fruit of Spirit intertwine to build you up as a believer, so too do the PPRSs, spirit-world realities, the works of the flesh, the lusts of the heart with emotional strongholds interweave to torment and cause suffering and confusion to all of humanity—believers and nonbelievers alike. Unfortunately, the armor of God, gifts of the Spirit, fruit of the Spirit, and Holy Spirit baptism are only available to those who repent, receive Jesus Christ as Lord and Savior, and "ask" to get baptized in the Holy Spirit. Many spirits mimic the gifts, fruit, and the Holy Spirit of God trying to deter you from the truth, sending you rather onto spiritual rabbit trails in search of other places for answers like science, academia, astrology, gurus, mystics, and false religious traditions, all searching for truth. That's why your confession of faith and the baptism of the Holy Spirit with all the gifts of the Holy Spirit are so critical for your spiritual growth and your walk in the Spirit. Let's pray this confession of Jesus again with our request for the baptism of the Holy Spirit as the Bible states regardless of church affiliation, denomination or tradition.

Dear Heavenly Father God in heaven, I come to you believing that Jesus Christ died on the cross for my sins. I open my heart and invite Jesus to come in and be my personal Lord and Savior. Jesus forgive me of all of my sins and cleanse me from all unrighteousness. Teach me God's Word and fill me with the power of the Holy Spirit. Give me knowledge, wisdom and the ability to heal my soul. Show me how to live a victorious life that brings glory to only You. Thank you Jesus because I am born again and saved through Your shed blood on the cross of Calvary".

"Heavenly Father I now ask You to fill me with your Holy Spirit. I receive Him by faith in the name of Jesus Christ of Nazareth. I thank You Father, for filling me with the power and anointing of the Holy Spirit. Now, I can and will speak in other tongues as the Spirit gives me the language in Jesus name, ANEN!"

Without the gifts of the Spirit, Satan has deceived millions of people to ignore or reject the true Word of God and the laws that He has provided for all believers as they enter His kingdom to rule and reign with Jesus. Religious leaders, academics, and authorities of different sects of orthodox Christianity have cherry-picked parts of Scripture that they've been taught and can personally accept or understand, while ignoring repeated spiritual warnings, promises, and gifts to all believers in Jesus. Most if not all organized denominations have only a small understanding of biblical Scripture as it applies to their traditions and customs alone, projecting them as gospel teachings but having no real power or biblical authority to validate their positions.

Without godly direction in power, truth, and love, there is no joy, peace, longsuffering, gentleness, goodness, faith, meekness, or temperance, and in their place is the complete opposite. For love there is hate and fear of godly retribution; in place of joy there is depression, bitterness, and rejection; in place of peace there is accusation and condemnation; instead of gentleness and meekness are envy and jealousy; faith is an addiction and obligation trying to escape life full of doubt and unbelief in their trying and attain salvation doing works; goodness is occultism and the deception of the paranormal or a mystical religious dogma; longsuffering in love is rejection and negative responses that destroy individuality with the superiority and authority of a selected few; and finally temperance, which is the unloving spirit and lack of self-control that lead people to physical and spiritual destruction through these selfish, biblically ignorant practices.

For every fruit of the Spirit, there are multiple diabolical spirit-world realities that draw in all sorts of foul spirits, unclean spirits, spirits of infirmities, spirits of fear and bondage, and seducing spirits. These foul and unclean spirits have a primarily satanic purpose that includes any immoral and lewd sexual act that defiles a man or woman's mind and body to the complete elation of Satan. This includes adultery, which is the breaking up of your spiritual vows mentally or physically with your covenant mate. Also included is fornication or illicit sexual relations between two unmarried people, which can include homosexuality, pedophilia, bestiality, and lasciviousness where there is no restraint in their actions and desires but only excesses that relish in the evils coming from the heart to satisfy emotional, intellectual, or fleshly desires.

Biblical Scripture alone deals with virtually every thought or deed a person can do in their lifetime. Thank God for Jesus and the Holy Spirit so that we can reclaim lost territory and be restored spiritually. Fear and depression had monopolized my entire life after I fell at work and lost the vision of my left eye due to the MS. I was terrified to eat anything and would not sit outside in the heat for fear of overheating. I would not drive or climb any stairs because of the imbalance and fatigue I felt. Fear had gripped my entire being. One of the things I did find out was that any foods I ate that had monosodium glutamate (MSGs) or any excitotoxins in it adversely affected my body. After learning this, I avoided anything with MSG, artificial sweeteners, and artificial coloring, and I didn't get as sick anymore once I stopped eating them. What really hurt me the most was that if I didn't eat anything all day, I got sick so I couldn't fast at all. This put me into a deeper depression, and seclusion gripped my life. I tried everything involving natural healing from honeybee sting therapy to UV light blood transfusions to a vegetarian diet to vitamins and pH level controls, but nothing really worked. Then it hit me that I was treating the symptoms and not the root cause of the disease. God has provided these medical therapies to help alleviate the pain, but the treatments didn't remove the disease; they only pacified them, masking the root for a while. The root issue was still there causing doubt and unbelief to manifest.

Prayer for destroying spirit-world realities and associated works of the flesh that have damaged my soul was the first step to restoration and spiritual healing. Instant healing by an evangelist is only a stopgap and may not be permanent because of soul wounds and deep root issues. Yes, it is valid and true to go to an evangelist because it happened to me when I went to a Todd Bentley revival in Florida. After being prayed for, all the excruciating pain in my legs was gone, and I could walk longer distances, climb staircases, and drive again. But..... I had gotten my partial healing off of someone else's gifting and blessing. It's like I had adopted someone else's miracle. The rotten roots of bitterness, guilt, self-hatred, and anger were still there, and some of the imbalance and fatigue returned.

God has provided these spiritual gifts to many gifted preachers, evangelists, and anointed people for sure, but He doesn't want us to rely on the gifts given to anointed people alone. He has given the ability to *all* believers, and God wants you and me to do it on our own. For my faith to grow I had to TRUST in Him alone, I had to release my trust in what I could see, hear, taste, smell, or touch and trust in the promises of His Word. Not that trusting in the Word alone is wrong, but it can't supersede common sense and medical treatments completely. There has to be balance in spirit, soul, and body. When people grab hold of a nugget of God's truth and base their whole life and doctrine around it without considering the spiritual or intellectual ramifications, then you will see failure. Man's partial grasping onto God's truths from creation only validates His Word. What I had to do was plant a spiritual seed with prayer and the Word of God into my spiritual womb to remove each individual problem. I prayed and meditated on the Word of God in Isaiah 53:5: "But he was wounded for our transgressions, he was bruised for our iniquities: the chastisement of our peace was upon him; and *__with his stripes we are healed__*." I had to plant this spiritual seed of my healing in my spiritual womb and believe God. I had to confess things that are not, as though they were.

> Before him whom he believed, even God, who quickens the dead, and calls those things which be not as though they were. (Romans 4:17)

Every believer, male and female, has a spiritual womb that can conceive miracles, some can be physical but I believe the majority of my infirmities and most believers ailments are spiritual and are rooted in the soul. You have to conceive miracles in your mind first and then you take God's promises in

His Word and plant them in your heart where the healing is eternal and not only for the body that is corruptible and dies.

> Being born again, not of corruptible seed, but of incorruptible, by the word of God, which lives and abides forever. (1 Peter 1:23)

I had to take these incorruptible seeds and plant them in my heart. Most believers don't know how to believe for their own miracles; they think that they have to go chasing after someone who will do it for them. We need to walk in faith daily on our own. God wants you to conceive your miracle in your spiritual womb with God's Word, bear it, and deliver it, giving birth to your miracle to your soul first. As with my miracle, it has taken a long time to deliver it completely because of all my deep self-inflicted soul wounds, and there have been many trials and difficulties in the process stemming from the manifested emotional strongholds to my soul. Yes I am saved, sanctified, and filled with the Holy Spirit, but my soul wounds stop me from living in Christlikeness daily in every situation. My miracle was planted the first time I read the Word of God and planted these seeds in my heart. His promises are true.

> Who his own self bare our sins in his own body on the tree, that we, being dead to sins, should live unto righteousness: by whose stripes *you were healed*. (1 Peter 2:24, emphasis added)

> But he was wounded for our transgressions; he was bruised for our iniquities: the *chastisement of our peace* was upon him; and *with his stripes we are healed*. (Isaiah 53:5, emphasis added)

> *For as he thinks in his heart, so is he.* (Proverbs 23:7, emphasis added)

Only when you ask the Holy Spirit will He chastise you, which means that He will instruct you as a child is educated and instructed by their parent's loving direction, and Jesus with the Holy Spirit will help us through them. The difference between being an infant child and you as an older person is that you have to ask specifically for His help. Correcting, disciplining, and chastening of the areas influenced by these spirit-world realities, works of the flesh, emotional strongholds and lusts of the heart that can only occur when you specifically ask the Holy Spirit.

But to believe that just because you've accepted Jesus as Lord and Savior you're never ever going to have issues of depression, anxiety, fears, and worry, again is simply foolishness on our part. By voluntarily requesting the Holy Spirit to specifically point out areas of concern of the damaged fruit of your soul, it then is identified for healing and restoration. You have to want it, and you have to verbally ask for the Holy Spirit for assistance and instructions. This chastisement of your peace is only uncomfortable to your fleshly dominated soul. This painful admonishment only leads to loving correction with wonderful results visible to friends and family alike as they notice something different in you.

Like I said before, the obstacles and hindrances are primarily self-induced and likewise can only be self-corrected. Just as you had to change your mind and repent at your salvation experience with Jesus Christ, so too now you have to make adjustments to your natural and worldly lifestyle and change your actions to heal your soul with the Holy Spirit. God's not going to do it for you. He's already done His part; now it's up to you to act by removing manifested strongholds for self-repairing of damaged fruit to begin. When an issue or situation comes before you and you feel irritated or aggravated, take that thought captive, resist your habitual fleshly reaction of fight or flight. Loose it from your mind by taking authority over it then we are to bind the appropriate godly fruit of the Spirit to our soul and replace the fleshly instincts with a godly fruit reaction for that situation in its place. It has to be a conscious effort on your part to stop the thought in your mind from reaching your mouth, stop talking and shut that big fat mouth of yours; it will only cause more pain to you and those around you.

> Submit yourselves therefore to God. Resist the devil, and
> he will flee from you. Draw nigh to God, and he will draw
> nigh to you. Cleanse your hands, ye sinners; and purify your
> hearts, ye double minded. (James 4:7–8)

Yes, you're probably right about the reasons and consequences to a problem in your life, but you ain't right about really resolving the issue at hand unless you specifically remove the thoughts and actions from your fruit. What God's Word says to do is to draw close to Him, submit with your spirit, and stop sinning. Resist the Devil with your acquired spiritual gifts and resist the works of the flesh of anger, resentment, jealousy, bitterness, un-forgiveness, and hatred which ultimately leads to accusation with an unloving spirit that severs the ability to form relationships and causes violent murder with the words you speak (sometimes with seemingly irreparable damage done to the other person's soul). Only you can forgive and heal your Love gate and walls. Only you can stop your anger and prune the prejudice, anti-Semitic thoughts, and racism from your fruit-bearing trees. Only you can heal your wounded soul fruit and begin to bear the godly spirit of love.

I had reacted defensibly with anger and cynicism so often that it had become and still is a part of my personality and character unless I control it. The Holy Spirit showed me my soul wounds and the results caused by them, but only after I asked Him to through prayer and fasting. He showed me the specific instance that caused the wounds. I asked why I was so angry and mean all the time, having such a short fuse over the dumbest little things that not only embarrassed my wife and family with my fallen countenance, but misrepresented my Jesus. I had used anger and cynicism, coupled with off-color humor, as a way to protect me from the pain of rejection, un-forgiveness, resentment, self-guilt and bitterness I had placed on myself.

God has given His only begotten Son who shed His blood to redeem us. He sent His Holy Spirit to help heal and mend our broken soul's walls so we can rehang our gates as the fruit of the Spirit and be who we were designed from the foundation of the world to be. Only after I asked Him to show me my failures and after I acknowledged them as areas of my wounded soul as a born-again believer was the Holy Spirit able to reveal my issues related to all the fruit of the Spirit. I heard a Georgia preacher preach a sermon explaining my wounded fruit exactly. My anger evolved into rage in every one of my fruit, and I lashed out at any perceived discontent and irritation that occurred. He called it "rage-aholism" and I was a full blown "rage-aholic"—my anger was ridiculous.

As I tried to control it, my countenance that was the recipient of my anger left me unable to hide my frustration. Once I identified the impending reaction, I was able to recognize the trigger points that would begin my tirades. This is where our private prayer language is used under our breath, and our mind quietly captures that thought, takes it captive, and evicts it before it has a chance to infect us. Then I was able to defeat and evict anger and hate in my mind. I was able to consciously remove them from all my fruit and actually show joy in love.

Realize that issues like anger, hate, bitterness, un-forgiveness and a false sense of religious superiority not only contaminates all nine Fruit of the Spirit of your soul, but they originate from one specific issue, which has to be rooted out for healing to begin. If you're not careful, any of the seven emotional strongholds will latch onto spirit-world realities or the works of the flesh, coupled with bitterness and un-forgiveness in your heart (even as a born-again Christian).

These high level demons can open the door to demonic infestation (demonized) and spiritual destruction of your soul's walls.

From the fall of Adam and Eve to the resurrection of Jesus Christ of Nazareth with the gift to us of the Holy Spirit, it has taken six thousand–plus years for us to be where God created us to be. At His incarnation created in the image of the living God Jehovah (Christlikeness), we look to Yeshua (Jesus) His only begotten Son. A Jew from a line of Jews (Matthew1:17) on His mother's side whose lineage kept the laws and precepts of the Hebrew God Jehovah. A Priest after the order of Melchizedek (Hebrews 5) from the line of David (Matthew 1:18–25) on His step-father's side, Jesus was and is the Messiah who will come back for His church (1 Thessalonians 4:13–18). One who is without spot or wrinkle, prejudice or pride, bigotry or racism, hate or anger, religion or denomination but one based and grounded in the love of Jesus.

As born-again believers (John 3:3), sanctified and filled with the Holy Spirit we have to adjust our lives and allow the Holy Spirit to heal our spiritual fruit of love. The same love that is the foundation to all the other eight fruit of the Spirit. Then the Holy Spirit can begin to heal and repair our protecting souls walls as well as assist us to grow in Christlikeness and learn to walk in all nine fruit the Spirit daily.

Chapter 21

FRUIT OF LOVE

*L*ove is the first and most important of the nine fruit; it is the foundation of all nine walls and gates of our soul. This love fruit is not independent of the other eight fruit but dependent on them to represent our ability to love and ultimately show who we are as a person. Man's love is a many-faceted emotion that is given to all men and women at birth and is very easily perverted and distorted if not administered in godly purity. Love is a very complicated and confusing feeling if not given without considering the other eight fruit. In its purist form it is given in complete and utter innocence, it is selfless and desires nothing but love in return. All nine fruit work together in perfection in Christ to strengthen your heart and soul.

Love is not only the greatest of the commandments of God, it is the easiest and first fruit Satan attacks. The reason is because of its far-reaching effects on the other fruit as their common foundation for all of them. Satan's first line of attack is ambiguous and somewhat difficult to understand. He will not assault your fruit of love directly but rather very subtly seeking access through our soul's fruit foundations using hate, errant rationale, sexual enticements, fear of the unknown, and false religious conclusions that compromise biblical Scripture to appease the fleshly desires of the PPRSs of Ephesians 6:12.

You can start out with some pretty good intentions, but if not in the will of God, you end up offending all those around you with your religiosity, delivery, and sharp hateful tongue. The point I'm trying to make is that our scripturally correct point of view is usually muted by our poor countenance and self-righteous delivery that pretty much gets it shot down before it ever gets out. I have learned that whether it's with my wife and kids or other family members at a family function, it's the delivery that shuts people down and usually not what I'm saying.

Even a person you're talking to about politics or religious doctrine will shut you out because of the tone and word inflections given with anger, condescension, arrogance, pride, or self-righteousness. Your tone will destroy and make impotent the point you're trying to make. The Holy Spirit taught me something that I've adopted as my rule of discourse when discussing how to put the Word of God into practice, and it's the title of this book: "You might be right but … you ain't right with the Word of God." Anything and everything we do must be done to the glory of God and in love. People just tune you out and really don't hear a word you're saying, acknowledging that you might be right but you aren't right with the way you say or portray it.

The heart redeemed by love can't do anything but reciprocate with the same love given it, and only that love can bear the fruit of the Spirit—*God's love.* God's love is shed abroad in our hearts by the Holy Spirit, the same Spirit who when you ask Him to show you the cause of an issue you're battling with, will show you the root causes. The Holy Spirit will reveal to you any and all things that are displeasing to the Father or what you're doing wrong in your life. He will show you. Acting in a godly manner to people you do love is no great accomplishment, but acting with a compassionate, considerate, and truly sincere attitude toward those you don't even know or don't like is behaving in Christlikeness. How can we possibly act short or cross to a family member let alone a stranger and still profess our Christianity? Love is behaving contrary to your fleshly desires and considers the needs of others before themselves. Too many times, we can get in the habit of just being mean-spirited and get out of the habit of showing God's love.

> A new commandment I give unto you, That ye love one
> another; as I have loved you, that ye also love one another.
> By this shall all men know that ye are my disciples, if ye have
> love one to another. (John 13:34–35)

The word *love* is profaned, vulgarized, and almost completely desensitized by the world today, and in its place a flesh-oriented replica of what God designed it to be is common. Constantly trying to find love, people have tried to find it by fulfilling love with the lust of the flesh. Satan has equated sex with love, leaving an empty void in the hearts of millions of people. Still the word *love* best characterizes Christianity and the teachings of Jesus Christ. During His ministry, Jesus had expressed ideas that were virtually unknown in the Middle Eastern culture. Actually the Greek words used to define and explain the different distinctive meanings attributed to the word *love* have been either ignored or perverted in today's English language. Love has become an ambiguous definition that is often misrepresented and distorted to include inanimate objects and the act of premarital and promiscuous sex.

As a fruit of the Spirit, the two Greek words for love—*agapao* and *phileo*—are used to describe God's attitude toward His Son Jesus and all those who believe He is the Christ. Too often this misrepresentation of *phileo* love is used by homosexuals to justify their perversion. Not that their love isn't real between them, because I believe that it is, but that the act of making love between a man and a woman married to each other is not the same as two people of the same gender making *"love"* the way God designed it. This perverted spirit is a very high-ranking demon and its lies pervert the very essence of who God created man and women to be. The very acts of sex have been so demeaned and perverted that the identity of God's greatest creation is lost in the charade. Just as demonic spirits roam the earth looking for open doors in a person, so too do they look for families that are susceptible to these perversions. This greatest distortion of love has destroyed the purest of intentions and confused the minds and souls of millions of people that just want to show *"agapao"*. The God of creation has clearly shown His love for all humanity; first He gave us a free will and the freedom to choose to believe in Him, and secondly He sent His only begotten Son Jesus Christ of Nazareth to become a curse for us and die, taking our sin to the cross.

And I have declared unto them thy name, and will declare it: that the love wherewith thou hast loved me may be in them, and I in them. (John 17:26)

In this was manifested the love of God toward us, because that God sent his only begotten Son into the world, that we might live through him. (1 John 4:9)

Ye are my friends, if ye do whatsoever I command you. Henceforth I call you not servants; for the servant knoweth not what his lord doeth: but I have called you friends; for all things that I have heard of my Father I have made known unto you. (John 15:14–15)

But as touching brotherly love ye need not that I write unto you: for ye yourselves are taught of God to love one another. (1 Thessalonians 4:9)

The love expressed here as a fruit of the Spirit can only be seen as a gift of His perfect Son to an utterly unworthy subject—us. God's love to us, Jesus' love to us, our love to other believers in Jesus Christ, affectionate love to a son or a close friend, or for an inanimate object all have a specific Greek word and "love" can lose its particular meaning if not specified in context. Love is one ingredient that must be found in every fruit of the spirit and is what every block of our walls is set with. Love is the foundation of our walls and the frame of our side posts; compassion, mercy, and grace are the cement; sand and water bind the building blocks all together. Works done no matter their intent are useless to a loving God without true love. First Corinthians13:1–3 confirms the importance of our love walk when done correctly.

Though I speak with the tongues of men and of angels, and have not charity (love), I am become as sounding brass, or a tinkling cymbal. And though I have the gift of prophecy, and understand all mysteries, and all knowledge; and though I have all faith, so that I could remove mountains, and have not charity (love), I am nothing. And though I bestow all

my goods to feed the poor, and though I give my body to be
burned, and have not charity (love), it profits me nothing.

These first three verses declare the futility of boasting of the gifts of the Spirit
and that they are but only clanging noise without love (charity). Speaking in
tongues is only a noise without love. Good works, service, tithing, and sacrifice
profit us nothing if done without love. In verses 10 and 11, Paul tells us that
childish chatter and lip service may have to be put up with for a short time,
but the Holy Spirit will soon make us embarrassed over childish things we've
said and done. Remember, Jesus referred to you and me as fruit-bearing trees,
and if our branches are fruitless (without love), they will be pruned off and
burned as useless waste.

> But God, who is rich in mercy, for his great love wherewith
> he loved us, Even when we were dead in sins, hath quickened
> us together with Christ, (by grace ye are saved ;) And hath
> raised us up together, and made us sit together in heavenly
> places in Christ Jesus: That in the ages to come he might
> show the exceeding riches of his grace in his kindness toward
> us through Christ Jesus. (Ephesians 2:4–7)

> But God commended his love toward us, in that, while we
> were yet sinners, Christ died for us. (Romans 5:8)

> Love not the world, neither the things that are in the world.
> If any man loves the world, the love of the Father is not in
> him. For all that is in the world, the lust of the flesh, and the
> lust of the eyes, and the pride of life, is not of the Father, but
> is of the world. (1 John 2:15–16)

Besides love, the other eight fruit of the Spirit are *joy, peace, longsuffering,
gentleness, goodness, faith, meekness, and temperance* all should be based in love.
All must be spoken of in the plural as relying upon each other in Christ's
perfection. When confronting an issue, it must be approached with our soul's
fruit each having taken on the qualities of Christ. Then in Christlikeness,
you put on the whole armor of God to deflect any spiritual attacks. Each
one of your fruit must be girt about with truth, putting on the breastplate of

righteousness to protect your heart from being wounded, your feet shod with the gospel of peace for wherever you tread, the shield of faith to squelch all fiery darts that come your way, the helmet of salvation to remind you that you belong to Jesus, and the sword of the Spirit (gifts of the Spirit) to defeat the plots and plans of Satan. So your soul's fruit that surround your born-again Spirit are each equipped with all of God's armor (Ephesians 6:11–17) so that you may be able to stand in His love.

We will now go through each of the fruit of the Spirit individually binding the Godly attributes of Christ along with the armor of God, utilizing the gifts of the Spirit (1 Corinthians 12) to us. Then praying a prayer with your understanding and with your personal prayer language in the Spirit (1 Corinthians 14:15) we will loose on earth as in heaven with the keys of the kingdom given to all believers (Matthew 16:18) all the scripturally quoted works of the flesh, spirit world realities and the lusts of the heart that have become emotional strongholds in our lives.

Pray this prayer as you read it out loud for your love gate and the foundations of all nine fruit of the Spirit to be healed. There is power in the spoken Word!

Heavenly Father God,

I come to You to bind and loose spiritual issues that are affecting the Love gate and foundation of the other fruit of my soul. According to Your Word in Matthew 16:19

And I will give unto thee the keys of the kingdom of heaven: and whatsoever thou shalt bind on earth shall be bound in heaven: and whatsoever thou shalt loose on earth shall be loosed in heaven.

Therefore I have been given the keys to the kingdom of heaven, and by the authority of Jesus Christ of Nazareth, I loose all the spirit-world realities, works of the flesh, emotional strongholds and lusts of the heart as I loose all chains, fetters, and bindings on all generational curses, word curses, and self-curses cast upon me, my children, and my ancestors on my mother's side and my *father's side, all the way back to Adam and Eve that have bound me, causing pain and deep soul wounds to my Love foundation, walls, and gate.*

I now loose all principalities, powers, rulers of darkness, and spirits of wickedness that have tormented me and my family with uncontrollable anger, rage and hatred. I loose all un-forgiveness, resentment, and any retaliation caused by envy or jealousy for love; I loose all gossip, lying hatred, violence, and murder in word or deed for love. I loose all separation, bitterness, accusation to deflect any shame or embarrassment for actions that have been done for perceived love, and I loose all spirits of addictions and dabbling in occultism, looking for love. Lastly, I loose all works of the flesh, and I take responsibility in my generation and the generations on my mother's side and on my father's side, all the way back to Adam and Eve for the spirits associated with worry and distrust that could influence others to commit adultery, fornications, uncleanness, lasciviousness, idolatry, witchcraft, hatred, variances, emulations, wrath, strife, seditions, heresies, envyings, murders, drunkenness, and revelings related to love or the lack of love.

I am now loosed and free from all chains and fetters that had me bound in generations past and present, and I now bind to myself in their place the spirit of godly love. I bind godly love as God designed love to be—full of grace and mercy—to my Love gate. I bind godly charity, contentment, and courage to me in love, and I bind faith with forgiveness, hope, and hospitality full of grace and mercy. I ask the Holy Spirit to bind honesty and humility on all the remaining eight fruit of the Spirit; joy in brotherly love; and to promote peace in my relations to all mankind in humility. I bind the spirit of endurance, patience, forbearing with restraint in longsuffering to my soul's walls and gates. I now bind gentleness in kindliness and sympathy, with compassion in civility and respect in the face of adversity, and goodness as a quality of virtue and morality. I further bind godliness and reliability with honor and integrity, I bind faith in fidelity toward God, dispelling all doubt and unbelief and meekness with a humble submissiveness to God and His will, and to divine revelation by the Holy Spirit. And finally, I bind temperance to stand firm in the face of temptation with a dedicated determination to place the glory of God ahead of every fleshly desire by means of self-control, self-restraint, self-denial, self-discipline, moderation, composure, abstinence, sobriety, and that God's protection and righteousness be imputed to me in the name of Jesus Christ of Nazareth. Amen and amen!

Love is to be taken care of and loved by the living God regardless of our failures, and we reciprocate with thankfulness in our worship and praise. His love is unconditional. It is more readily seen in action than defined by words, just as ours should be also. Each fruit of the Spirit is illuminated with love, like a ray of light through a prism which results in the separation of that light into the different colors of the rainbow representing each individual fruit of the Spirit. So too should we as ambassadors of Christ walk in that Spirit. After forming the foundation for the walls and side posts of each gate, this foundation of love transcends each of the nine fruit and becomes a part of our individual personalities, character, and integrity. Each individual gate color represents a separate fruit of the Spirit and each layer rising vertically represents that particular fruit throughout the soul wall of the other eight fruit.

In our quest to become Christlike, we must first adhere to the basic tenets that Jesus represented as priest and teacher of the Jewish faith. These ten tenets were an established fundamental belief system accepted by all Israel, especially when relating to religion, life in general, and politics. Each one was constructed and formed by the precepts established and practiced through the Ten Commandments given to Moses. These principals are eternal, and they cross ethnic, denominational, and racial lines to bring glory to the creator of everything through His Son Jesus Christ.

Loyalty: "Thou shalt have no other gods before me" (Exodus 20:3). We are to love Him above all else, worshipping and serving Him only.

Faithfulness: We are to make no graven image or likeness unto God with which to share our worship, serving Him only.

Reverence: We are to hold His name in awe with godly fear and respect. There is to be no dismissiveness or glib familiarity with the holy creator God.

Holiness: We are to keep the entire Sabbath day holy as our soul rests in Christ.

Respect of mother and father: We are to respect and honor the authority from a heart of love with an appreciative obedience to law and order.

Respect of life: There will be no killing by murder of the innocent, which includes the unborn and elderly.

Purity: There will be no adultery, fornication, or uncleanness, but only pure thoughts and actions to all people.

Honesty: You will not steal or cheat; you will keep your word.

Truthfulness: You will not bear false witness in court or out; there will be no lying one to another, be it in word or deed, in business or taxes.

Contentment: We are to be content with what we have been given, either money, property, or position; there will be no covetousness, selfishness, or self-serving at the expense of others (Rosenthal).

Failure in any one of these tenets doesn't necessarily inhibit your entry into heaven, but it will limit your receiving your crowns and rewards as a child of the living God in the new Jerusalem. I do believe that you will be relocated to the outer courts of the new temple and the outskirts of the city with the unbelieving in Christ Hebrews and with the unaccepting of the Holy Spirit baptism believers.

Biblically the fruit of love as not only one of the gates to our spirit but also the foundation to all the other eight fruit forming our protective soul and visible personalities with the countenance that we each portray. Again these PPRSs are powers, principalities, rulers of darkness, and lastly, spiritual wickedness in high places, and they are high-level demonic forces that affect every aspect of love in our lives with the lusts of the heart and the pride of life. The demonic powers that be have great abilities to coerce us using our natural religious desire to love God and to be loved by God; this includes self-love and self-affirmation. These actions of acting in the name of nationalism and religious devotion are not only truly genuine commitments, but also the fulfilling of our fleshly desires and perceived emotional needs. They affect all our sensibilities and show great influence over our emotions and sense of reason by perverting all obligations to family and country with a myriad of spirit-world realties and emotional strongholds. In trying to meet false expectations of self-worth, nationality, and religious obligations, we open doors to religious high-level demons that are deep-seated and all-consuming. Principalities and perceived powers that have the ability to control a territory or area of our being are actually ruled by a spiritual prince that influences our every thought and action with a work of the flesh through some form of addiction to religious works. Jesus in Luke 16:15 said to them, "Ye are they which justify you before men; but God knows your hearts: for *that which is highly esteemed among men is abomination in the sight of God"* (emphasis added)

Pride, ego, and self-indulgences are justified by us to only satisfy our self-esteem and fleshly desires. Each one of these PPRS's play on your ability to love and be loved. God's warnings are throughout Scripture, and He has given us these four separate main areas of concern about love that we as believers need to be aware of. These warnings are a generalization of topics of concern for everyone saved or unsaved alike; each one needs to be addressed because of their ability to spread to all the other fruit of the Spirit in our life.

Bible Scripture alone gives examples and methods to remedy and eliminate these soul wounds that affect every relationship we have. When an individual has been traumatized or rejected in love by someone from whom they expect to receive love, then the power to love is compromised. These four areas of concern with love are *Un-forgiveness, bitterness, jealousy,* and *rejection,* and each of these can be instilled by a mother, father, or some other role model to that person. This can retard or even work against their ability to love or be loved.

If there is any real love, it is usually distorted and overly protective to the point of being obscene and unnatural. The other eight fruit of the Spirit are joy, peace, longsuffering, gentleness, goodness, faith, meekness, and temperance. These are all based on a foundation of love as well and can be perverted and influenced by not only these four perversions of love, but equally influenced by any combination of lusts of the heart, spirit-world realities, plus any of the works of the flesh we face in this life.

Let's take a look at the leaders and authority figures in our life and see if they have in any way allowed any spiritual principalities and powers to pervert any of the nine fruit with any of these four emotions. Pray specifically for the person who first comes to mind and pray the TRUST prayer for revelation of the situation that caused your soul wounds that make you act the way you do and feel the way you feel. Many of the spirit-world realities and the lusts of the heart are precursors and enticements to justify your feelings and emotional reactions. You might be right about each feeling, but you ain't right with God. Remember that His ways are not our ways, and God's Word alone speaks of most of these spirit-world reality emotions in the example of lusts of the heart in the first twelve chapters of the book of Genesis. God's Word alone discusses the various ranges of sinful emotions evident in a family, and only His Word shows us the correct responses to each of them.

James the half-brother of Jesus, tells us in his epistle of the same name that *"lust"* is to desire to possess something we do not or cannot have. The word is defined as "with great eagerness and enthusiasm," but if it is obtained through the motivated flesh, it is of no avail with God. As a matter of fact, your worldly, fleshly acquisitions are anathema (object of loathing) to God.

> Ye lust, and have not: ye kill, and desire to have, and cannot obtain: ye fight and war, yet ye have not, because ye ask not. Ye ask, and receive not, because ye ask amiss, that ye may consume it upon your lusts. Ye adulterers and adulteresses know ye not that *the friendship of the world is enmity with God?* Whosoever therefore will be a friend of the world is the enemy of God. (James 4:2–4, emphasis added)

It is very simple to receive the fruit of the Spirit as long as you're in the will of God and your desires are righteous and pure in the sight of Jehovah God. Your acquisition of material things along with financial wealth are God's desire for you as His children. Understand that worldly reproductions of the fruit of the Spirit, especially love, can be forced upon a family member, country, or population as national pride and family obligation but is a perversion at its core and is rotten. Your sense of obligation toward family, church, and the ruling hierarchy is artificial and rooted with the wrong tree or vine, producing rotten fruit. All counterfeit fruits are spiritually rooted alongside dormant good fruit and need to be recognized as idols in our life that constantly produce rotten or unproductive results. The God of the Bible doesn't force joyous adulation, love, praise, or worship upon Himself like the kings and rulers of this world, but rather, He heaps it upon those who really love Him and blesses all His children for their obedience.

> These things have I spoken unto you, that my joy might remain in you, and that your joy might be full. (John 15:11)

> I will greatly rejoice in the LORD, my soul shall be joyful in my God; for he hath clothed me with the garments of salvation, he hath covered me with the robe of righteousness, as a bridegroom decks himself with ornaments, and as a bride adorns herself with her jewels. (Isaiah 61:10)

Remember that the Law was given not only to direct us in this life, but the Word in Romans 8:2–4 tells us that the Law is weakened by the flesh and unable to overcome evil and sin, and even when done with the best intentions, we will reap from the seeds sown. Reciprocity is reiterated throughout Scripture as either planting seeds of strife, bitterness, and un-forgiveness or as blessings planting seeds of godly love, mercy, and grace. Either way, God's Word tells us that we shall reap what we sow here in this life or reap them in the next. Moral weaknesses and ethnic hatred are the root cause to most of the issues that we face in the world today, and these evil seeds of hatred reverberate throughout history. God's warnings of their eternal consequences are only found in the Bible. Only the Bible is based in love, and only the God of Israel gives of Himself for all of mankind, affording any and all salvation only through His Son Jesus Christ the incarnate Word of God.

> For God so loved the world, that he gave his only begotten Son, that *whosoever* believeth in him should not perish, but have everlasting life. (John 3:16, emphasis added)

And not only this, He gives us His Spirit to assist us on our quest to Christlikeness:

> But the Comforter, which is the Holy Ghost, whom the Father will send in my name, he shall teach you all things, and bring all things to your remembrance, whatsoever I have said unto you. Peace I leave with you, my peace I give unto you: not as the world gives, give I unto you. Let not your heart be troubled, neither let it be afraid. (John 14:26–27)

> For all have sinned, and come short of the glory of God; Being justified freely by his grace through the redemption that is in Christ Jesus: Whom God hath set forth to be a propitiation through faith in his blood, to declare his righteousness for the remission of sins that are past, through the forbearance of God; To declare, I say, at this time his righteousness: that he might be just, and the justifier of him which believeth in Jesus. (Romans 3:23–26)

Propitiation refers to the sacrifice required by God to atone for man's sin. An offering that would pay the sin debt in full. It is God who is "propitiated" by the vindication of His righteous and holy character through His Son, Jesus Christ, where He deals with sin and shows mercy on the believing sinner. God made by Himself a provision for any man or woman, free or bond, rich, poor, white, red, black, or yellow who chooses Him. Whereby removing their guilt and the remission of their sins through the sacrifice of His Son, Jesus Christ. Jesus Christ fulfilled every requirement of the Old Testament; this is truly God's love to us by a holy God. In Luke, Jesus speaks of Himself.

> And beginning at Moses and all the prophets, he expounded unto them in all the scriptures the things concerning himself. … And he said unto them, These are the words which I spake unto you, while I was yet with you, that all things must be fulfilled, which were written in the law of Moses, and in the prophets, and in the psalms, concerning me. (Luke 24:27, 44)

Wherefore the law was our schoolmaster to bring us unto
Christ, that we might be justified by faith. (Galatians 3:24)

God, who at sundry times and in divers manners spoke in
time past unto the fathers by the prophets, Hath in these last
days spoken unto us by his Son, whom he hath appointed
heir of all things, by whom also he made the worlds; Who
being the brightness of his glory, and the express image of his
person, and upholding all things by the word of his power,
when he had by himself purged our sins, sat down on the
right hand of the Majesty on high. (Hebrews 1:1–3)

Halleluiah! From His divine glory and kingship, His deity and redemptive
ministry, to the power as the God-Man "Jesus" with His sacrificial ministry
and His sinless humanity atoning for all mankind, Jesus the Christ is the
Way, the only way. His resurrection and position seated shows us that the
work is completed. It is finished, and He has shown us the way to heal our
souls to ultimately reach our spiritual potential for eternal life. This is "the
good news" preached and proclaimed to all of mankind, and love is the key.

Regardless if you've received Jesus as Lord or not, salvation doesn't preclude
you from satanic attack. Your emotions and thoughts are still susceptible to
spiritual provocation, irritation, and aggravation, as well as instances where
your heart is wounded and your soul's love foundation is breached. Jesus only
guarantees our salvation when we receive Him as Lord and Savior. Not that
our life will be trouble free; in fact, life gets harder and more difficult as Satan
tries to hinder you from your decision to serve Christ.

Every human who has ever lived is affected by Satan's devices, and when you
receive Jesus as Lord of your life, he no longer has you and he then tries to
get you back to live for him. When your name is not written in the Lamb's
Book of Life, you're already Satan's and all that happens to you is the normal,
natural consequences of the fall of Adam and Eve. If Satan has lost your spirit
to Jesus, he will employ every demon in hell that fits into the open doors you've
legally given him access to by your thoughts and actions. The actions that
you partake in allow principalities, powers, rulers of darkness, and spiritual

wickedness to have free rein with your thoughts and emotions, and love is his primary target.

I reiterate there are three types of love that Scripture teaches us in the New Testament: agape, eros, and philio. *Agape* is the word that most closely represents the English translation of "love," with "brotherly love" representing true friendship a close second. But all forms of love are open fodder for satanic manipulation and destruction. Eros love or erotic love has been maligned and confused with the God-ordained marriage covenant between a male (husband) and a female (wife) with every sexually promiscuous act done outside of marriage as sin. Each one of these can be perverted and demonically influenced to destroy any relationship we have, and if we allow Satan access through our soul's walls, he comes in seeking to destroy and devour you through your thoughts first. Pornography is today's fantasy machine spewing out filth to both male and female alike, planting seeds of dissatisfaction, unhappiness, and frustration in the privacy of your own mind—love has nothing to do with it.

> I love them that love me; and those that seek me early shall find me. (Proverbs 8:17)

> He that loves his brother abides in the light, and there is none occasion of stumbling in him. (1 John 2:10)

> Beloved, if God so loved us, we ought also to love one another. No man hath seen God at any time. If we love one another, God dwelleth in us, and his love is perfected in us. (1 John 4:11–12)

> Seeing you have purified your souls in obeying the truth through the Spirit unto unfeigned love of the brethren, see that ye love one another with *a pure heart* fervently. (1 Peter 1:22, emphasis added)

> Put on therefore, as the elect of God, holy and beloved, bowels of mercies, kindness, humbleness of mind, meekness, longsuffering; Forbearing one another, and forgiving one

another, if any man has a quarrel against any: even as Christ
forgave you, so also do ye. (Colossians 3:12–13)

Peace be to the brethren, and love with faith, from God
the Father and the Lord Jesus Christ. Grace be with all
them that love our Lord Jesus Christ in sincerity. Amen.
(Ephesians 6:23–24)

It also is very important for you to realize that there is no real order, rules,
or regimen to Satan's attacks. He uses any and every opportunity to entice,
squirm, and finagle his way into your life, Christian or not. The "rulers of
darkness" are not heavenly but spirit powers of this world that seek only to
dishonor and bring degradation to every man or woman created in the image
of the living God. Satan's use of "spiritual wickedness," extreme immorality,
sexual perversion, and deviant evil lawlessness deliberately cause harmful
actions to humiliate and disgrace people into feeling that they're just another
animal and that they haven't any control over their fleshly urges (not true).
If you are a believer, then his tactic is to convince you to believe that you're
unworthy and too dirty for God to love, forgive, and be used for His purposes
(again, not true). This is the sole desire and goal of Satan: your repudiation
of God the Father, God the Son, or God the Holy Spirit—the triune God
of the Bible.

Understand that you can be right about how terrible your actions were in your
life, but you aren't right about His forgiving you of your sins or His undying
love for you despite what you may have done in the past. True repentance
and the shedding of the blood of Jesus on the cross covers any and every
sin you may have committed, as long as you stop doing it and change your
mind (repent). You can be right about who creator God (Elohim) is, but you
aren't completely right about who God really is (Jewish faith). You can be
right about who the Son of God is (Jesus), but you aren't completely right
about God if you ignore and discount the Jewish roots by your particular
denomination. You can be equally right about the Father and Son, but you
ain't right when putting on denominational spiritual blinders when it comes
to the Holy Spirit. The Holy Spirit is the third person of the Trinity (God).

> For there are three that bear record in heaven, the Father, the
> Word, and the Holy Ghost: and *these three are one.* (1 John
> 5:7, emphasis added)

Any exclusion of any one of the three that make up the triune God limits your access to the throne room of the King and also hinders your ability to do battle with the demonic PPRSs as *they* try to capture and ultimately destroy your spirit through your soul. Because of doctrinal bias and dogmatic religious ignorance of the Word of God that "is" given to all men regardless of racial or ethnic persuasion, Jehovah is the God of all humanity and the unadulterated Judeo-Christian Bible (1611 version KJV or NKJV) has all the answers to this life's final exam we all will take once we reach the deadline and meet our maker. Not knowing this truth about who the Father, Son, and Holy Spirit are only complicates and detracts from the simplicity of what God has given to all of mankind in His Word.

Since Satan is the god of this world, he uses every inch of what we legally give him permission to use to sway us into participating in any of the works of the flesh or any of the spirit-world realities and get us to lust in our heart for them. Using the rational that "you only live once," "the one with the most toys when you die wins," or "try it, you'll like it" are again only derived from fleshly works and are very cleverly laid-out plots and plans by Satan to get you to dabble "only a little bit" in them. These justifications and rationales are spiritually motivated and are very harmful and destructive to your eternal well-being, and if you open a door, it's very difficult if not impossible to close it again without God's help. You can choose not to sin ... not to have sex; not steal, do drugs, drink or lie but it's a choice "you" must make.

This fruit of love is critical to every other fruit and is indicative of *who* we really are. You being hateful and mean to family and fellow believers in the Messiah ain't right with God. As I remember the vision I had of the perfect God-Man Jesus, love is not only the foundation of all the other fruit, it is what binds the bricks of our soul walls together. It transitions from one fruit color to the next almost seamlessly while strengthening and bringing stability to all of the other eight fruit with love vertically. Joy with love brings peace, giving us the ability to be longsuffering with temperance for those we love and pray for. The love derived from faith gives us the strength in meekness to show goodness and a godly gentleness as a witness and testimony to a spiritually dying people.

Love is the crown jewel of all we can ever reach or hope to attain in this life, with the exact opposite being an unloving spirit. An unloving spirit works in us to destroy any and every avenue where God's true unadulterated pure love can be revealed. Self-righteousness and religious legalism is the most common method used to destroy and pervert God's plan to show mercy, grace, and compassionate love to a lost people. You can be right with your opinion about the way people have acted in the past, about how they dress and how they might continue to mess up in your eyes, but you ain't right with Jesus. God's grace transcends all superficial and religious standards and traditions with mercy and the love of Christ trumps all that the world has to offer.

Remember that this "life- choice" is a gift from the living God Jehovah. Only through the cross of the only begotten Son, Jesus Christ of Nazareth is that eternal life-choice given freely to all who ask. The obvious consequences being the fruit of the Spirit as we walk daily in that spirit, a born-again new creature. Walking in the Spirit of God by exemplifying Jesus as we walk in the fruit of the Spirit and should be our goal and daily testimony. As we model Jesus in the way we walk, talk, and act through each of the nine fruit in our lives, we become a living, breathing ambassador of our Lord and Savior Jesus Christ.

> For what the law could not do, in that it was weak through the flesh, God sending his own Son in the likeness of sinful flesh, and for sin, condemned sin in the flesh: That the righteousness of the law might be fulfilled in us, who walk not after the flesh, but after the Spirit. (Romans 8:3–4)

> This I say then, Walk in the Spirit, and ye shall *not* fulfill the lust of the flesh. ... *If we live in the Spirit, let us also walk in the Spirit.* (Galatians 5:16, 25; emphasis added)

We shall all live and work for eternity in one of two resultant positions because of the choices we have made in this life. The first is to believe in the Word of God—the Bible—adhering to its precepts by choosing to try to live in obedience to that Word daily, where you have complete control over the physical, mental, and emotional situations you have been offended in. The other is to constantly walk in the flesh dominated self-righteous indignation of a religious denominational zealot that preaches religion over relationship with Jesus.

For instance, we can be offended by the responses by a coworker or family member's sarcastic and foul comments and you can respond in one of two ways. Either ignore it altogether and allow it to snowball and accumulate with their other offences or you can deal with it here and now. If then the offender refuses to acknowledge your obvious discomfort, you need to limit your contact with them. Forgive, forget, and forego any future contact as much as possible if you can by not allowing your disapproval with their actions to be a source of conflict or strife. Be the bigger person. This is a hard one for me and my countenance. I know that I have learned to shut my mouth when offended now I need to show Christ in my discomfort.

The Word of God in Colossians 3:12–14 says,

> Put on therefore, as the elect of God, holy and beloved, bowels of mercies, kindness, humbleness of mind, meekness, longsuffering; Forbearing one another, and forgiving one another, if any man have a quarrel against any: even as Christ forgave you, so also do ye. And above all these things put on charity, which is the bond of perfectness.

There are better ways to deal with family insolence and coarse jesting made entirely out of ignorance or disrespect. Either way, our response is the territory of where the spiritual battle is fought. Depending on our reaction and response, one of two things will occur: we can then first return volley with the same attitude of a self-righteous attitude and anger, or we can under our breath pray in the spirit, taking full control of our emotions and resolving the situation at least in our mind so we can respond in a Christlike manner. Longsuffering, gentleness, and love reiterates the moral and ethical stance you profess while your life exemplifies Jesus through all your trials and tribulations. To walk in the Spirit in every situation and circumstance is to have power, control, and authority in Jesus' name over the pain of seeing blatant sin or feeling the hurt of physical and emotional wounds.

One of my greatest difficulties as a man of God is keeping my big fat mouth shut, especially when I know I'm right about something, and I'm justified in responding with what I believe is righteous indignation either in moral or ethical instances—but I ain't right with God. I have learned that coarse jesting or blaspheming God's name can be handled quite effectively if done calmly and reasonably sternly. Especially with family who constantly do and say things to deliberately try to offend and cause strife with you just to see you react so they can justify their opinions of your hypocrisy.

My fallen countenance was the next area I needed to work on, knowing where the fiery dart originates from and with my learning to look past the offences I needed to show Christ in spite of my natural desires for retaliation and retribution. Even though we are saved and will live in a state of peace for the rest of eternity, if we choose to live in rebellion to the Word of God because of our inability to overcome an issue because of pride or haughty arrogance, we are going to be in a state of separation from the God of the Bible for eternity *in that area* of offence that we can't deal with. Regardless of how long we've been a Christian, our fallen countenance and our mean-spirited, self-righteous rage will not be permitted in the presence of a Holy God. Yes, we have made the eternal decision for Jesus, but we ain't right with God with all the excess baggage that we bring along in our spiritual fruit, and it still needs to be removed. Then the real work begins for us as ambassadors of Jesus Christ once we begin acknowledging and repairing our damaged walls. Our life will then show whose we are—either God's or the world's—by the fruit we bear. Matthew here repeats the metaphor that Jesus used to explain a believer's works and actions as they progress in their Christian walk.

> Either make the tree good, and his fruit good; or else make the tree corrupt, and his fruit corrupt: *for the tree is known by his fruit.* ... A good man out of the good treasure of the heart brings forth good things: and an evil man out of the evil treasure brings forth evil things. But I say unto you, That every idle word that men shall speak, they shall give account thereof in the day of judgment. *For by thy words thou shall be justified, and by thy words thou shall be condemned.* (Matthew 12:33, 35–37; emphasis added)

I believe that the judgment Jesus is speaking of here is not only confirmation of our salvation "being saved" which is a fee gift, but it is in the rewards that a believer shall receive at the mercy seat ("bema") that are earned by our words and works done after we are saved.

> For we must all appear before the judgment seat of Christ;
> that every one may receive the things done in his body,
> according to that he hath done, whether it be good or bad.
> (2 Corinthians 5:10)

Yes our decision for Christ is eternal, but so too is our walk in the Spirit, and this is where I believe many sincere, loving, born-again (all Jesus) believers are robbed of their eternal rewards if not their salvation altogether because of their continual biblical disobedience and ignorance of the Word. Not only are many newly converted believers deceived in their salvation experience with their continued sinful lifestyles (backslidden), but people have been deceived into thinking that since they were baptized as infants, go to church, or belong to a particular denomination that their eternity is secured. Nothing could be further from the truth.

The Word of God continually reasserts our need to repent daily, change our minds daily, and walk in the Spirit daily to continue the process of sanctification with spiritual growth in humility and love throughout our Christian walk. I believe many people are duped into thinking that the onetime salvation experience or their church attendance and affiliation makes them immune from the normal trials and tribulations due to our Adamic nature that was given to all humanity at our individual birth.

> Many will say to me in that day, Lord, Lord, have we not
> prophesied in thy name? and in thy name have cast out
> devils? and in thy name done many wonderful works? And
> then will I profess unto them, I never knew you: depart from
> me, ye that work iniquity. (Matthew 7:22–23)

So-called Christians who belong to organized denominations are, I believe, some of the most confused about their escape from damnation. The relationship we now have with God the Father, Jesus the Messiah, and the power we receive after the Holy Spirit comes upon us is imperative for our daily walk. I do believe that many professing believers in Jesus are living their Christian life ignorant to the Word of God and I was one of them, living contrary to its dictates. Therefore I do believe deliverance and restoration through prayer is needed immediately after your confession of faith to Jesus. In order to accomplish this soul restoration, I have provided a prayer for dedication or rededication to Jesus. Romans 10:9–10 and I have provided an individual prayer for each individual fruit of the Spirit similar to the prayer given in the last chapter on the Fruit of love.

To bind and loose any and every hindrance to your ability to walk in the fruit of the Spirit as you grow in Christlikeness (Matthew 16:19).

Through these next eight chapters pray the TRUST prayer with me out loud

Jesus answered and said unto him, Verily, verily, I say unto thee, Except a man be born again, he cannot see the kingdom of God. for each of the fruit in your natural language, and in your personal prayer language for identification of spots, wrinkles, and blemishes of the fruit you bear and prepare for eternity with Jesus as His bride.

Too often we think that God will understand our situation because we really aren't as bad as the next guy. The fruit produced by my walk was rotten and putrid. I was arrogant and self-righteous in virtually every aspect of my life, even after I was born again. I now know and realize as I look back on those days that I deserved the scorn and ridicule I had gotten from my coworkers, neighbors, and family members for my obvious hypocrisy and double-mindedness. From my Greek heritage and Greek Orthodox religious arrogance to my perceived socioeconomic financial standing, my opinions and prejudices about the "other" people were always evident in my countenance and condescending mannerisms. As with most of today's society, I too was compromising what little of God's Word I thought I knew with good works and miniscule financial donations. As a young man, immoral sexual practices, fornicating, and adulterous thoughts were there with every woman I saw, and I had a very liberal self-taught misinterpretation of Scripture. Along with the pride and a sense of superiority that I was raised with, my meager church offerings were negated along with any good works because my heart wasn't really in it. Youthful indiscretions are not an excuse but only a way to pacify selfish and ignorant actions and attitudes that I knew deep down were wrong, but I did them anyways. Thinking God judges people on a curve eased my conscience and many people (myself included) justified my actions of rage and anger with an "it is what it is" nonchalant attitude of self-righteous indignation.

Chapter 22

THE FRUIT OF JOY

*J*oy and joyfulness are the feelings of great pleasure or delight with happiness, gladness, and gratefulness in the thrill and delight of life. Of all the billions of people alive today, only a very small few are truly happy—and I wasn't one of the few. The antithesis (exact opposite) of joy is depression and without a real grasp on who we are or knowledge of the true purpose for our lives, then what occurs is senseless and hopelessness to our existence that invades our thoughts. The reality of despair, sorrow, and depression even to believers is so prevalent that we need to reiterate how much God loves us even at our lowest points. Even when we have destroyed every semblance of the magnificence of a creation created in the image of the living God "man," God still loves us and there is still hope.

You have to remember that although there is no sin that God will not forgive you for, that doesn't give you justification or the freedom to blatantly sin, thinking God will still forgive you. This is especially true today when most secular educators and commentaries are of the "anything goes" type with literally no real hope of happiness, let alone purpose for this life. This may be the reason for the desperate desire to accumulate more and more toys or stuff, trying to pacify the never-ending need for spiritual fulfillment with instant gratification.

Of the seventeen works of the flesh, idolatry is the greatest killjoy of the fruit of the spirit "joy." Idolatry is when we elevate someone or something above the importance of God, usually in money, work, or sports. I am guilty of ruining the day for my whole family because of my countenance falling due to my favorite team losing the football game on a Sunday afternoon. Because of this, none of my three boys really want to watch a game with me, and they have lost complete interest in sports because of my stupidity. I had made an idol out of my city's sports teams and had gotten into too many bad moods for my sons to enjoy watching a "game" with me. If it wasn't sports, it was work. If it wasn't work, it was the business. And if any combination of them was not meeting up to my expectations, it would trigger an angry outburst of cursing and angry banter (rage-aholic). I'm embarrassed to admit it happened even after I was saved.

The spirit-world realities of these lower-level demons had influence over me, introducing thoughts of resentment, accusation, rejection, and separation that in my anger, usually ended in bitterness and fear to those I unleashed my wrath on. Whether it was an employee, coworker, acquaintance, or family member, I had a short fuse and my displeasure of whatever my unattained expectations were was quite evident. Too many nights I had to collapse on the couch from mental and emotional exhaustion due to that day's stresses. Depression, anger, and negativity were what always seemed to be evident in my countenance, and it was overlooked by my wife and family and excused because I worked so hard. Even when on family vacations, the plant or the business employees would call on the cell phone because of some emergency that absolutely had to be addressed immediately I had to answer.

Many nights I had to stay late at my second job for fear that my employees were stealing from me (which they were). At the same time, I was heavily involved with the men's group at the church and my wife was leading the women's group. Everything was wonderful from the outside: we had lots of money (debt), lots of friends (we paid for a lot), we were leaders at church (spiritually unfulfilled), and at home we were living the American dream (charade). I remember asking God one night in prayer the summer of 1998 why I didn't feel content or was as happy as I thought I should be. The self-imposed pressures to succeed began to affect me, and I felt like a failure.

This is when I first prayed the TRUST prayer. I asked the Holy Spirit to reveal the reason for my discontent, and I wasn't ready for the answer. He told me that my whole life was upside down. By the amount of my time spent in each area I knew the answer. My business was number one, my job number two, my family was next, and God was last. What He then told me was that I had to reverse the order and put God first, my family next, the job third, and my business last. I didn't understand it completely at the time, but over the next six months of trials and tribulations, I would come to really understand His unconditional, unmerited, undying love, and provision through Jesus Christ and the Holy Spirit of the living Lord of Hosts.

Then … I was diagnosed with MS a couple of months later in November 1998. I told my boss, and the company terminated me within a month for a purchasing mistake I had made on the job. I also have come to understand that my poor attitude was probably the real reason I was let go. I did make the mistake but my disrespectful and obstinate countenance was evident to all who saw me at staff meetings. What a terrible ambassador for Christ I was, and I apologize to all the men and women that I worked with. Ken, Steve, Dave, Hank, Norberto, and Olek: I am sorry and please forgive me for my hypocrisy. In that same six-month time frame that I lost my job at the factory, I found one of my employees dead from a heroin overdose in the workshop at my business. Then another employee took the gas card and purchased $500 worth of cigarettes to resell for crack money. My other employee took the company van and went on a four-day drinking binge, selling some of the company tools for drugs and alcohol, and I had to search the ghettos looking for the business van. To top it all off, the guy I bought the business from threatened to take my house in order to pay for the remainder of the debt that I wasn't able to pay for the business because of my inability to work.

My whole world came crashing down. In a six- to seven-month period after I was diagnosed with an incurable disease, I lost my job, my business was failing, and I was being threatened with $250,000 lawsuit for my house. Why? Why did God let this happen to me? I didn't remember the warnings from God that He had told me only a couple of months earlier. I was a Christian, so

I thought. I cried out to God and asked Him to show me what I had done wrong. As I prayed and prayed and prayed, still nothing …

It has taken over ten years of me trying to fix my health in the flesh that I came to realize that I was damaged goods and I carried a lot of useless baggage that was of no use to God. Even saved and filled with the spirit, working in the church and teaching classes, I was still a mean, stinking thinking, foul-mouthed (mostly under my breath), rage-aholic. As a representative of the Lord Jesus Christ, I realized that in spite of Him, what was happening to my body, life, and family was the result of my past actions and rotten fruit seeds sown years earlier. I was reaping the fruits of forty years of rotten seeds sown even after I was saved. My anger towards my fifteen year old son Matthew with his disrespectful attitude caused me to punch the wall instead of him. After explaining the situation and cast on my right hand to my Pastor he told me I could not teach until I resolved my anger issues. The embarrassment and shame I felt as I explained my stupidity to parishioners was the last straw.

If I desired different results (good fruit), I had to cut down all the trees and vines that were producing the bad fruit and anger in my life and plant new good ones. I then had to accept all my failures, acknowledge all my hates and all my prejudices that were deeply rooted in who I was, and find out where they were in my past. That's when the Holy Spirit revealed my rotten fruit of joy and the inability for me to show love and true happiness because of it. I learned through the Word that I could eradicate these works of the flesh and lusts of the heart, re-till the grounds of my heart and soul, and plant good seed through the Word of God. If I wanted to produce good fruit, I had to plant good seed. As I humbled myself before God, I had begun to capture these outbursts and change my mind before I acted out my thoughts. Over the next ten years of trial and error, I accepted the consequences for my actions by word and deed and began to heal my damaged soul.

I realized that the majority of my issues were self-imposed and self-induced and that I had to deal with these consequences as the Holy Spirit revealed each one of them to me. There are no easy ways out of facing and dealing with your newly revealed failures as a child of the living God. Many Christians don't understand that the law of reciprocity or of seeds sown will return to you and come to fruition either in this life or the next, whether saved or not.

Only through Jehovah God, His written Word, and the shed blood of Jesus Christ at the cross could we overcome these issues.

As I prayed in the Spirit to Jesus and meditated upon His Word, the Holy Spirit gave me the acronym TRUST as I explained earlier in chapter 6. I thanked Him and I asked Him to reveal to me why and what was it in my fruit that I was doing or, better yet, not doing that inhibited my growth and healing of my soul. What He did was remind me of what He had said to me years earlier in the summer of 1998 that my whole life was upside down. I had to re-walk the actions of my life leading up to my diagnosis. I had to pray and I had to figure out why my business was number one, my work was number two, my family was number three, and God was last. Not in importance, but in priority—priority with the most valuable thing we all have in this life: our time.

God was last and my wife and kids were right before Him. The most important things in my life were given the least of my time, and the time I really spent with God and my family confirmed my priorities. Not that I made a conscious decision to neglect God or my wife and kids, because I really justified my neglect of them by convincing myself that it was all for them. That's what I told myself: "it's for my family." I asked when these perverted seeds of love and joy got planted in my soul? Most of what I did in my life was done because that's what I thought was expected of a family man to do. Work, work, work; be successful and make as much money as I can, then I'll be happy when I retire.

What I thought was joy was very planned and expected because that's what you do when you get married and have kids. Go to Disney World, go camping or to a baseball game, buy all the stuff your wife and kids want. You're supposed to "enjoy" it and have fun and be happy. All I ever really did was buy fun times at the expense of true happiness by working so hard I missed the most important things in life so I could go to supposed fun places trying to find supposed joy and supposed happiness. Going to these places and buying these things truly only left minimal satisfaction and no real joy with my life because I always had to do more, make more, and buy more. I can't remember a time that I actually laughed without making jokes with sexual overtones or ridiculing at the expense of someone else's appearance or actions. That was all I ever did—tease and make fun of other people. There was no joy, and my very existence was filled with depression, fear, and anger and that was only exacerbated with my newly diagnosed condition. Thank God I knew enough to go to His Word, the Bible, and search for answers. Even though it took ten years, I still went to the Word. He gave me these verses:

> Trust in the LORD with all thine heart; and lean not unto thine own understanding. In all thy ways acknowledge him, and he shall direct thy paths. Be not wise in thine own eyes: fear the LORD, and depart from evil. It shall be health to thy navel, and marrow to thy bones. (Proverbs 3:5–8)

> To whom your love is given, though you have not seen him; and the faith which you have in him, though you do not see him now, gives you joy greater than words and full of glory. (1 Peter 1:8)

> Beloved, think it not strange concerning the fiery trial which is to try you, as though some strange thing happened unto you: But rejoice, inasmuch as ye are partakers of Christ's sufferings; that, when his glory shall be revealed, ye may be glad also with exceeding joy. (1 Peter 4:12–13)

I was comforted by these words by Solomon and Peter, but there was still this contradiction in my life. I knew that I was eternally secure with Jesus, but the more I read the Bible, the more I realized that I needed to change my entire outlook on my life. I knew that God's Word differentiated the spirit from the soul, and my soul was very different from what I read was expected of a true man of God (that I thought I was).

> For the word of God is quick, and powerful, and sharper than any two edged sword, piercing even to the *dividing asunder of soul and spirit*, and of the joints and marrow, and is *a discerner of the thoughts and intents of the heart*. (Hebrews 4:12, emphasis added)

I also knew that my spirit was the part of me that was saved when I received Jesus and that spirit was as perfect as it would ever be for eternity. If my spirit was perfect, why was it divided asunder from the soul and for what purpose would God look at the two differently? Could the soul of a man be the part that backslides and is the reason why Jesus would say on judgment day, "Depart from me you worker of iniquity, for I never knew you"? I believe this warning is for all professing Christians today.

> And then will I profess unto them, I never knew you: depart from me, ye that work iniquity. (Matthew 7:23)

> But he shall say, I tell you, I know you not whence ye are; depart from me, all ye workers of iniquity. (Luke 13:27)

As I meditated on this Word, I realized that just saying the words wasn't enough to assure eternal salvation; it only gives you a ticket to the dance so to speak. What the Holy Spirit was revealing to me was that each of us as an individual believer who partakes and indulges in the worldly excesses that are afforded us in this life is walking a very tight line. God says He is a discerner of the thoughts and intents of the heart, and when I read that, I knew that I was in trouble. I thought if God was going to judge me on my every thought and intent, I ain't going to make it. The possibility that I could have very easily replaced the worship of the one and only true God I was reading about in the Bible with these worldly indulgences, prejudices, and my unmet expectations, I knew I had fallen short in my daily walk. That the desire to succeed in financial status and position in this life had become everything to me with the most valuable thing we all have: time devoted to thoughts and prayer. What are you doing? Why are you doing it? Is there something you really want for doing it? What are you expecting in return for your actions, for your time, your love, your money?

The more I read, the less complicated the Word really got. Once you remove the gray areas in your actions and your thoughts, compromising choices became clearer. Even after being saved, I had to learn that it's not religion, its relationship, and I could see in Scripture that my soul was the visible part of who I really was in God's eyes and my soul was what everyone else could see as my testimony. That every thought can become the lusts of the heart is a very real possibility to even the very staunchest of religious Christians.

This is the same darkness that I saw in the vision of the people's hearts as the exact opposite of the movie *Pleasantville*: instead of turning Technicolor, the people were turning black-and-white with each work of the flesh that they entertained. This is what the Holy Spirit was revealing to me: that this was exactly what I had become, and God could see all my motives and intents. I had become a very dark, cynical, and negative person who saw perversion and ulterior nasty motives for everything done. Who I was, was not a very good person or a very good representation of Jesus. Like I had said earlier, while you're still breathing, you can change and spiritually heal your soul wounds to become more Christlike. After you die, it's too late and the consequences of your actions and intents will be revealed, and you will be without excuse. I needed to catch my soul and body up to where my spirit was in Christlikeness. So I began over the next ten years to make it my quest to resolve the many issues of anger, hatred, and skepticisms toward all other Christians as I could.

As I searched the Scriptures for answers as to why this was happening to me physically, I discovered that not only was my body sick, but the more I read I discovered that my whole personhood was messed up. My love gate and foundation affecting my ability to love other Christians was nonexistent. I could see how I was incapable of showing real joy either. Not only was my eternity based on my decision for Christ through my confession of faith, but everything I did and why I did it would be determining my rewards—or if I even would get any rewards. I continued to pray for my lack of real joy in my life, and as I looked at my gate and walls of the fruit of Joy, I could see that my Love foundation for Joy had been destroyed so badly that there couldn't be any real joy because of it. I was depressed for not reaching the goals I had set for myself. This had only added to my despair as another self-imposed goal was not met. This added more stress and aggravation to an already perplexed mind.

Cynicism and anger for all the reasons I was rejected as a child and teenager, to why I didn't meet my life goals and other people's expectations in my life were always evident as part of my personality. I could see that my way of resolving and dealing with soul wounds was by my showing indifference and an unwillingness to commit to any real relationship. Hence the reason I had such a hard time telling my soon-to-be wife that I loved her until after we were married. Cynical, coarse jesting toward everyone I came into contact with was my method of communicating my feelings, and the joyless miserable man that I had become had to make jokes to hide how I really felt. I concluded that once I dealt with the four PPRSs of my Love foundation and gate, I could then begin to work on my fruit of Joy and rebuild its walls. True joy expresses itself in so many ways that its better shown in actions and deeds than in words like *love*. Joy unspeakable and full of glory is what Jesus did for us at the cross, and the joy we feel is born in our hearts at salvation.

> And the angel said unto them, Fear not: for, behold, I bring you good tidings of *great joy*, which shall be to *all* people. For unto you is born this day in the *city of David a Savior, which is Christ the Lord*. (Luke 2:10–11, emphasis added)

What did I need to be saved from now? .... Myself!

We are our own worst enemies, and the devils in this world spend *our* lifetime trying to convince us there is no God, and if there is a God, He doesn't care about us. Despair, dejection, and a cloud of sadness looms over our life's future with no hope. So often we try to create our own source of joy trying to convince ourselves we have joy, but it's fleeting and doesn't last. When we look to the Scriptures in Galatians 5:22–24, we see that the fruit of joy is listed between the fruits of love and peace, being closely related and influencing each other. It is easy to see how my soul couldn't experience real joy without love, or peace with God. Romans 14:17 tells us, "For the kingdom of God is not meat and drink; but righteousness, and peace, and joy in the Holy Ghost." If we believe that Jesus died for our sins, then Romans 15:13 tells us that joy springs out of us by believing in the promises of God and hope then motivates peace, love, and joy if we believe in the promises of God.

The power of the Holy Ghost is available to *all* that believe in Jehovah God and trust in Jesus Christ as our Savior. Power is given to us to teach us, deliver us, heal us, and restore all that has been stolen from us. Through life in general, our joy has been stolen from us through failures and disappointments, and most of the time we really don't know how or when it was taken. If we allow certain circumstances to envelop our life, then we become a product of the situation and live defeated and depressed lives. Nehemiah 8:10 states, "The joy of the LORD is your strength." Isaiah 51:11 and 55:12 say that God is our source of strength and if we seek Him, He will provide.

> And he said unto me, My grace is sufficient for thee: for my strength is made perfect in weakness. Most gladly therefore will I rather glory in my infirmities, that the power of Christ may rest upon me. Therefore I take pleasure in infirmities, in reproaches, in necessities, in persecutions, in distresses for Christ's sake: for when I am weak, then am I strong. (2 Corinthians 12:9–10)

Infirmities, reproaches, and distresses are all the results of sin in this life; the issue or malady is not the focus, but rather what we do because of it. How do we respond to the problems we now face? As we look to Jesus as the perfect example of the perfect soul, we see that He is our true strength by becoming a servant. Paul says of Jesus in Philippians,

> Holding forth the word of life; that I may rejoice in the day of Christ, that I have not run in vain, neither laboured in vain. Yea, and if I be offered upon the sacrifice and service of your faith, I joy, and rejoice with you all. For the same cause also do ye joy, and rejoice with me. (Philippians 2:16–18)

The reason that we don't experience lasting joy in this life is because it is derived from temporary things, and because they don't last, we feel empty and let down continually seeking joy. Disappointment and sadness are the precursors to some of the spirit-world realities which lead directly to the works of the flesh. The joy that lasts has its roots firmly planted in the love of God, and again only the Bible speaks to these issues as the fruit of the Spirit in our quest to attain eternal life. This idea of eternal life has but one source: the Messiah Jesus Christ. Through salvation in Jesus and the indwelling of the Holy Ghost in our hearts, joy is the natural reaction and response—"good news." Because the Holy Spirit will always glorify Jesus, the fruit of joy is the fruit He will bear in our lives first. Remember that we can hinder our spiritual growth by harboring resentment, un-thankfulness, un-forgiveness, jealousy, and bitterness which limit His operation in our lives. Along with love, your joy is the next area of attack Satan's minions try to breach.

Again, we have been given the keys to the kingdom to bind and loose the PPRSs, the works of the flesh, the spirit-world realities, and the lusts of the heart that influence us to hinder our walk in the Spirit in joy. Pray with me out loud;

> *Heavenly Father God,*
>
> *I come to You to bind and loose spiritual issues that are affecting the Joy gate and Love foundation of the fruit of my joy. According to Your Word in Matthew 16:19:*
>
> > *And I will give unto thee the keys of the kingdom of heaven: and whatsoever thou shalt bind on earth shall be bound in heaven: and whatsoever thou shalt loose on earth shall be loosed in heaven.*
>
> *Therefore, I have been given the keys to the kingdom of heaven and by the authority of Jesus Christ of Nazareth, I loose all the spirit-world realities, works of the flesh, and lusts of the heart. I loose all chains, fetters, and bindings on all generational curses, word curses, and self-curses cast upon me, my children, and my ancestors on my mother's side and my father's side, all the way back to Adam and Eve that have bound me, causing pain and deep soul wounds to my Joy walls and gate.*
>
> *I now loose all principalities, powers, rulers of darkness, and spirits of wickedness that have tormented me and my family. I loose all un-forgiveness, resentment, and any retaliation for joy. I loose all anger, hatred, violence, and murder in word or deed for joy. I loose all separation, bitterness, accusation, envy, and jealousy that has been done for perceived joy, and I loose all spirits of addictions and dabbling in occultism looking for joy. Lastly, I loose all works of the flesh, and I take responsibility in*

my generation and the generations on my mother's side and on my father's side, all the way back to Adam and Eve for the spirits associated and influencing adultery, fornications, uncleanness, lasciviousness, idolatry, witchcraft, hatred, variances, emulations, wrath, strife, seditions, heresies, envyings, murders, drunkenness, and revelings relating to joy or the lack of joy.

I am now loosed and free from all chains and fetters that had me bound in generations past and present, and I now bind in their place the spirit of godly joy to me. I bind godly joy as God designed joy to be full of grace, mercy, and happiness to my Joy gate. I bind godly charity, contentment, and courage to me in joy, and I bind faith with forgiveness, hope, and hospitality full of grace and mercy. I ask the Holy Spirit to bind honesty, humility, and happiness on all the remaining eight gates of the fruit of the Spirit; to give joy in brotherly love; and to promote peace in our relations to all mankind in humility. I bind the spirit of endurance, patience, forbearing with restraint in longsuffering to my soul's walls and gates. I now bind gentleness in kindliness and sympathy, with compassion in civility and respect in the face of adversity, and goodness as a quality of virtue and morality. I further bind godliness and reliability with honor and integrity. I bind faith in fidelity toward God, dispelling all doubt, unbelief, and depression with a humble submissiveness to God and His will, and to divine revelation by the Holy Spirit. And finally, I bind temperance to stand firm in the face of temptation with a dedicated determination to place the glory of God ahead of every fleshly desire by means of self-control, self-restraint, self-denial, self-discipline, moderation, composure, abstinence, sobriety, and that God's protection and righteousness be imputed to me in the name of Jesus Christ of Nazareth. Amen and amen!

Chapter 23

THE FRUIT OF PEACE

he fruit of peace can only be built on the foundation of Love, and without the Spirit's power, it is futile if not virtually impossible to find peace. The bigger questions for people to ask are, How do I find peace with God without compromising His Word? And Are my actions and attitude to other so-called Christians really in accordance with His Word? It seems to me that the religious Christians of today will put up with anything to avoid controversy and will appease the lifestyles of most pastors, priests, church elders and parishioners for the right price and to keep the pews filled. True peace with a holy God requires propitiation and reconciliation, and only through our kinsman Redeemer Jesus Christ, our sinless Advocate do we find peace with God. Propitiation is the sacrifice required by God to atone for man's sin that would pay the sin debt in full, not like the Old Testament law where the high priest had to offer up a sacrifice first for his own sins and then he could offer up one for the people's sin. For this, God did it once and for all when Jesus offered up Himself, the perfect undefiled sacrifice for all of mankind.

For such an high priest became us, who is holy, harmless, undefiled, separate from sinners, and made higher than the heavens; Who needeth not daily, as those high priests, to offer up sacrifice, first for his own sins, and then for the people: for this he did once, when he offered up himself. (Hebrews 7:26–27)

Since God made Himself the sacrifice in the person of the Son Jesus Christ, He cannot allow or ignore the actions of well-intended (good) people offering token appeasements and good works for their sinful actions thinking that they in some way can remove sin by their good works. Paul reiterates in his Epistles that reconciliation is needed from Him to us and that other than believing in the risen Christ, anything we do affords us nothing.

For all have sinned, and come short of the glory of God; Being justified freely by his grace through the redemption that is in Christ Jesus: Whom God hath set forth to be a propitiation through faith in his blood, to declare his righteousness for the remission of sins that are past, through the forbearance of God; To declare, I say, at this time his righteousness: that he might be just, and the justifier of him which believeth in Jesus. (Romans 3:23–26)

Paul tells us in the following verses:

Therefore if any man be in Christ, he is a new creature: old things are passed away; behold, all things are become new. And all things are of God, who hath reconciled us to himself by Jesus Christ, and hath given to us the ministry of reconciliation; To wit, that God was in Christ, reconciling the world unto himself, not imputing their trespasses unto them; and hath committed unto us the word of reconciliation. (2 Corinthians 5:17–19)

And, having made *peace* through the blood of his cross, by him to reconcile all things unto himself; by him, I say, whether they be things in earth, or things in heaven. And you, that were sometime alienated and enemies in your mind by wicked works, *yet now hath he reconciled* In the body of his flesh through death, to present you holy and unblameable and unreproveable in his sight. (Colossians 1:20–22, emphasis added)

For if, when we were enemies, we were reconciled to God by the death of his Son, much more, being reconciled, we shall be saved by his life. And not only so, but we also *joy* in God through our Lord Jesus Christ, by whom we have now received the atonement. Wherefore, as by one man sin entered into the world, and death by sin; and so death passed upon all men, for that all have sinned. (Romans 5:10–11, emphasis added)

The love, joy, and now peace can only be attained through our Lord Jesus Christ and Him crucified. Only through Jesus can we really see the condition of our soul and spirits. The consequences of sin in our lives can only be reversed by the shed blood of Jesus at the cross. His blood and His blood alone fulfill every requirement of the Old Testament; in His lineage as a man, our kinsman Redeemer; and as High Priest, after the order of Melchizedek. Believing and confessing the risen Christ affords us the privilege and authority to heal and mend the damaged walls of our souls. Being reconciled and redeemed by the love, joy, and peace of the living God only emboldens us as believers to utilize the gifts of the Spirit with the keys to the kingdom to fulfill our destiny as kings, priests, and coheirs in the kingdom of God.

By understanding and receiving the free gift of forgiveness and eternal salvation through the Messiah Jesus Christ of Nazareth, true peace is evident only in the forgiven soul and real peace is achieved and found only in the sinner's reconciliation to God. Without repentance and reconciliation to God, one can never find true contentment and peace in this life. True peace is contentment with self with no aspirations to achieve fleshly desires, but rather to fulfill each one of our individual godly destinies. None of us can ever meet the conditions required by a Holy God with our fleshly nature, thus we need the guidance and direction of the third person of the Trinity, the Holy Spirit. Peace as a fruit of the Spirit like love and joy transcends each one of the other fruit of our souls. Because love is the foundation of all the fruit, peace based on love is best explained as our admonition in Hebrews 12 which is to keep our eyes on Jesus and to be holy as He is holy.

> Follow *peace* with all men, and holiness, without which no man shall see the Lord: Looking diligently lest any man fail of the grace of God; lest any root of bitterness springing up trouble you, and thereby many be defiled. (Hebrews 12:14– 15, emphasis added)

The tranquility and harmony of people living or working side by side can only be achieved when both parties are living or led by the Spirit of God; if not, then your actions are to ignore the comments to the best of your ability, keeping your opinions to yourself and keeping your mouth shut. Show the peace of Christ with mercy and grace even though every fiber of your being wants to explode. Not adhering to the precepts of Christ in your observable day-to-day walk only leads one or both parties to feeling taken advantage of or worse yet, a sense of hypocrisy that leads to many spirit-world realities as noted earlier. The more you overcome adversity instance by instance, the easier the next episode will be and you will be able to defeat it in your mind first and then in your responses.

Family living in the same house is a perfect example of all nine fruit portrayed in the life of an individual, and any failure to control your mouth and actions only diminishes your testimony. The annoyance and aggravation of an unhappy mate or with your disrespectful child is a small test in our ability to love and show the godly fruit of peace in unity with the other eight fruit of the Spirit. Again, you can be right about an issue or circumstance, but you ain't right with God or with the seeds sown in you're trying to prove a point. The Devil is the prince of this world and is devoted to destroying our testimony and witness at home. Satan is in constant opposition to the Prince of Peace in your heart. He started his earthly war against God in the Garden of Eden, and he continues to this day stealing peace and tranquility and is not above using your righteous indignation or your church's denominational doctrines to do it. We have to depend on the Holy Ghost to identify and help us learn to live in love, joy, peace, longsuffering, gentleness, goodness, faith, meekness, and temperance. Galatians 5:17–18 tells us,

> For the flesh lusteth against the Spirit, and the Spirit against the flesh: and these are contrary the one to the other: so that ye cannot do the things that ye would. But if ye be *led of the Spirit*, ye are not under the law. (emphasis added)

The first step to restoration and healing your Peace gate and walls is to identify the root causes of the issue or problem of not having peace and living contently with those around you by nailing it to the cross of Christ. When you ask the Holy Spirit specifically to show you the issue stealing your peace and inhibiting your growth, He will tell you in prayer exactly what the issue is and you can then eliminate that thought that inhibits your peace. I believe that only through this spiritual identification of an issue through the Holy Spirit can true personal peace be attained with the living God of all creation. He wants to heal you … yes, *you*! He wants you to be healed spirit, soul, and body from the Adamic nature that influences us all from birth.

> Likewise *the Spirit also helpeth our infirmities*: for we know not what we should pray for as we ought: but the Spirit itself maketh intercession for us with groanings which cannot be uttered. And he that searcheth the hearts knoweth what is the mind of the Spirit, because he maketh intercession for the saints according to the will of God. (Romans 8:26–27, emphasis added)

The spirit heals our *infirmity* which in the English translation doesn't really identify all the aspects of the word. There are three different Scriptures with three different meanings, but the same English word *infirmity*: (1) Romans 8:26 "weakness"; inability to produce results, (2) Luke 13:11 "spirit of infirmity"; directly influenced by Satan, and (3) Romans 15:1 those thoughts which arise from weakness of faith that weaken self-restraint. The word *infirmities* is used to either mean physical ailments or for moral weaknesses which causes the soul and mind to be troubled causing peace to be short-lived.

Both need to be explained in context. Nothing we can do in the flesh or mind will fill that void. Only the intercessory assistance of the Holy Spirit as we humble ourselves to pray for the helper in our personal prayer language can we learn the root causes of our problems. Once the root is discovered, we can then begin identifying the PPRSs, the spirit-world realities, the emotional strongholds and the works of the flesh that are in our peace fruit that need restoration, deliverance, and healing through the blood of Jesus. Then true peace with God will increase the peace in our countenance that is visible to all those around us as well as we develop our ability to love and show godly joy with peace in this life to all.

> Follow peace with all men, and holiness, without which no man shall see the Lord: Looking diligently lest any man fail of the grace of God; lest any root of bitterness springing up trouble you, and thereby many be defiled. (Hebrews 12:14–15)

I had asked myself so often what I did that caused me to have to go through this debilitating disease that only until I began writing this book was I able to admit that doubt and disbelief, anger and frustration had entered my soul building larger strongholds to an already damaged soul. Not until I asked the Holy Spirit why this happened to me was I able to understand and see that what was happening was self-imposed and that these emotions needed to be nailed to the cross of Jesus and defeated. When the vision of Jesus' perfect walls and gates was given to me in one night, I didn't think about how bad my love, joy, and peace were and the effects they had to every relationship I ever had. It has taken me these last two years to explain and write down what I now understand to be the true causes of my maladies.

When I compared His perfection to my failures, I realized that this infirmity was not only a physical one, but it was primarily a spiritual one and was only the consequence of my own actions and thoughts as a person. Through these actions of prejudice, hate, and anger, I had given Satan a way that he could attack me and cause me to question my faith. These spiritual attacks through the open doors I legally gave him through my attitudes, prejudices, racism, and hate were still with me even after I was saved. I gave Satan and his minion's legal access to my body, emotions, and mind through my soul, and these physical attacks to my immune system were the consequences of poor and ignorant choices that wounded my soul with even more deep soul wounds. I only found true peace with the diagnosis when the Holy Spirit reminded me that *everyone* dies, but that the spirit and soul never die. Because of this, as long as I'm breathing I have a chance to heal and restore the damaged areas of my soul I had injured through my prejudices and self-righteous thoughts. My spirit is renewed with Romans 10:9–10.

> That if thou shalt confess with thy mouth the Lord Jesus, and shalt believe in thine heart that God hath raised him from the dead, thou shalt be saved. For with the heart man believeth unto righteousness; and with the mouth confession is made unto salvation.

My soul is renewed with these verses:

> He that believeth on me, as the scripture hath said, out of his belly shall flow rivers of living water. (John 7:38)

> Be not deceived; God is not mocked: for whatsoever a man soweth, that shall he also reap. For he that soweth to his flesh shall of the flesh reap corruption; but he that soweth to the Spirit shall of the Spirit reap life everlasting. (Galatians 7:38)

My body is renewed with 1 John 3:2–3.

> Beloved, now are we the sons of God, and it doth not yet appear what we shall be: but we know that, when he shall appear, we shall be like him; for we shall see him as he is. And every man that hath this hope in him purifieth himself, even as he is pure.

We as believers are all destined to be renewed spirit, soul and body.

Psalm 17:15

As for me, I will behold thy face in righteousness: I shall be satisfied, when I awake, with thy likeness.

First Cor. 15:49

And as we have borne the image of the earthy, we shall also bear the image of the heavenly.

Phil. 3:20-21,

That I may know him, and the power of his resurrection, and the fellowship of his sufferings, being made conformable unto his death; If by any means I might attain unto the resurrection of the dead.

Rom 8:28-30, And we know that all things work together for good to them that love God, to them who are the called according to his purpose. For whom he did foreknow, he also did predestinate to be conformed to the image of his Son, that he might be the firstborn among many brethren.

I am convinced that writing this book is the purpose for my life and that I'm to warn all my brothers and sisters in Christ as soon as possible of the deception perpetrated upon an unprepared believing people. We are to prepare as the five wise virgins and not the five unwise. We as Christians must come together, not conforming to any denominational church's doctrine but only in reading the Bible, studying it and changing your minds and becoming Christlike as you walk in the Fruit of the Spirit daily. In healing your souls, there can't be any hate, prejudice or racism toward any fellow believers in the risen Christ no matter how much of the Word they accept after confessing Romans 10:9-10.

There are many who profess Jesus but don't know Him, and many who if they were to die because of this lack of love, joy and peace would go to hell for the life they're living that is outlined only in the Word of God as sin. Look and find out that there is no expiration date with the Holy Spirit and He is available to all who receive Jesus as Lord and Savior. Either you believe that the Bible is true or you don't! You can't cherry-pick parts you don't like to fit your narrow-minded church bylaws or sinful lifestyle. God is good and He is longsuffering and waits for us to receive His blessings, but He is holy and will not reward you for your sinful thoughts or hateful actions to fellow believers in Jehovah God, Jesus Christ, or the Holy Spirit.

> Therefore thou art inexcusable, O man, whosoever thou art that judges: for wherein thou judges another, thou condemns thyself; for thou that judges does the same things. (Romans 2:1)

> But now in Christ Jesus ye who sometimes were far off are made nigh by the blood of Christ. For he is our peace, who hath made both one, and hath broken down the middle wall of partition between us; Having abolished in his flesh the enmity, even the law of commandments contained in ordinances; for to make in himself of twain one new man, so making peace; And that he might reconcile both unto God in one body by the cross, having slain the enmity thereby: And came and preached peace to you which were afar off, and to them that were nigh. For through him we both have access by one Spirit unto the Father. (Ephesians 2:13–18)

> And the peace of God, which passes all understanding, shall keep your hearts and minds through Christ Jesus. (Philippians 4:7)

Receive assurance and peace in Jesus Christ for eternity as you pray this prayer out loud again to declare with your mouth what you believe in your heart and the promises of God's words which call those things which be not as though they were to His glory using you as a living testimony and witness to expand His kingdom in love, joy, peace, and longsuffering.

> *Heavenly Father God,*

> *I come to You to bind and loose spiritual issues that are affecting the Peace gate and foundation of this fruit of peace to my soul. According to Your Word in Matthew 16:19*

And I will give unto thee the keys of the kingdom of heaven: and whatsoever thou shalt bind on earth shall be bound in heaven: and whatsoever thou shalt loose on earth shall be loosed in heaven.

Therefore I have been given the keys to the kingdom of heaven, and by the authority of Jesus Christ of Nazareth, I loose all the spirit-world realities, works of the flesh, and lusts of the heart to my Peace gate. I loose all chains, fetters, and bindings on all generational curses, word curses, and self-curses cast upon me, my children, and my ancestors on my mother's side and my father's side, all the way back to Adam and Eve that have bound me, causing pain and deep soul wounds to my Peace walls and gates.

I now loose all principalities, powers, rulers of darkness, and spirits of wickedness that have tormented me and my family for generations. I loose all un-forgiveness, resentment, and any retaliation for wanting to show peace with my Jewish brothers. I loose all anger, hatred, violence, and murder in word or deed for peace with all races of fellow believers in the risen Christ. I loose all separation, bitterness, accusation, envy, and jealousy that has been done for perceived peace, and I loose all spirits of addictions and dabbling in occultism looking for peace. Lastly, I loose all works of the flesh in peace, and I take responsibility in my generation and the generations on my mother's side and on my father's side, all the way back to Adam and Eve for the spirits associated and influencing adultery, fornications, uncleanness, lasciviousness, idolatry, witchcraft, hatred, variances, emulations, wrath, strife, seditions, heresies, envyings, murders, drunkenness, and revelings relating to peace or the lack of peace.

I am now loosed and free from all chains and fetters that had me bound in generations past and present, and I now bind in their place the spirit of godly peace to me. I bind godly love, joy, and true peace as God designed these gates to be full of grace, mercy, and happiness to my soul. I bind godly charity, contentment, and

*courage to me in peace, and I bind faith with forgiveness, hope,
and hospitality full of grace and mercy. I ask the Holy Spirit
to bind honesty, humility, and happiness in peace on all the
remaining gates of the fruit of the Spirit; to give peace in brotherly
love; and to promote peace in our relations to all mankind in
humility. I bind the spirit of enduring, patience, forbearing with
restraint in longsuffering to my soul's walls and gate of Peace. I
now bind gentleness in kindliness and sympathy, with compassion
in civility and respect in the face of adversity, and goodness as
a quality of virtue and morality. I further bind godliness and
reliability with honor and integrity. I bind faith in fidelity toward
God, dispelling all doubt, unbelief, and depression with a humble
submissiveness to God and His will, and to divine revelation by
the Holy Spirit. And finally, I bind temperance to stand firm
in the face of temptation with a dedicated determination to
place the glory of God ahead of every fleshly desire by means of
self-control, self-restraint, self-denial, self-discipline, moderation,
composure, abstinence, sobriety, and that God's protection and
righteousness be imputed to me in the name of Jesus Christ of
Nazareth. Amen and amen!*

Chapter 21

THE FRUIT OF LONGSUFFERING

Love suffers long, and is kind; love envies not; love vaunted not itself, is not puffed up, Doth not behave itself unseemly, seeks not her own, is not easily provoked, thinks no evil; Rejoices not in iniquity, but rejoices in the truth; Bears all things, believeth all things, hopeth all things, endureth all things. (1 Corinthians 13:4)

The Lord is not slack concerning his promise, as some men count slackness; but is longsuffering to us-ward, not willing that any should perish, but that all should come to repentance. (2 Peter 3:9)

Here are two aspects of longsuffering that we should be aware of in this Scripture. First is in God's forbearance with humanity as a whole after the flood and His promise not to destroy the earth with water again after the multiple failures of man. The longsuffering of God is incomprehensible to this instantly gratifying people of today.

> Then Jesus answered and said, O faithless and perverse
> generation, how long shall I be with you? how long shall I
> suffer you? (Matthew 17:17)

His patience and refraining from utterly destroying all of mankind again is a testament of His love for us and is exemplified through the incarnation of His Son Jesus Christ the Messiah.

Secondly, longsuffering is the aspect of our character that is improved as we grow in Christlikeness. It is in our patient longsuffering with those we love and care for as we mature as Christians praying for answers. Remember that God has provided us with His Holy Spirit to intercede for us when all our fleshly attempts to overcome an issue have failed and we don't know what or how to pray anymore. It is through our supplication and intercessory prayers that we receive relief and comfort through answered prayer found only in His Word. As we submit and quit with our natural instincts of fighting or running away from confrontation, our prayers will begin to see victories.

To our own detriment, living in an instantly gratified society not receiving answers immediately after asking, we often give up and succumb to defeat when we should be nailing our flesh to the cross (figuratively speaking). This defeatist attitude of "it is what it is" or "oh well" attitude only produces doubt and unbelief, further solidifying failure. The Holy Spirit knows our needs and knows the desires of our hearts, and He will intercede on our behalf when our words seem inadequate and fall short (personal prayer language). Because we don't know the hindrances to unanswered prayers completely, the omniscient God of all creation has given us His Holy Spirit to stand in the gap and carry everything in our personal prayer language to God the Father. He will show you ... but only if you ask and only if you are willing to change your mind. Remember, you can be right about an issue and resolution seems impossible, but you ain't right about your reaction in sticking with your lousy countenance when their name is mentioned. God's Word along with your travailing prayers will tear down strongholds and rebuild damaged walls, but you have to want to.

Synonyms for *longsuffering* are *patience, endurance, tolerance, restraint, forgiving, accommodating,* and *selflessness,* not in confrontation but in prayer for the offender and your hard heart. I am continually amazed at the arrogance and the level of self-importance many liberally minded so-called pastors and church leaders have tolerated for the sake of numbers of "paying" parishioners in the pews. My stomach turns as televangelists beg and promise the ungivable for filthy lucre on television. Only the Judeo-Christian God has the remedy for pain caused by deep soul wounds and hateful mean people who don't even know how to be nice.

Unless forced to go to church as children or introduced to the Lord Jesus as a last resort, most people in this fleshly dominated world will suffer physically and perish spiritually. The message of becoming an overcomer is lost in feel-good sermons and coddling seminars instead of getting to the root of the damaged soul issue. Many hurt brothers and sisters in Christ put on a phony, happy Christian charade but inside are suffering and have put up an impregnable soul wall barricade because of being hurt in the past. The ignorant youth of today think it folly to follow a four-thousand-year-old book with its outdated rules and unfair regulations, but only the cross of Jesus and God's longsuffering patience can fill that void and loneliness. It's much easier to ignore the spiritual influences to our battered soul than to believe in the demonic war we face as believers. We believers are the ones who need to be longsuffering in our prayers for offenders and/or offences to our damaged soul fruit. Again, we need to come to the Lord with the offence in private prayer, audibly taking that offence captive and defeating it by nailing it to the cross of Jesus.

Uncertainty of the historic hope of maybe making it by being a good enough person or giving enough offerings will help you end up in a good place. All I know is that in my personal face with death three times that nothing but the blessed assurance of Jesus the Christ makes this life bearable, giving me peace with my maker in the hope of spending eternity in His presence.

Heavenly Father God,

I come before You to bind and loose spiritual issues that are affecting the Longsuffering gate of my life and its influences to all the other fruit of my soul. According to Your Word in Matthew 16:19,

And I will give unto thee the keys of the kingdom of heaven: and whatsoever thou shalt bind on earth shall be bound in heaven: and whatsoever thou shalt loose on earth shall be loosed in heaven.

Therefore I have been given the keys to the kingdom of heaven and by the authority of Jesus Christ of Nazareth, I loose all the spirit-world realities and works of the flesh. I loose all chains, fetters, and bindings in all generational curses, word curses, and self-curses cast upon me, my children, and my ancestors on my mother's side and my father's side, all the way back to Adam and Eve that have bound me, causing pain and deep soul wounds in my unwillingness to accept delays when necessary to repair my walls and gates of patient waiting and suffering long until my prayers are answered.

I now loose all principalities, powers, rulers of darkness, and spirits of wickedness that have tormented me and my family with impatience and frustrations. I loose all un-forgiveness, resentment, and any retaliation to those I love. I loose all anger, hatred, violence, and murder in word or deed for not meeting my selfish unwarranted expectations. I loose all separation, bitterness, accusation, envy, and jealousy that have been done for my perceived intolerances, and I loose all spirits of addictions and dabbling in drugs, looking for relief affecting my countenance and my gate and walls of Longsuffering. Lastly, I loose all the works of the flesh, and I take responsibility in my generation and the generations on my mother's side and on my father's side, all the way back to Adam and Eve for the spirits associated and influencing adultery, fornications, uncleanness, lasciviousness, idolatry, witchcraft, hatred, variances, emulations, wrath, strife, seditions, heresies, envying's, murders, drunkenness, and revelings relating to my patience or the lack of tolerance.

I am now loosed and free myself from all chains and fetters that had me and my family bound for generations past and present with the Longsuffering gate and walls, and I command them to go to the dark, dry places of the universe to await judgment by Jesus. I now bind in their place the spirit of Godly patience to me. I bind Godly love, joy, peace, and longsuffering as God designed my soul to be full of grace, mercy, and happiness to all my soul gates. I bind godly charity, contentment, and courage to me in longsuffering, and I bind faith with forgiveness, hope, and hospitality full of grace and mercy. I ask the Holy Spirit to bind honesty, humility, and contentment on all the remaining eight gates associated to the fruit of longsuffering in spirit. I bind restraint in brotherly love and to promote peace in all relations to all mankind in humility. I bind the spirit of enduring patience, forbearing with restraint in longsuffering to my soul's walls and gates. I now bind gentleness in kindliness and sympathy, with compassion in civility and respect in the face of adversity, goodness as a quality of virtue and morality binding godliness and reliability with honor and integrity. I bind faith in fidelity toward God, dispelling all doubt, unbelief and depression with a humble submissiveness to God and His will, and to divine revelation by the Holy Spirit. And finally, I bind longsuffering in selfless patience to stand firm in the face of temptation with a dedicated determination of perseverance to the glory of God ahead of every fleshly desire by means of self-control, self-restraint, self-denial, self-discipline, moderation, composure, abstinence, sobriety, and that God's protection and righteousness to be imputed to me in the name of Jesus Christ of Nazareth. Amen and amen!

Chapter 25

THE FRUIT OF GENTLENESS

Kindness, tenderness, and gentleness are not very sought-after traits in this ruthless cutthroat world we live in. History bears out these facts as to how cruel and ruthless man is to his fellow man in word or deed. Whether fellow Christians or a secular non-religious person the reality of what is done in order to achieve their own personal, national, or church goals is anything but Christlike. You would think that the Christian of other denominations would have advanced in civility, mercy, and grace toward each other, especially toward other believers let alone people in the same church pew where they attend Sunday service. It is a shame and anathema to God how many believers in the risen Christ would murder and go to war over who is in power and authority in ignorance of Scripture and never really learning the truth of how to live daily with Godly love like Jesus taught. These satanic-inspired conflicts would be completely alleviated if the truth of the gospel teachings of the Bible were taught as they should.

When Jesus spoke to the people, He spoke with words as a man who had power, authority, and a distinctive quality of an educated man in the Law as He spoke of the religious man's hypocrisy and about hell awaiting the religious zealots. Jesus represented Himself as the Good Shepherd who loved His sheep and whose sheep loved Him and were not afraid of Him. His method of proclaiming the love of the Father to His children was given to them with an example most of the hearers would be familiar with. Not only did He compare Himself to a shepherd, but He compared the people to the sheep and said that if not ministered to properly with love, joy and peace they could be led astray and lost. In Psalm 23, King David speaks some 950 years before of the same shepherd that the apostle John was witness to in the New Testament Gospels. In John 10:1–2, Jesus is that good shepherd.

> *The LORD is my shepherd*; I shall not want.
> He maketh me to lie down in green pastures: he leadeth me beside the still waters.
> He restoreth my soul: he leadeth me in the paths of righteousness for his name's sake.
> Yea, though I walk through the valley of the shadow of death, I will fear no evil: for thou art with me; thy rod and thy staff they comfort me.
> Thou preparest a table before me in the presence of mine enemies: thou anointest my head with oil; my cup runneth over.
> Surely goodness and mercy shall follow me all the days of my life: and I will dwell in the house of the LORD for ever. (Psalm 23, emphasis added)

> Verily, verily, I say unto you, He that entereth not by the door into the sheepfold, but climbeth up some other way, the same is a thief and a robber. But he that entereth in by the door is *the shepherd of the sheep*. (John 10:1–2, emphasis added)

Only if you look past your prejudices of the Jew and read Scripture in its entirety, Old and New Testaments together, do you see these two very different men. King David and the apostle John speak of the same shepherd—the Lord Jesus Christ the Messiah.

DIMITRI YANULI

In Matthew, Mark, Luke, and John, Jesus is the essence of gentleness. He represented Himself as "the good Shepherd who loved His sheep, and whose sheep loved Him and were not afraid of Him (Know Your Bible Series, 60–62).

Hear His invitation in Matthew 11:28–30.

> Come unto me, all ye that labor and are heavy laden, and I will give you rest. Take my yoke upon you, and learn of me; for I am meek and lowly in heart: and ye shall find rest unto your souls. For my yoke is easy, and my burden is light.

Paul wrote the following:

> Be kindly affectionate one to another with brotherly love; in honor preferring one another. (Romans 12:10)

> Put on therefore, as the elect of God, holy and beloved, bowels of mercies, kindness, humbleness of mind, meekness, longsuffering; Forbearing one another, and forgiving one another, if any man have a quarrel against any: even as Christ forgave you, so also do ye. And above all these things put on charity (love), which is the bond of perfectness. And let the peace of God rule in your hearts, to the which also ye are called in one body; and be ye thankful. (Colossians 3:12–15)

It is more admirable to point out your own failures and shortcomings than to ridicule and mock those who are less fortunate or knowledgeable than you, and to use these instances in retrospect fully acknowledging them as a way to review and grow in Christlikeness. Forgiving oneself of past failures is key to your ability to showing gentleness without being short or condescending especially to those you love.

> *Heavenly Father God,*

> *I come to You to bind and loose spiritual issues that are affecting my Gentleness gate and foundation of the fruit of my soul. According to Your Word in Matthew 16:19*

And I will give unto thee the keys of the kingdom of heaven: and whatsoever thou shalt bind on earth shall be bound in heaven: and whatsoever thou shalt loose on earth shall be loosed in heaven.

Therefore I have been given the keys to the kingdom of heaven, and by the authority of Jesus Christ of Nazareth, I loose all the spirit-world realities and works of the flesh. I loose all chains, fetters, and bindings on all generational curses, word curses, and self-curses cast upon me, my children, and my ancestors on my mother's side and my father's side, all the way back to Adam and Eve that have bound me, causing pain and deep soul wounds to my Gentleness walls and gates.

I now loose all principalities, powers, rulers of darkness, and spirits of wickedness that have tormented me and my family. I loose all unforgiveness, resentment, and any retaliation for compassion's sake. I loose all anger, hatred, violence, and murder in word or deed for kindness. I loose all separation, bitterness, accusation, envy, and jealousy that have been done for perceived kindliness, and I loose all spirits of addictions and dabbling in occultism looking for serenity. Lastly, I loose all works of the flesh, and I take responsibility in my generation and the generations on my mother's side and on my father's side, all the way back to Adam and Eve for the spirits associated with and influencing adultery, fornications, uncleanness, lasciviousness, idolatry, witchcraft, hatred, variances, emulations, wrath, strife, seditions, heresies, envyings, murders, drunkenness, and revelings relating to gentleness or the lack of tenderness and gentleness.

I am now loosed and free from all chains and fetters that had me bound in generations past and present, and I now bind to myself in their place the spirit of godly gentleness. I bind godly gentleness as God designed to be gentle and to be full of grace, mercy, and happiness to my Gentleness gate. I now bind godly charity, contentment, and courage to me in tenderness, and I bind faith with forgiveness, hope, and hospitality full of grace and mercy.

I ask the Holy Spirit to bind honesty, humility, and happiness on all the remaining eight gates of the fruit of the Spirit; to give joy in brotherly love; and to promote peace in our relations to all mankind in humility. I bind the spirit of endurance, patience, forbearing with restraint in longsuffering to my soul's walls and gates. I now bind gentleness in kindliness and sympathy, with compassion in civility and respect in the face of adversity, goodness as a quality of virtue and morality. I further bind godliness and reliability with honor and integrity. I bind faith in fidelity toward God, dispelling all doubt, unbelief, and depression with a humble submissiveness to God and His will, and to divine revelation by the Holy Spirit. Finally, I bind gentleness to stand firm in the face of temptation with a dedicated determination to place the glory of God ahead of every fleshly desire by means of self-control, self-restraint, self-denial, self-discipline, moderation, composure, abstinence, sobriety, and that God's protection and righteousness be imputed to me in the name of Jesus Christ of Nazareth. Amen and amen!

Chapter 26

THE FRUIT OF GOODNESS

*G*oodness, *goodly, good* in the context of the Scriptures: both Old and New Testaments refer to character traits as the constitution of the makeup of a person's spiritual health. This spiritual health of goodness as a fruit of the Spirit is born and established in the heart of the person by the Holy Spirit at the moment confession is made and Jesus is declared Lord and King of their life. Goodness as a spiritual fruit is what men see in their daily walk and conversation that gives value to what they say. The attributes of a truly good person is when Jesus comes into their heart and they act and do without fanfare to receive recognition. A truly good person doing good works for the right motives and intentions is explained by Jesus for all believers in Matthew 25:34–40.

> Then shall the King say unto them on his right hand,
> Come, ye blessed of my Father, inherit the kingdom
> prepared for you from the foundation of the world: For
> I was an hungered, and ye gave me meat: I was thirsty,
> and ye gave me drink: I was a stranger, and ye took me
> in: Naked and ye clothed me: I was sick, and ye visited

me: I was in prison, and ye came unto me. Then shall
the righteous answer him, saying, Lord, when saw we
thee an hungered, and fed thee? or thirsty, and gave
thee drink? When saw we thee a stranger, and took
thee in? or naked, and clothed thee? Or when saw we
thee sick, or in prison, and came unto thee? And the
King shall answer and say unto them, Verily I say unto
you, *Inasmuch as you have done it unto one of the least of
these my brethren, you have done it unto me.* (emphasis
added)

This character trait of goodness is the one fruit that most contradicts the
natural instincts of the flesh in our daily walk. This is where the abiding
Spirit prompts the believer to respond to meet a need and stand alongside
to help and not ridicule or condemn the person's obvious need, regardless
of their condition. Jesus expounded upon this eternal truth in this same
chapter verses 41–46 to believers as He spoke of the religiously self-
righteous and pious believers in Jehovah who loved mammon and status
more than benevolence. Jesus gave mankind a new way of thinking and
a way to live a godly life in love as one body with many parts. The rich
young ruler best exemplifies the futility of good works to gain eternal life,
and his inquiry to Jesus only validates the dissatisfaction, frustration, and
hopeless struggle anyone has who puts their eternal destination solely
on the works of the flesh, whether it be in a denomination or a religious
ideology.

Obviously this scenario is no longer applicable to believers in the Messiah
Jesus Christ, for we live under grace and not the law, but I do believe this story
applies to our eternal rewards as goodness is seen in our daily walk. Goodness
must be founded on the foundation of Love and must contain a portion of all
the fruit of the Spirit as a person exemplifies virtue, godliness, benevolence,
kindness, reliability, and compassion as we grow in Christlikeness. It is
best witnessed as a selfless, gracious word or deed that will return as fruit
in a bountiful harvest for the kingdom of God. God is omniscient and
omnipresent. He knows our intents and He sees what we do in secret and
will reward us accordingly.

Heavenly Father God,

I come to You to bind and loose spiritual issues that are affecting the gate of Goodness and foundation of the fruit of my soul. According to Your Word in Matthew 16:19

> *And I will give unto thee the keys of the kingdom of heaven: and whatsoever thou shalt bind on earth shall be bound in heaven: and whatsoever thou shalt loose on earth shall be loosed in heaven.*

Therefore I have been given the keys to the kingdom of heaven, and by the authority of Jesus Christ of Nazareth, I loose all the spirit-world realities and works of the flesh. I loose all chains, fetters, and bindings on all generational curses, word curses, and self-curses cast upon me, my children, and my ancestors on my mother's side and my father's side, all the way back to Adam and Eve that have bound me, causing pain and deep soul wounds to my walls and gates of goodness.

I now loose all principalities, powers, rulers of darkness, and spirits of wickedness that have tormented me and my family. I loose all unforgiveness, resentment, and any retaliation for any goodness. I loose all anger, hatred, violence, and murder in word or deed for goodness. I loose all separation, bitterness, accusation, envy, and jealousy that has been done for perceived goodness, and I loose all spirits of addictions and dabbling in occultism looking for good things to happen. Lastly, I loose all works of the flesh, and I take responsibility in my generation and the generations on my mother's side and on my father's side, all the way back to Adam and Eve for the spirits associated with and influencing adultery, fornications, uncleanness, lasciviousness, idolatry, witchcraft, hatred, variances, emulations, wrath, strife, seditions, heresies, envyings, murders, drunkenness, and revelings related to goodness or the lack of goodness.

I am now loosed and free from all chains and fetters that had me bound in generations past and present, and I now bind to myself in their place, the spirit of godly goodness. I now bind godly goodness as God designed goodness to be full of grace, mercy, and happiness to my Goodness gate. I bind godly charity, contentment, and courage to me in goodness, and I bind faith with forgiveness, hope, and hospitality full of grace and mercy. I ask the Holy Spirit to bind honesty, humility, and happiness on all the remaining eight gates of the fruit of the Spirit; to give joy in brotherly love; and to promote peace in our relations to all mankind in humility. I bind the spirit of endurance, patience, and forbearing with restraint in longsuffering to my soul's walls and gates. I now bind gentleness in kindliness and sympathy, with compassion in civility and respect in the face of adversity, and goodness as a quality of virtue and morality. I further bind godliness and reliability with honor and integrity. I bind faith in fidelity toward God, dispelling all doubt, unbelief, and depression with a humble submissiveness to God and His will, and to divine revelation by the Holy Spirit. And finally, I bind temperance to stand firm in the face of temptation with a dedicated determination to place the glory of God ahead of every fleshly desire by means of self-control, self-restraint, self-denial, self-discipline, moderation, composure, abstinence, and sobriety, that God's protection and righteousness be imputed to me in the name of Jesus Christ of Nazareth. Amen and amen!

Chapter 27

THE FRUIT OF FAITH

But now the righteousness of God without the law is manifested, being witnessed by the law and the prophets; *Even the righteousness of God which is by faith of Jesus Christ unto all and upon all them that believe: for there is no difference:* For all have sinned, and come short of the glory of God; Being justified freely by his grace through the redemption that is in Christ Jesus: Whom God hath set forth to be a propitiation through faith in his blood, to declare his righteousness for the remission of sins that are past, through the forbearance of God; To declare, I say, at this time his righteousness: that he might be just, and the *justifier of him which believeth in Jesus.* Where is boasting then? It is excluded. By what law? of works? Nay: but *by the law of faith.* (Romans 3:21–27, emphasis added)

Faith is to have trust in the God of the Old Testament (Torah) and in His Son Jesus Christ whom He sent to dwell in the hearts of whosoever will receive (Him) as Lord and Savior. It baffles and disturbs me at the same time how so many professing Christ believers can be so adamant about the church and her rules with men's traditions, yet be so ignorant of the Word of God and God's new command. I in my limited "theological" knowledge know that evil comes from the heart and that the desires of the flesh only feed into its perversion. Again, Scripture is not hard or a secret that is too difficult to understand, which is precisely why its simplicity has been so misrepresented and mystified to so many so as to confuse the common man. The gospel is the good news for every human being, regardless of ethnicity, sex, or race, and Jesus Christ shed His blood for the remission of sins for every man, woman or child of any sin committed. Jehovah God, Jesus Christ, and the Holy Spirit are all-inclusive and not exclusive to a select few.

> For God, who commanded the light to shine out of darkness, hath shined in our hearts, to give the light of the knowledge of the glory of God in the face of Jesus Christ. (2 Corinthians 4:6)

> That the God of our Lord Jesus Christ, the Father of glory, may give unto you the spirit of wisdom and revelation in the knowledge of him. (Ephesians 1:17)

> For if these things be in you, and abound, they make you that ye shall neither be barren nor unfruitful in the knowledge of our Lord Jesus Christ. ... For if after they have escaped the pollutions of the world through the knowledge of the Lord and Savior Jesus Christ, they are again entangled therein, and overcome, the latter end is worse with them than the beginning. ... But grow in grace, and in the knowledge of our Lord and Savior Jesus Christ. To him be glory both now and forever. Amen. (2 Peter 1:8; 2:20; 3:18)

The Greek word for "faith" (*pistis*) is used as an action taken by an individual as personal trust, prayer, hope in the unseen, and confidence in the work of Jesus on the cross for our eternal salvation apart from what the world theorists claim. You must believe in something, and if you claim you believe in nothing, the reality of your trusting in your own accomplishments proves this point. Your personal trust in the Father, Son, and Holy Spirit crosses and intertwines every aspect of your being, and only the Word of God clarifies our individual eternal purpose for this life. Hebrews 11:1 says, "Now faith is the substance of things hoped for, the evidence of things not seen."

By walking in the Spirit, your spirit-led walk becomes a fruit of the Spirit as a natural outworking of your accepting Jesus into your heart. Producing visible fruit on the tree or vine of your life becomes so natural that your personality DNA is transformed the instant you receive Jesus and begin to walk in Christlikeness.

This faith walk that we travel becomes easier and easier as you identify each issue and defeat any of the individual spirit-world realities, works of the flesh or lusts of the heart that may have been planted in your soul's foundation, walls, or gates. Understand that just because you're saved doesn't mean that you're immune to attacks or traumatic situations, and it doesn't mean that your prejudice, anger, or mean attitude toward other believers will be accepted into the presence of a Holy God. Satan knows that if he can introduce doubt and unbelief into this particular fruit of faith through the natural consequences of this life, then he weakens all the other fruit as well and his ultimate plan to destroy us begins. Deep soul wounds in any of your other fruit can and will affect your faith fruit if for no other reason than because of the doubts that arise by trials, tragedies, and tribulations in this world.

Satan is the god of this world, and the longer pains, tragedies, and natural calamities are blamed on the God of heaven, the easier it is for him to plant doubt in your mind and heart about who he is. The longer we physically suffer and have no answers for these pains, the more futile and senseless our faith and prayer seem. Satan's number one tool to dissuade and discourage our belief in God and our prayer life is through self-imposed defeatism and doubt in a loving God. When we don't see immediate answers to trials, our natural response is to question God and doubt Him. This is why travailing prayer of a believer is compared to a mother who works especially hard while giving birth naturally—the more it hurts, the closer the contractions are; and the closer the contractions are, the closer the birth of the child is.

This is exactly how I believe our faith works: the more we have troubles, the closer we are walking in the spirit, we just don't realize the peril we were in before we committed to Jesus. I do know that the second you put all your faith in the risen Christ, every open door to the spirit-world realities and the lusts of your born-again spirit/soul will rise up in your thoughts. As these trials and disappointments in this life increase, our faith must increase as well, and every issue that conflicts with your Christlikeness must be addressed. It seems to me that every one of these instances of a trial regardless of how small will occur in our life to put doubt in our faith in God. It doesn't seem fair, but these pains and hurts are a consequence of the fall of Adam, and there is no other way to prove to yourself that you are an overcomer other than by taking these thoughts captive and dispelling them. The apostle Paul declared that faith comes by hearing, and hearing by the Word of God. Later he states in Hebrews that without faith it is impossible to please God, for he that comes to God must believe that He is (exists) and that He is a re-warder of them that diligently seek Him. This compilation of these seemingly unattainable Scriptures is the reason for most if not all unanswered prayers.

If doubt and unbelief enter your mind or heart through science or worldly rationale, then every fruit of the Spirit will be infected by them and your decision-making processes will be skewed. Your thoughts or mental hard drive is tainted by these questions, and doubts about God and your purpose for having to endure such pain and misery makes every motivation and intent of doing good and showing love suspect. If you don't believe that the Jewish God of the Torah is the Father of Jesus or that He is the prophesied Messiah of the Old Testament, then your faith is tainted with prejudice. If you have a hard time believing that Jesus spoke only to the Jew in the Gospels or that Jesus fulfilled every requirement outlined in Torah, then your heart is tainted in one of the fruit of the Spirit with a spirit-world reality or lust in the heart.

This faith fruit of the Spirit isn't the most important—that title belongs to the fruit of love—but its importance is derived in the fact that it activates the other eight fruit and leads you on the right path to Christlikeness. If you believe that Jesus was doing the Father's will; that He died, was buried, rose again and is alive seated at the right hand of the Father interceding for all mankind regardless of race, denomination or nationality, yet you still hate the Jewish people or people of color, then you hinder many of God's blessings from occurring in your life. Yes, your faith in Jesus saves your spirit and soul forever, but your reluctance to give up the works of the flesh inhibits your spiritual growth and entrance to the inner courts, let alone the Holy of Holies. If you don't diligently seek after Him in the Word and you don't fear the true judgment of His Son Jesus, then how do you expect a holy, righteous God to hear your prayers while you are in rebellion and still in sin? Jesus not only claimed His divinity, but also proclaimed that without faith, it was impossible to please God and that without repenting and changing your mind, your salvation is in question. This faith that is in your being can't help but come out as an outpouring of His love, but a love steeped in tradition and denominationalism nullifies what Jesus taught, and your faith and prayers are impotent just like the Pharisees of Jesus day.

Listen to what Jesus says Matthew.

> Enter ye in at the strait gate: for wide is the gate, and broad is the way, that leadeth to destruction, and many there be which go in thereat: Because strait is the gate, and narrow is the way, which leadeth unto life, and few there be that find it. Beware of false prophets, which come to you in sheep's clothing, but inwardly they are ravening wolves. Ye shall know them by their fruits. Do men gather grapes of thorns, or figs of thistles? Even so *every good tree bringeth forth good fruit*; but a corrupt tree bringeth forth evil fruit. A good tree cannot bring forth evil fruit, neither can a corrupt tree bring forth good fruit. Every tree that bringeth not forth good fruit is hewn down, and cast into the fire. *Wherefore by their fruits ye shall know them.* (Matthew 7:13–20, emphasis added)

Your beliefs determine what tree or vine you are. The type of fruit you are determines the seeds you plant in this life, and the fruit your orchard bears determines your access and privilege to work in the Kingdom of heaven. Your faith fruit grounded in the love of Jesus nurtures the other fruit of your soul as you grow in Christlikeness.

You have not chosen me, but I have chosen you, and ordained you, that you should go and bring forth fruit, and that your fruit should remain: that whatsoever you shall ask of the Father in my name, he may give it you. (John 15:16)

Heavenly Father God,

I come to You to bind and loose spiritual issues that are affecting the Faith gate and faith of my soul. According to Your Word in Matthew 16:19

> *And I will give unto thee the keys of the kingdom of heaven: and whatsoever thou shalt bind on earth shall be bound in heaven: and whatsoever thou shalt loose on earth shall be loosed in heaven.*

Therefore I have been given the keys to the kingdom of heaven, and by the authority of Jesus Christ of Nazareth, I loose all the spirit-world realities and works of the flesh. I loose all chains, fetters, and bindings on all generational curses, word curses, and self-curses cast upon me, my children, and my ancestors on my mother's side and my father's side, all the way back to Adam and Eve that have bound me, causing pain and deep soul wounds to my Faith walls and gates.
I now loose all principalities, powers, rulers of darkness, and spirits of wickedness that have tormented me and my family. I loose all unforgiveness, resentment, and any retaliation for faith. I loose all anger, hatred, violence, and murder in word or deed for faith. I loose all separation, bitterness, accusation, envy, and jealousy that has been done for perceived faith, and I loose all spirits of addictions and dabbling in occultism looking for faith. Lastly, I loose all works of the flesh, and I take responsibility in my generation and the generations on my mother's side and on my father's side, all the way back to Adam and Eve for the spirits associated with and influencing adultery, fornications, uncleanness, lasciviousness, idolatry, witchcraft,

hatred, variances, emulations, wrath, strife, seditions, heresies, envyings, murders, drunkenness, and revelings relating to faith or the lack of faith.

I am now loosed and free from all chains and fetters that had me bound in generations past and present, and I now bind in their place the spirit of godly anointed faith to me. I bind godly faith as God designed faith to be full of grace, mercy, and happiness to my Faith gate. I bind godly charity, contentment, and courage to me in faith, and I bind this faith with forgiveness, hope, and hospitality full of grace and mercy. I ask the Holy Spirit to bind honesty, humility, and happiness on all the remaining eight gates of the fruit of the Spirit; to give joy in brotherly love; and to promote peace in our relations to all mankind in humility. I bind the spirit of endurance, patience, forbearing with restraint in longsuffering to my soul's walls and gates. I now bind gentleness in kindliness and sympathy with compassion in civility and respect in the face of adversity, goodness as a quality of virtue, and morality. I bind godliness and reliability with honor and integrity, I bind faith in fidelity toward God, dispelling all doubt, unbelief, and depression with a humble submissiveness to the God of creation and His will, and to divine revelation by the Holy Spirit. And finally, I bind faith to stand firm in the face of temptation with a dedicated determination to place the glory of God ahead of every fleshly desire by means of self-control, self-restraint, self-denial, self-discipline, moderation, composure, abstinence, sobriety, and that God's protection and righteousness be imputed to me in the name of Jesus Christ of Nazareth. Amen and amen!

Chapter 28

THE FRUIT OF MEEKNESS

here are a number of examples of the fruit of meekness "in action" with men in Scripture that we can look at. The first Scripture really doesn't do justice to our understanding of the character of meekness, and if anything, dilutes his strength by its definition.

> Now the man Moses was very meek, above all the men which
> were upon the face of the earth. (Numbers 12:3)

Meekness is defined as "to follow mildness" or "quietness of nature," "showing submissiveness". It is sometimes seen as a lack of initiative or will. Again, like with so many of the fruit of the Spirit, meekness is connected to and associated with mildness and submissiveness, which could not be further from the truth. When we look at the story of Moses, I'm struck with the way he learned how to control his anger and self-righteous indignation through the consequences of his actions. He was right about the mistreatment of the Hebrew slave, but he wasn't right about how he dealt with his perceived form of justice and the consequences of his thoughts and actions.

He had an attitude of superiority and privilege replaced with fear as he reflected on the loss of his position and status in that he learned to serve in humility. As he tended the flocks of Jethro the priest of Midian for forty years guilt and shame of what he had done had plucked his once-proud cock feathers and prince's scepter and replaced them with a shepherd's staff and Hebrew slave status. His fear of the penalty for killing an Egyptian forced humility and a timidity not usually seen in a prince. He knew of the prejudice, cruelty and injustice of slavery to the Hebrew people and this process he was going through was necessary to till his heart to receive what was to be revealed to him. These spiritual attributes would have been seen as weakness in a future king. He had time to think and reflect on his actions and at the same time was preparing spiritually for the task he would soon face as the leader of the Hebrew slaves and scripter of the Ten Commandments from God. By learning the spirit of gentleness with tenderness as he tended the sheep meekness was the result.

As a shepherd, he learned patience in the time necessary to raise, shear, and take to market the sheep; there was no other way to rush the process of removing his pride and ego from his soul's fruit. He learned submissiveness, mildness, and humility as the one-time prince of Egypt became a shepherd, and he fell from worldly greatness by defeat, fear, and shame for murdering a fellow Egyptian. There was no other way for Moses's heart to change except for his actions and resultant consequences. With this revelation, he grew to spiritual greatness even though he suffered from the same disease that I and many other people suffer from: "rage-aholism" (Exodus 2 to Joshua 1). As with us, God doesn't hurry to answer our prayers or fulfill our wants, because He loves us and understands that in our successes in the flesh, some of our expectations and prayers are not in His will and we are susceptible to the lusts of the heart and the pride of life if we received what we asked for.

> Ye lust, and have not: ye kill, and desire to have, and cannot obtain: ye fight and war, yet ye have not, because ye ask not. Ye ask, and receive not, because ye ask amiss, that ye may consume it upon your lusts. (James 4:2–3)

As Saul and even David started out in God's perfect will, we read that both experienced spiritual failures because of believing everything people told them and opening the doors of their soul to spirit-world realities and the works of the flesh. Any of our self-willed arguments or justifications for our actions avail nothing with the Lord, and we need to leave the controls of this life in the hands of the Holy Spirit. Know that you might be right about all your situations and conclusions, but you ain't right about your responses to them.

First Samuel tells us that Saul was anointed king and that after only two years this humble, strong, and modest man became presumptuous, self-absorbed, and unresponsive to God's direction—so much so, that God rejected him and selected David as his successor because of their respective hearts. Saul in his heart became so jealous and insecure that he sought to kill David, and we see in David's heart a respect and honor toward Saul because he feared God more than he feared Saul. He did not kill him even when he was justified in doing so and had multiple opportunities. Similarly as with us today, when we take issues into our own hands, misunderstandings, accusations, and stresses occur and we can become unbearable.

Put on therefore, as the elect of God, holy and beloved, bowels of mercies, kindness, humbleness of mind, meekness, longsuffering; Forbearing one another, and forgiving one another, if any man have a quarrel against any: even as Christ forgave you, so also do ye. (Colossians 3:12–13)

Meekness is one of the natural attributes of the Holy Spirit as being one with the Father and the Son. The Spirit was depicted as a dove at Jesus' baptism. We think of the dove as the sweetest-natured of all birds-possibly because of this depiction on so sacred an occasion. We just do not think of the dove being "at home" in anything other than a peaceful setting. Even the nations of the world understand the symbolism of the dove with the olive leaf in its beak as an emblem of peace. It is seemly, then, to consider the Holy Spirit as the bearer of "meekness" in every temple He indwells *you and me*.......Meekness is no "go to the meetin" or "go to the holy church" in your Sunday best attire. Meekness is the "work clothes" of our daily walk. The apostle Peter "...Yea, all of you be subject one to another, and be clothed with humility: for God resisteth the proud, and giveth grace to the humble." 1 Peter 5:5

And Paul says in Colossians 3:12 "Put on therefore, as the elect of God, holy and beloved, bowels of mercies, kindness, and humbleness of mind, meekness, longsuffering;"

There are many things all around us to undermine our meekness. We must beware of these things. Paul put it well in his first letter to Timothy, admonishing to flee these things

(Know Your Bible Series, 91-93,96-97)

Heavenly Father God,

I come to You to bind and loose spiritual issues that are affecting the gate of Meekness and foundation of the fruit of Meekness to my soul. According to Your Word in Matthew 16:19,

And I will give unto thee the keys of the kingdom of heaven: and whatsoever thou shalt bind on earth shall be bound in heaven: and whatsoever thou shalt loose on earth shall be loosed in heaven.

Therefore I have been given the keys to the kingdom of heaven, and by the authority of Jesus Christ of Nazareth, I loose all the spirit-world realities and works of the flesh. I loose all chains, fetters, and bindings on all generational curses, word curses, and self-curses cast upon me, my children, and my ancestors on my mother's side and my father's side, all the way back to Adam and Eve that have bound me, causing pain and deep soul wounds to my Meekness walls and gates.

I now loose all principalities, powers, rulers of darkness, and spirits of wickedness that have tormented me and my family. I loose all unforgiveness, resentment, and any retaliation for the fruit of meekness. I loose all anger, hatred, violence, and murder in word or deed for meekness. I loose all separation, bitterness, accusation, envy, and jealousy that has been done for a perceived spirit of meekness, and I loose all spirits of addictions and dabbling in occultism looking for the fruit of meekness. Lastly, I loose all works of the flesh, and I take responsibility in my generation and the generations on my mother's side and on my father's side, all the way back to Adam and Eve for the spirits associated with and influencing adultery, fornications, uncleanness, lasciviousness, idolatry, witchcraft, hatred, variances, emulations, wrath, strife, seditions, heresies, envyings, murders, drunkenness, and revelings relating to modesty or the lack of showing a meek heart.

I am now loosed and free from all chains and fetters that had me bound in generations past and present, and I now bind in their place the spirit of godly humility to me. I bind a spirit godly meekness as God designed meekness to be full of grace, mercy, and happiness to my Meekness gate. I bind godly charity, contentment, and courage to me in humility, and I bind faith with forgiveness, hope, and hospitality full of grace and mercy. I ask the Holy Spirit to bind honesty, humility, and happiness on all the remaining eight gates of the fruit of the Spirit; to give meekness in brotherly love; and to promote peace in our relations to all mankind in humility. I bind the spirit of endurance, patience, forbearing with restraint in longsuffering to my soul's walls and gates. I now bind gentleness in kindliness and sympathy, with compassion in civility and respect in the face of adversity, and goodness as a quality of virtue and morality. I further bind godliness and reliability with honor and integrity. I bind faith in fidelity toward God, dispelling all doubt, unbelief, and depression with a humble submissiveness to God and His will, and to divine revelation by the Holy Spirit. And finally, I bind temperance to stand firm in the face of meekness with a dedicated determination to place the glory of God ahead of every fleshly desire by means of self-control, self-restraint, self-denial, self-discipline, moderation, composure, abstinence, and sobriety, and that God's protection and righteousness be imputed to me in the name of Jesus Christ of Nazareth. Amen and amen!

Chapter 29

The Fruit of Temperance

Self-control ... abstinence ... restraint. Temperance in character is likened to the fruit of love in that temperance binds all the fruit together and is a sort of blend of them all. When temperance is the bond of a person's disposition, that person is able to live temperately in every situation. When a person is wholly surrendered to God, they are able to be helped by the Holy Ghost. It is to restrain your natural passions having complete control of ones conduct and temporal desire relating to earthly appetites. A person who puts no restraint on their fleshly passions will soon be carried away by them regardless if they're saved or not. When walking in the spirit of temperance, all the walls of the fruit are securely in place, and temptations are identified as plots and plans and discarded. The undisciplined and unregenerate person is a depraved creature with an inbred Adamic sin nature that needs to be redeemed, and only the shed blood of the resurrected Jesus Christ can pay the price of sin in full. Only through the indwelling of the Holy Spirit can a man live uprightly and be in control of his fleshly desires. The fruit of temperance like the fruit of longsuffering is the natural visible out pouring of the Holy Spirit and if you're not in control of your own temper then who is: you, God or Satan?

This attribute of the indwelling of the Third Person of the Trinity will bear that fruit of loving temperance the more securely we are attached to Christ. Only the gospel has redeeming power to deliver the enslaved soul from the hands of the great deceiver. Only the 1611 King James Version of the Judeo-Christian Bible speaks of the pitfalls of the natural man, and only the Word of the living God tells all who ask how to rebuild their damaged fruit walls and rehang the gates with a loving, temperate soul. Finally there is no person or any church denomination that can separate the truly repentant heart from confessing Jesus and receiving the gift of eternal life promised in Romans 10:9-10. Just as there is no person or church that can assure your salvation unless you personally confess Jesus as Lord, believe in His resurrection from the dead and change your mind and lifestyle to live as the unadulterated 1611 King James Version or New King James Version of the Bible states for those who don't like the thee's and thou's.

Heavenly Father God,

I come to You to bind and loose spiritual issues that are affecting the Temperance gate and foundation of the fruit of my soul. According to Your Word in Matthew 16:19

And I will give unto thee the keys of the kingdom of heaven: and whatsoever thou shalt bind on earth shall be bound in heaven: and whatsoever thou shalt loose on earth shall be loosed in heaven.

Therefore I have been given the keys to the kingdom of heaven, and by the authority of Jesus Christ of Nazareth, I loose all the spirit-world realities and works of the flesh. I loose all chains, fetters, and bindings on all generational curses, word curses, and self-curses cast upon me, my children, and my ancestors on my mother's side and my father's side, all the way back to Adam and Eve that have bound me, causing pain and deep soul wounds to my Temperance walls and gates.

I now loose all principalities, powers, rulers of darkness, and spirits of wickedness that have tormented me and my family. I loose all unforgiveness, resentment, and any retaliation for temperance. I loose all anger, hatred, violence, and murder in word or deed for self-restraint and temperance I loose all separation, bitterness, accusation, envy, and jealousy that has been done for perceived temperance, and I loose all spirits of addictions and dabbling in occultism looking for temperance. Lastly, I loose all works of the flesh, and I take responsibility in my generation and the generations on my mother's side and on my father's side, all the way back to Adam and Eve for the spirits associated with and influencing adultery, fornications, uncleanness, lasciviousness, idolatry, witchcraft, hatred, variances, emulations, wrath, strife, seditions, heresies, envyings, murders, drunkenness, and revelings relating to joy or the lack of temperance.

I am now loosed and free from all chains and fetters that had me bound in generations past and present, and I now bind in their place the spirit of godly temperance to me. I bind godly temperance as God designed temperance to be full of grace, mercy, and happiness to my Temperance gate. I bind godly charity, contentment, and courage to me in temperance, and I bind faith with forgiveness, hope, and hospitality full of grace and mercy. I ask the Holy Spirit to bind honesty, humility, and happiness on all the remaining eight gates of the fruit of the Spirit; to give temperance in brotherly love; and to promote peace in our relations to all mankind in humility. I bind the spirit of endurance, patience, forbearing with restraint in longsuffering to my soul's walls and gates. I now bind gentleness in kindliness and sympathy, with compassion in civility and respect in the face of adversity, and goodness as a quality of virtue and morality. I further bind godliness and reliability with honor and integrity. I bind faith in fidelity toward God, dispelling all doubt, unbelief, and depression with a humble submissiveness to God and His will, and to divine revelation by the Holy Spirit. And finally, I bind temperance to stand firm in the face of temptation with a dedicated determination to place the glory of God ahead of every fleshly desire by means of self-control, self-restraint, self-denial, self-discipline, moderation, composure, abstinence, and sobriety, and that God's protection and righteousness be imputed to me in the name of Jesus Christ of Nazareth. Amen and amen!

Chapter 30

BE BATTLE TESTED

"This know also, that in the last days perilous times shall come. For men shall be lovers of their own selves, covetous, boasters, proud, blasphemers, disobedient to parents, unthankful, unholy, Without natural affection, trucebreakers, false accusers, incontinent, fierce, despisers of those that are good, Traitors, heady, high minded, lovers of pleasures more than lovers of God;Having a form of godliness, but denying the power thereof: from such turn away. For of this sort are they which creep into houses, and lead captive silly women laden with sins, led away with divers lusts, Ever learning, and never able to come to the knowledge of the truth. (II Timothy 3:1-7)

"*T*his know also, that in the last days perilous times shall come. For men shall be lovers of their own selves, covetous, boasters, proud, blasphemers, disobedient to parents, unthankful, unholy, Without natural affection, trucebreakers, false accusers, incontinent, fierce, despisers of those that are good, Traitors, heady, high minded, lovers of pleasures more than lovers of God; Having a form of godliness, but denying the power thereof: from such turn away. For of this sort are they which creep into houses, and lead captive silly women laden with sins, led away with divers lusts, Ever learning, and never able to come to the knowledge of the truth.

The spirit and soul never dies, and depending on your soul's condition, it will determine your eternal destination and rewards, providing of course, you've made the decision to follow Jesus Christ, the Jewish Messiah, as Lord and Savior. My desire as a simple man is to take the Bible as I believe it was intended to be given to all of mankind—Jew and *all believing Gentiles* alike. That includes all the physical warnings with all the spiritual preparations and promises as outlined in scripture needed to endure these last days. We believers grafted into the Jewish root are not to be influenced by any self-elevating denominational, racist, or ethnic superiority that is prejudiced by them, but instead we are to receive with a complete understanding of who the Father, Son, and Holy Spirit are and our relationship with them. We must believe in the Hebrew Father, the Messianic Jewish and Gentile believers Jesus and the Pentecostal's full Bible believers of the Holy Spirit that prepares us all completely in spirit, soul, and body in these last days. I do not believe that there is any difference in the Messianic Jewish believer and the born again Jesus believing Gentile regardless of denomination and only the Third Person of the Trinity the Holy Spirit differentiates there location and duties in the kingdom.

If the Lord were to come today, wonderful—I'm ready to go because I believe over the last fifteen years I've been able to correct many of my anger, racist, prejudice and anti-Semitic issues with the help of the Holy Spirit. But, the real question to all believers if Jesus tarries is; would you be ready to go through what Jesus said was to happen in these last days? This is my desire for my children, my family, and all my brothers and sisters in Christ; that we all be ready, spirit, soul and body no matter when He comes for us or if we die. Like my pastor friend Bev Hills always said: pray for the peace of Jerusalem, always tell the truth rightly dividing the Word of God, and prepare both physically and spiritually in anticipation of our departure or the Lord's arrival. Would you be ready if things got worse and we had to live through some tough times like Jesus said or would you be one of the ones praying for the rocks to fall on them? Which of the ten virgins would you be: the five foolish or the five wise? Why did Jesus place this parable after He explained life after the resurrection in Matthew 22:28–32, following it with the most important command from the Father in verses 37–40 which is to love thy neighbor as thyself? Then Jesus warns of the last days' coming woes as the beginning of sorrows (tribulations) that are the precursor of the great tribulation. We all will live through the four horsemen before being taken out in the rapture as I believe is described in Revelation 7:9–12 after the seven seals but before the seven trumpets in Revelation 8 and His wrath is poured out on all mankind.

I do believe that this is the purpose of the baptism of the Holy Spirit with your personal prayer language, the nine gifts of the Spirit, the armor of God, and the nine fruit of the Spirit—that are for you to do spiritual battle in these last days. Every breath we breathe is an opportunity to correct, rebuild, and fortify our soul walls, becoming battle tested through this brief life we live. If Jesus were to come, wouldn't He come before the great day of His wrath stated in Revelation 6:17 and not before with the sound of a voice as some pre-tribulationists believe (Revelation 4:1)? Any way you look at Scripture, the time is near for all believers to come together and prepare individually for our coming Bridegroom "Jesus the Christ." Whether with the rapture or with death our fruit walls must be repaired and we must be as Christ-like as possible to not only enter the kingdom but also to receive as many rewards as we can while alive. Because like we said earlier once you cross that dead-line you can't come back and fix your fruit. (Luke 16:19-31)

I don't mean to offend you with this warning; I just want to warn my brothers and sisters in Christ that they can't be full of prejudice, hate, racism, anti-Semitism or a false sense of security of a pre-tribulation rapture, completely ignorant of the impending trials and oppressions coming. Why else would Jesus record in Matthew 24:45–51 and Luke 12:41–48 of the faithful and unfaithful servant if the Lord tarries? He can't be talking about unbelieving Jews; He's got to be talking to us "last day's believers" in the Messiah. As believers we must be prepared for any situations or circumstance that we find ourselves in.

Sun Tzu (512 BC) said in his book called *The Art of War*, which is still being taught today in the physical battles we face in the flesh.

So it is said that if you know your enemies and know yourself, you can win a hundred battles without a single loss. If you only know yourself, but not your opponent, you may win or lose. If you know neither yourself nor your enemy, you will always endanger yourself.

If you know your enemy and know yourself you will win a hundred battles without losing a single one

Know yourself but not your enemy you lose half the time

Know your enemy and not yourself, again you lose half the time

Applying these same principles of war to the spiritual warfare works very well too.

If you don't know who you are as a believing Christian with your entire spiritual weapons available to you with the baptism of the Holy Spirit you will lose half the time.

If you don't know all the plots, plans and schemes that your spiritual enemy throws at you with Powers, Principalities, Rulers of darkness and Spirits of wickedness in high places again you will lose half the time!

But if you know who you are in the risen Christ with the power through the baptism of the Holy Spirit and you know your spiritual enemy with all his plots, plans and schemes you WIN!!

We are in a war over our eternal spirits, and our soul's condition with its proximity to Christlikeness determines our eternal position and rewards in the kingdom.

Sun Tzu, one of the world's greatest military tacticians quoted above, taught a principle that is not only relevant for hand-to-hand combat in war, but is the same approach we individually must take in spiritual warfare as believers in Jesus. We should not only know the strengths and weaknesses of our enemy (Satan), but we should admit and identify our own strengths and weaknesses. Through our personal confession of faith in Jesus and our willingness to conform to His Word, we are destined to rule and reign as His eternal bride.

This is why it is so vitally important for us to know and understand who God is from eternity past to eternity future, who we are in God's plans with our spiritual weapons, and finally to know who and what the enemy of our spirit and soul is. We are to know who our enemy is and what our spiritual potential is as we do spiritual battle in this life in preparation for any future demonic attacks whether the Lord tarries or not. It is incumbent upon each one of us to be battle tested as we encounter, identify, and defeat the enemy of our souls that is only outlined in the Judeo-Christian Bible, and only in the entire unadulterated 1611 King James Version. Finally, my greatest fear is with all my brothers and sisters in Christ that have allowed a false sense of security and immunity to trials and tribulation because they've accepted Jesus as Lord or belong to a particular Christian denomination.

> My people are destroyed for lack of knowledge: because thou
> hast rejected knowledge, I will also reject thee, that thou
> shalt be no priest to me: seeing thou hast forgotten the law
> of thy God, I will also forget thy children. (Hosea 4:6)

Yes, the God of the Old Testament was speaking to the Hebrews in this verse, but because of their unbelief in Jesus as Messiah, we Gentiles were grafted in. Likewise, because of our unbelief of the whole New Testament explaining the gifts of the Spirit and the armor of God, we could potentially lose our eternal rewards as well.

I do believe that as we become battle tested with every spiritual victory we face in this life using the gifts of the Spirit, so to shall we as godly warriors be utilized in these last days to increase the kingdom of God. If we don't acknowledge and prepare our souls and spirits to the warnings Jesus Himself warned us about in His Word, not only can we become an unwise servant, but we could be left behind. We should be leading the battle cry, being used as spiritual witnesses and spiritual warriors against the demonic hordes influencing the unbelievers in power with fasting and prayer.

My understanding of eschatology is that we are in the last days and that it isn't one of escaping tribulation or oppression for our beliefs, because we live in spiritual oppression now and it's only going to get worse. Because of each of these trials we face with increased oppression, we become stronger and wiser to the plots, plans, and deceptions that Satan uses to make us give up and doubt the God of the Bible. Nowhere does it say that we Gentiles replace the Jews, but only that we are grafted in because of their unbelief in the promised Messiah and we Gentiles are added to the already established root system and not replacing it.

You may not agree with my pre-wrath rapture assertion that we as believers are in today, because I too had reservations with this basically mid-tribulation conclusion. The distinction and definition of the word *tribulation* that must be made to fully understand and prepare for these last days is defined as "great difficulty, affliction or distress" and is not to be designated or assigned only to a post-rapture date or time frame. Again, we as believers must believe that Jesus is the Messiah prophesied with the first advent with His virgin-born incarnation and His death, burial, and resurrection from the grave, redeeming all of mankind with His shed blood. We must also believe in His second advent as the time mentioned in Matthew 24:21, 29; Mark 13:19, 24; Luke 21:21–23; and Revelation 6 and 7 as yet to occur. As Gentiles grafted into the Hebrew root, we then will encounter the future trials and oppressions as we try to convert the unbelieving pagans, gentiles and practicing Jews into Christianity.

Again, we can't cherry-pick only the pleasant promises of God and think we are exempt from man's wrath; God only promises to exempt us from His wrath and not man's wrath. The cosmic disturbance introduced with the opening of the seals of Revelation chapter six only make sense if you take your selective denominationally inspired blinders off and read the Word of God without prejudice. The anti-Semitic replacement theologians have tried to make the Christ-believing church exempt from what the Bible clearly teaches will occur in the last days. These satanically inspired roots of hate and prejudice toward the Jews and fellow Christians of other denominations is what I believe the Word of God states will occur immediately prior to the rapture of the church in Revelation 7:9–13 (Rosenthal, 153, 184–186).

To preempt the great falling away and the loss of your eternal rewards is the purpose of this book, and if I'm wrong, then okay—I'm wrong; no harm no foul, and you get your soul walls and gates as close to Christlikeness as possible. But if I'm right and we live through the six seals of war, famine, pestilence, martyrdom, antichrist, and the cosmic disturbances as explained as the beginning of sorrows before the great tribulation, then we will be ready for that too. Either way, we should be ready and not offended by this assertion.

Remember, Jesus, the Son of the Jewish God Jehovah, practiced all of the seven holidays given to Israel on Mount Mariah (Exodus 23:14–17 and Deuteronomy 16:16). Jesus acknowledged and participated in at least three of these holidays as recorded in the New Testament—Passover, Pentecost, and Tabernacles—and all three were a central part of His ministry. As a professing Christian, you can't ignore His Hebrew lineage as being integral for mankind's eternal salvation. We as believers in the resurrected Christ can't discount the Old Testament prophecies of Psalm 118; Isaiah 53; and Zechariah 9:9, or that believing the Jewish Messiah is the Lord of our lives. We must also take into account Isaiah 13:6–10; Daniel 9; Joel 2:30–31; 3:14–15; Zephaniah 1:7; and Malachi 3:2, as well as New Testament warnings of impending deception and tribulations prophesied in Matthew 24; Mark 13; Romans 1:18; and 2 Peter 3:9.

Know that we as believers can't enter into the presence of a holy God with this religious prejudice and this false sense of superiority that many Christian denominations have toward each other. You are an island unto yourself, and your eternal destination is determined by no one else other than you and your actions in this brief life that you live here on this planet. It is incumbent for each of us as believers to grow in Christlikeness as we walk in the fruit of the Spirit daily, showing the love of God through the shed blood of His Son, Jesus the Christ. We believers are to be ambassadors of Christ, representing Him in whatsoever we eat, whatsoever we drink, and whatsoever we do to the glory of the Father, regardless of denomination or worldly flesh-dominated traditions man has contrived.

God the Father has not only paid the price for our salvation through the innocent shed blood of His only begotten Son Jesus Christ of Nazareth, but He has given us the power and authority for each of us to accomplish our God-given destiny and receive complete restoration through the baptism of the third person of the Trinity, the Holy Spirit. This path is only outlined in the written Word of the living God in the King James Bible, from the written account of Moses in Genesis to the Revelation of the apostle John on the

Isle of Patmos in Revelation. Your newly "saved" temple is protected by your restored and rehabilitated soul walls, and they alone determine your eternal rewards—not your salvation, but your rewards.

Let us now travel together through this life journey as we examine our soul walls for restoration, deliverance, and spiritual healing that only the Bible explains. We are each created in the image of the living God and all have a spirit, soul, and body.

First the *spirit* can only be redeemed through the resurrection of Jesus Christ of Nazareth from the grave alone.

> Verily, verily, I say unto thee, Except a man be born again, he cannot see the kingdom of God. (John 3:3)

> That if thou shalt confess with thy mouth the Lord Jesus, and shalt believe in thine heart that God hath raised him from the dead, thou shalt be saved. For with the heart man believeth unto righteousness; and with the mouth confession is made unto salvation. (Romans 10:9–10)

The soul can then be restored through the process of sanctification and growing in Christlikeness through the fruit of the Spirit.

> My little children, these things write I unto you, that ye sin not. And if any man sin, we have an advocate with the Father, Jesus Christ the righteous: And he is the propitiation for our sins: and not for ours only, but also for the sins of the whole world. (1 John 2:1–2)

The body will be renewed in the millennial kingdom to rule and reign with Jesus. We know that we will be like Jesus' glorious body.

> Beloved, now are we the sons of God, and it doth not yet appear what we shall be: but we know that, when he shall appear, *we shall be like him*; for we shall see him as he is. And every man that hath this hope in him purifieth himself, even as he is pure. (1 John 3:23, emphasis added)

Christ will be glorified in us.

> When he shall come to be glorified in his saints, and to be
> admired in all them that believe (because our testimony
> among you was believed) in that day. Wherefore also we pray
> always for you, that our God would count you worthy of this
> calling, and fulfill all the good pleasure of his goodness, and
> the work of faith with power: *That the name of our Lord Jesus
> Christ may be glorified in you*, and ye in him, according to the
> grace of our God and the Lord Jesus Christ. (2 Thessalonians
> 1:10–12, emphasis added)

> The Spirit itself bears witness with our spirit, that *we are
> the children of God: And if children, then heirs; heirs of God,
> and joint-heirs with Christ*; if so be that we suffer with him,
> that we may be also glorified together. For I reckon that the
> sufferings of this present time are not worthy to be compared
> with the glory which shall be revealed in us. For the earnest
> expectation of the creature waiteth for the manifestation of
> the sons of God. For the creature was made subject to vanity,
> not willingly, but by reason of him who hath subjected the
> same in hope. (Romans 8:16–20, emphasis added)

> Now the Lord is that Spirit: and where the Spirit of the Lord
> is, there is liberty. But we all, with open face beholding as
> in a glass the glory of the Lord, are changed into the same
> image from glory to glory, even as by the Spirit of the Lord.
> (2 Corinthians 3:17–18)

REVELATION GIVEN 7/1/2010

*T*he whole purpose of this life was and is to bring glory to the Father, and through this life's experiences, the walls and gates of our soul are formed or destroyed by the PPRS's, the works of the flesh, the spirit-world realities, and the lusts of the heart that we do or are the recipients of. These gates are represented by the fruit of the Spirit exemplified in Jesus Christ, and they are the primary way all people are judged after death in this life, regardless of when or where they lived. The nine fruit of the Spirit are universal and do not reflect sex, race, or socioeconomic standing, but they do reflect the thoughts and actions we have in this life. From Cain and Abel to now, only the innocent and the righteous of heart would be permitted to enter into the presence of the holy God of lights, *Yahweh*. Righteous Enoch and all the innocents of heart were permitted into the outer courts of the Holy of Holies where God is. From Abraham to Jesus, the Jewish people were separated from the rest of the world's populations and cultures while the laws and precepts of a civilized monotheistic people were established. Since the birth, death, and resurrection of Jesus Christ, the requirements for entry into the presence of Jehovah has become clearer and more specific. This includes born and unborn souls alike, or what the world calls naive fairy tales.

I woke up with a vivid picture of Jesus, and I understood that the whole purpose of this life was and is to bring glory to the Father. Through this life's experiences, the walls and gates of my soul were formed or destroyed by the PPRSs, the works of the flesh, the spirit-world realities, and the lusts of my heart, and I realized that I was the recipient of these consequences. These gates are represented by the fruit of the Spirit, built on the foundation of Love exemplified in Jesus Christ, and they are the primary way that all people are judged after death in this life regardless of when or where they lived. The nine fruit of the Spirit are universal and do not reflect sex, race, or creed, but they do reflect the thoughts and actions we have made in this life.

I had Cain's attitude and hatred toward Abel, and I saw that this anger and hatred was somehow in me. I could feel the intent and knew that only the innocent and the righteous of heart would be permitted to enter into the presence of the God of lights, *Yahweh*. Only the righteous and only the innocents of heart were permitted into the outer courts of the Holy of Holies where God is. From Abraham to Jesus, the Jewish people were separated from the rest of the world's populations and cultures while the laws and precepts of a civilized monotheistic people were then established.

Since the birth, death, and resurrection of Jesus Christ, all the requirements for entry into the presence of God have become clearer and more specific to me. The prejudice and racism that was evident in the church to the Jews and blacks was also evident and planted deep inside of me. The Holy Spirit revealed to me how deeply these seeds of superiority, pride, and hate were planted, and then He showed me such grace and patience with me until I could change and begin to heal my soul.

These individual dates are the days that I specifically asked the Holy Spirit to reveal revelation to me about my spiritual condition. With the TRUST prayer I was able to ask how to repair and restore my soul walls to re-hang my gates of the Fruit of the Spirit and protect my born again spirit temple and receive my greatest potential of rewards.

7/27/10 Fruit of the Spirit walls and gates of Jesus' perfection

8/19/10 Walking after the Spirit

12/27/10 Spirit-world realities

DIMITRI YANULI

1/22/11 Works of the flesh

9/27/11 Nimrod atheism; anti-Semitism

2/15/12 Rapture of the church (Revelation 7:9–12)

BIBLIOGRAPHY

America's Providential History. Beliles and McDowell College.

Berkowitz, Ariel and D'vorah. *Torah Rediscovered 1996 First Fruits of Zion.*

Conner, Kevin J. *The Tabernacle of Moses.1975, Bible Temple Publishing Portland, Or.*

Courtney, Howard P., and Vaneda H. Courtney. *The Baptism in the Holy Spirit.*

Hayford, Jack. *Rebuilding the Real You.* 2009 Charisma House. Lake Mary Florida

Know Your Bible Series. *A Study Course of the Fruit of the Spirit.* 1976, Church of God Bible Training Institute, BTI Publishing, Cleve. Tenn. pp.18, 25, 79, 96.

Meyer, Steven. *Signatures in the Cell DNA and the Evidence for Intelligent Design.* Philosophy of Science, Cambridge University. (Cofounder of the Intelligent Design Movement).

Prince, Derek. 1986.*Does Your Tongue Need Healing?* pp. 33–41.

Whitaker House, New Kensington, Pa

Prince, Derek. 2006, Chosen Books, Grabd Rapids, Mich.

Restoration Ministry of Ohio, pp. 9–10, 13, 16.

Rosenthal, Marvin. *The Pre-Wrath Rapture of the Church.*

Wright, Henry W. A More Excellent Way, 2005, Pleasant Valley Church, Inc. Thomaston, Ga.

Zodhiates, Spyros. *Hebrew Greek Key Study Bible,* King James Version.

AMG Publishers, Chattanooga, Tenn.

Sun Tzu, *The Art of War*